Second Wind

SECOND WIND

The Memoirs
of an
Opinionated Man

BILL RUSSELL
and
TAYLOR BRANCH

Random House · New York

Dedicated to my father
and to the memory of my
mother and my father's father

Library of Congress Cataloging in Publication Data
Russell, William Felton, 1934–
Second wind.
1. Russell, William Felton, 1934–   2. Basketball
players—United States—Biography. 3. Boston Celtics
(Basketball team) I. Branch, Taylor, joint author.
II. Title.
GV884.R86A35 796.32'3'0924 [B] 79-4780
ISBN 0-394-50385-6

Manufactured in the United States of America
24689753
First Edition

Authors' Note

This book could not have been written if there had been a gasoline shortage in 1978. Most of the research took place while we were puttering around in a golf cart with a tape recorder, or driving to and from a golf course. Sometimes it was quite a drive. At least three times we woke up in Seattle and decided to drive to a golf course in San Francisco. Once we drove from Seattle to Los Angeles and back.

We formed an odd partnership for such personal memoirs. At the beginning it was highly unlikely that the subject would even touch a typewriter or that the writer would ever put on golf shoes. Now one of us writes newspaper columns on his own brand-new typewriter, and the other messes up at golf. As in many worthwhile ventures, we started as strangers and ended as friends.

Contents

1

Family Heroes

My father is a strong man. My earliest memories of him come from days when our whole family played together in the fields near our home in Monroe, Louisiana. He worked hard in a paperbag factory, but he'd still come home full of energy and call out for my brother and mother and me. We would follow him to fields where the grass grew as tall as wheat, and the four of us would play hide-and-seek there, sneaking around and tackling, laughing and rolling around in the old hiding places. When it was time to go home, my father would reach down and pick me up under one arm, my brother under the other, lean down so my mother could crawl up on his back, and then run all the way home, carrying his whole family as if we weighed nothing. I remember bouncing along on his big forearm, laughing those long giggles the way a kid does when he's happy.

Mister Charlie was in charge. He had a deep rumbling voice, and he talked in proverbs. He loved to tell stories, spin yarns and visit his family. To all our kinfolk scattered across northern Louisiana, Mister Charlie was someone to count on for strength, wisdom and good humor. He was big—six feet two inches, over two hundred pounds and built like a heavyweight boxer—so people would have paid attention to him in any case, but he was also a source of warmth and laughter. People fussed if he didn't show up for a revival meeting or a family meal, and they fussed over him when he did. Mister Charlie was like a piece of rich soil, and everybody was looking to him to make something grow.

Not that he was perfect. Mister Charlie used to drink a little on weekends out with the boys back in the late 1930's, and I remember one time when he came home roaring that he could get along better by himself; he didn't need no marriage or no kids. My brother and I huddled terrified with our mother, and she told us it was this stuff he drank that made him like that, and not to pay him no mind. Which only baffled me more. All I understood was that something scary was happening to my father, and I felt all trembly the way I did during thunderstorms. The three of us went over to our grandfather's for the night, and when we got back next day everybody acted as though nothing had happened.

The very next weekend Mister Charlie came home all lit up again, but this time he laughed and hugged us and told loud jokes. Then suddenly he got mad again and started yelling about how he didn't need no marriage or no kids. My mother decided to stay with him, and she told us to run over to our grandfather's again. My father didn't like this, and he told my brother not to go and to make sure I didn't either. For a minute we were paralyzed between our parents, and then I took off, running in a panic. My brother was right behind me and grabbed me not far from the house. Panting, he told me to keep running and he'd pretend he couldn't catch me.

Our grandfather walked us back home after we fetched him. When we got there we saw our mother standing outside with an iron pipe in her hands. She was patting it lightly, and she had the beginnings of a smile on her face and wasn't angry any more. Mister Charlie was staggering around holding his head where our mother had whacked him. He was in pain, but not too much, and he said, "That woman sure do mean business."

The Old Man walked up to Mister Charlie and said, "You're wrong, son. You got no call to turn on the family you took and made yourself." From then on I never saw Mister Charlie act that way again, and he stopped boozing on weekends.

My brother and I had lumps in our throats through all this. I'm not sure it was possible for me to be any more in awe of my mother than I already was, but I remember being impressed that she didn't seem afraid of all the power Mister Charlie had stored up inside. I couldn't understand it then, and even looking back now, I think she was probably the only woman within a thousand miles who was a match for him. She was always amazing us with what she could do. One time, we were having trouble with the rats that came out of the swamp nearby to eat our chicken eggs. Mister Charlie spent a few afternoons waiting outside the hen-house to get a shot at them with us kids gathered around all excited, and once he gave the pistol to our mother more or less as a joke. I expected her to hand it back to him and say it wasn't woman's work, but just then, by chance, a rat came scurrying across the field toward the henhouse. Mother killed it with one shot, smiled and handed the gun back. The rest of us, including Mister Charlie, dropped our jaws so far we could have stepped on them. Not long after that, Mister Charlie got rid of that pistol. I think it made him nervous.

As forceful as my parents were in the town of Monroe, they were overshadowed in strength by my grandfather, Mister Charlie's father. He was stern. He had a mean streak, and the talk was that you couldn't get very far in this world without a little bit of the Old Man's mean streak. Everybody I knew had a special respect for him. He was a patriarch even to people outside the family—not so much as a wise man or counselor but as someone who never kowtowed to anybody. People borrowed a little dignity from the Old Man; he was like an oak tree.

He was the oldest living Russell that we knew of, the head of the line. The rest of the family had vanished when the Old Man's father ran off to Oklahoma back in the 1880's, abandoning him as a little boy. He had grown up without a father during the hard years in turn-of-the-century Louisiana. It had been even harder back then for a black man to survive without holding one of the selected "Negro jobs"—farmhand, janitor or the like. Mister Charlie's job in the bag factory was a "Negro job." But the Old Man never worked for anyone. He farmed on his own until farm credit squeezed him dry, around World War I, and after that he was a drayman. He drove a buckboard team for hire. Every day he waited down at his spot near the courthouse, where people knew they could find him. He'd haul logs, farm equipment, furniture or just about anything, and when he wasn't hauling he was busy trading at the railroad depot. The Old Man didn't have much money, but he was someone you could go to if you wanted to buy or sell some chickens, and he knew how to get a little cloth from Baton Rouge or a special kettle from St. Louis. He dealt in basics and staples, and would clear your land or find you a winter coat. He knew a lot of people, but he never worked for anybody except as a free agent; it was a point of pride with him that nobody had ever been in a position to fire him. He didn't like unexpected blows, and he believed that you could depend only on yourself.

The Old Man was lean and small compared with the later Russells. Only his hands were large, but they were really something. I remember touching them and studying them. They were smooth and hard like leather, and they seemed too large for his wrists. Those hands were known for what they could lift and carry. Everybody said that pound for pound he was the strongest man they knew.

The Old Man's reputation dated back to the old days when he was a champion logroller. Back before trucks and bulldozers came into use, black families in rural areas used to help each other clear land. On holidays or on Sundays, when the traveling preacher wasn't in town, all the men within ten or twenty miles would show up in the morning to clear somebody's land. There was a lot of tradition to it. They'd cut and strip the trees, and drag all the limbs into a big pile for burning. Nobody would burn all that timber now, but back then it was the only way to get rid of it. So the men would spend all day setting up this huge bonfire, leaving the trunks and big logs for last, and in the afternoon the women and kids would arrive for a big barbecue. While they were setting up the food, the men would have their logrolling. Two men would go to each end of a heavy log, slide strong sticks up under it and pick it up for carrying to the pile. There was a kind of competition about it. If you couldn't hold up your end of the stick with the man across from you, the log would roll right down on your hands and you'd have to drop it. Then somebody else could try to hold it up if he thought he was strong enough. It was in these contests that the Old Man showed his strength. They always put the biggest and strongest men opposite him, but he never dropped a log and never had one roll down on his hands. At least that's what I was told, and I believed it. The Old Man was celebrated around many a bonfire.

By the time I came along in 1934 the days of logrolling were gone, and soon the Old Man traded in his buckboard for an old pickup truck. All he had left from the buckboard team was a mule named Kate. He used Kate for odd jobs, like plowing his garden, but basically she just hung around. When I was four or five I loved nothing better than to tag along when the Old Man was out walking Kate somewhere; I might get a ride at the end of the day if he was in a good mood, and to me, riding Kate was like riding a horse. Besides, I simply liked walking along behind my grandfather. Most of the time he didn't say anything, but when he did, it was worth the wait.

I could tell that Kate and the Old Man understood each other. One day I was walking along with them when Kate decided to go off and stand in a ditch. Being an honest mule, she had a stubborn, mulish personality, and she stood there with this determined look on her face. It was as if Kate were saying, "Okay, I got you now. We're going to do this my way." The Old Man did everything he could to get Kate back up on the road. I watched him talk to her, and push, pull, shove and kick—a tough job, because there must have been nine hundred pounds of mule there. The Old Man would get Kate's front up on the road and be cooing into her ear, but when he walked around to pull up her tail end, the front would sidle back into the ditch again—so he'd take a deep breath and start over. I was taking all this in, and I couldn't believe that the Old Man didn't lose his temper.

After a long ordeal, Kate finally wound up back on the road. The Old Man looked exhausted, and the mule must have taken some satisfaction from all the effort she'd cost him. She looked fresh and relaxed, standing there as warm and lazy as the country air. The Old Man leaned on Kate and rested there for a minute or two; then out of nowhere he hauled off and punched her with his bare fist. Whack, just once, right in the side of the neck. The thud was so loud that I must have jumped a foot. The mule gently swayed back and forth groggily; then her front legs buckled and she collapsed to her knees. Then the hindquarters slowly buckled and settled down too. Kate looked all bent and contorted, like a squatting camel, as she sat there with a vacant stare in her eyes. I was dumbstruck. Right in front of my eyes the Old Man had knocked out a *mule* with one punch.

He never said a word to me or to the mule. He just let Kate sit there for a minute, and then he grabbed her by the head and picked her up. "Okay, let's go," he said quietly, and we started off again as if nothing had happened.

That sight stuck in my mind so vividly that I learned a practical lesson from it. I got into very few fights when I played for the Celtics, but every single one of them was in the last quarter, after the game was decided. You have to choose when to fight, and that is the time. The Old Man knew he'd have been in big trouble if he'd knocked that mule down in the ditch, so he waited until it didn't cost him anything. Then he relieved his frustration and gave Kate something to think about.

For someone descended from three powerful folks like my parents and the Old Man, I started out in life very weak. As a baby I was always sickly. My mother told me I had pneumonia twice before I could walk, and I was the only black baby in town who couldn't keep down either mother's milk or a formula; the doctor had to give me some sort of prescription medicine to mix in. While I was growing up I used to hear about all the medical emergencies I'd gone through, and about all the times I'd caused the relatives to gather anxiously at our house to pray over "the baby," as my mother called me until the day she died.

One of those crises has followed me ever since. At about the age of two, as I later picked up the details, I began running a strange fever that no medicine could arrest. No food of any kind stayed down. After a series of trips to the local doctor, who couldn't find anything wrong, I stayed at home for three or four days while the women of our extended family fluttered around and worried. I grew steadily worse, and finally my family took the desperate step of driving me to the big hospital for white people, on the road to Baton Rouge. There the doctors ran tests on me, but they couldn't find anything either.

It was a Catholic hospital, and one of the nuns came by to talk with my mother and Mister Charlie. They were all in knots, and things had reached the point that they were beseeching strangers in the halls for help. The nun listened, and promised to go off and pray. My parents didn't expect to see her again, but she came back not long afterward and told them to hold me upside down by my feet. That's all she said: "Hold him upside down by his feet." As crazy as it sounded, the nun had an air about her that made it seem like the thing to do, even with a very sick baby. Besides, my parents were ready to try anything. So Mister Charlie picked me up by my feet and held me over the bed. In less than a minute, they tell me, I coughed up a large piece of corn bread that had been stuck in my throat for days. Somehow it had lodged so that I wasn't aware of it and didn't choke, and the doctors had no way of knowing it was there. All my body's defenses had gathered to fight it, gradually draining my strength. The nun said a prayer of thanks and disappeared. My parents always said she had received a vision that saved my life.

Of course I don't remember what happened in that hospital, but I think it became part of a special bond between my mother and me. She told me the story over and over, and said that I carried a special blessing. I was marked, she believed, and destined for something special and precious. More than that, she told me that I was her favorite. Even today, when I think about my mother for any reason, what first jumps to mind are memories of her telling me that she loved me more than anyone in the world. She didn't care who knew it. Everybody knew that Katie Russell was sweet on me, and she stood by me like this fierce guardian. By custom and temperament, Mister Charlie wouldn't show much affection for his children, in order to set an example of respect, but my mother always cradled and hugged me, and told me I was the one she loved with all her heart. It was the best feeling there was.

My mother was a marvel because she could be so gentle and yet so tough. At the time I sometimes thought she was the best parts of a man and a woman, with none of the bad parts of either, and that these qualities were so big inside her that she might bust open. She was rich, tender and strong all at once. If I'd run into a king or queen, I would have been proud to show my mother off to them.

Once, when I was nine—just after we moved to West Oakland —a bigger kid walked by our project and slapped me across the face, then kept right on going. The local kids wanted to let me know that whatever I'd brought inside me from Louisiana didn't swing much weight with them. My mother saw me get slapped and came running out. She grabbed me and took off running until we caught the guy. There wasn't any doubt about what was going to happen: she made me fight him right there in front of her. I closed my eyes and went in swinging. While the little blows were flying, one of my opponent's friends cheered him on. In the heat of the fight this friend said something about me that offended my mother. So when the fight was over and I rushed to her for comfort, she just pointed at the friend and told me what he had said, so I had to fight him, too. I won the first fight and lost the second, but I didn't care. The scrapes and bruises were nothing compared with my mother's proud approval.

My mother made me feel so secure that I honestly believed nothing could hurt me. The feeling was pleasant and it was there all the time, no matter what, like a bridge between us. You could spit on it, kick it or drive a truck over it, and the feeling would still be there. Even though I remained a little sickly and was overshadowed by the accomplishments of my big brother Charlie, everything was okay; I could do what I wanted because I was certain that my mother would protect me. I would jump right in where other kids my size would know better.

I was always taking one step over the line into mischief, and my mother was partly to blame. The way she cooked was one of those magical bonuses that made her even more amazing. It was like that with her clothes, too. Whether she was cooking or putting on a scarf, she had style. After just a few easy motions on her part, everything seemed to fall into place. A complicated dish would come out just right before I'd even noticed she'd gone in the kitchen, and with just the brush of her hand she could put exactly the right folds and curves into her scarf. Everything seemed to take on a special feeling when it came near my mother.

The most seductive food was her banana pudding. It always seemed to work out the same way. She'd whip up a big round plate of banana pudding in the afternoon, leave it to cool on the table while she and Mister Charlie went out visiting, and I'd be left alone with it. Before leaving, she'd say, "Don't you eat none of that pudding. It's for supper."

Alone, I'd walk back and forth by the table, looking at it and wondering how it tasted. I knew how it tasted in general, but I wanted to know how this *particular* batch had turned out. Finally I'd say to myself, "Well, she was making this pudding for me anyway because she knows I love it so much, so I'll just have one little serving"—which would be gone in a flash, and I'd taste it all the way down to my stomach. When the last bite was gone I'd run outside to play, because I knew it was the only way to control myself. But after a while I'd come back to the house, and the pudding would still be there. So I'd eat a little bit as a reward for going so long without eating any more. I'd play awhile, and then eat another little bit. This serving, I decided, was my parent's fault instead of mine; they'd left me alone too long.

Pretty soon I'd have eaten about half the pudding, and then came the critical moment. I'd think long and hard, and finally I'd say to myself, "Hey, I'm gonna get a whipping anyway, so I might as well eat the rest."

There was always a kind of bittersweet taste to that last bite, as I suddenly became aware that nothing more lay between me and the whipping. What I had eaten would begin to feel heavy as a cannonball in my stomach, and I'd be sluggish just when I needed to be sharp to plan my strategy. Usually this was to lock myself in the house and not let the folks in when they came home. "Come on, son!" they'd yell. "Open up!"

"You been in that pudding again, ain't you, boy?" Mister Charlie would shout, and he'd start pounding his big fist on the door. I knew he'd set his own heart on some of that pudding, so he'd be extra mad. By this time I'd really be sweating.

"If I let you in, will you promise not to whip me?" I'd ask. There I'd be, negotiating with my parents over a whipping, all because of the banana pudding.

Occasionally, my mother would go against Mister Charlie on my behalf. Once she tried to buy me a set of electric trains that cost fourteen dollars, which back then was more than he earned in a whole week. She saved and worked, even taking extra jobs as a maid for the white folks, but the money was simply out of her reach. I'll always remember how hard she tried.

She agreed with Mister Charlie about the pudding, though. No matter how the negotiations proceeded, I always got a whipping.

But even whippings didn't bother me much. I had what they called a happy disposition, which meant that sometimes I was entertaining and other times a nuisance. I loved to kid around with people, even the Old Man.

My grandfather's house was a gathering place for relatives and neighbors alike. Kids would drop by just to watch him, or they'd rendezvous at "Old Mr. Russell's place" to play. Grownups stopped in to see him all the time, even when they were heading somewhere else. The Old Man lived by himself for the last thirty years of his life, after his wife died when I was very small. He didn't *marry* anybody else, but he did have a bunch of girl friends. In fact, his love life was always the subject of amusing gossip, as a long string of younger women took a fancy to him, way up into his seventies and beyond. When the Old Man was about eighty-two, Mister Charlie called me to laugh about how his father was afraid he was going to *have to* get married to a lady in her early forties, because some rabbit had died.

Mister Charlie loved it when his father bragged and complained about women at the same time, but he knew the Old Man could tell a whopper or two. Now that Mister Charlie is pushing up there in age himself, he's less skeptical of the Old Man's alleged feats; he draws hope from them. As a kid, I knew everybody admired the Old Man for the way he treated women. He'd shake his head and tell me, "Now it takes me all night to do what I used to do all night." I had no idea what he was talking about.

Anyway, what got me in trouble at the Old Man's house was the fruit. You could count on him to have some apples, bananas and oranges around the house for people who stopped by, and you could count on me to give it away to my friends like there was no tomorrow. Giving it away was one of those things the Old Man wouldn't tolerate. "You can eat all my fruit you want," he'd say. "You can eat it until you get sick. But don't give it away."

I was about seven years old, so happy and secure in my mother's love that I'd kid around with the Old Man. After he left the house one day, my friends had a fruit feast. We started gradually, but we built up momentum fast. When he came home there was nothing left but peels and cores. He walked right up to me. "You've been giving my fruit away," he said. "I'm gonna whip you."

The first thought that came into my mind was, "Uh oh, this is the same guy who knocked out the mule!" So I bolted and ran. It was a split-second decision; I knew I stood a chance of getting another beating just for running, and a third beating for not facing up to the first one. That's the way Mister Charlie would have figured it. But all I could think about was the sight of Kate sprawled on the ground, and I was *gone*.

Right in the yard I opened up a fifty-yard lead. Looking back over my shoulder, I saw him jump up and grab a branch off a tree as he went by, to use as a switch. That made me speed up. I zigzagged down to the fields of high grass where our family played, and dived into a clump of the really tall stuff. But when I heard the Old Man puffing up behind me, I changed my mind. I decided he might have seen where I jumped in, so I started crawling through the underbrush. When I'd gone a little way I heard him pull up at the edge of the grass and prowl around. I kept crawling, and by the time I got to the opposite side, I was rested and out of range.

I stood up and looked back at the Old Man still rummaging around back there, then sassily yelled back at him, "You know that old T-Model can't catch this Ford V-8!"

The Old Man didn't catch up with me until long after I'd gotten home. I noticed that he hadn't brought the switch with him, even though I was sure that on a matter of principle Mister Charlie would have let him use it right there in the house. But then the Old Man smiled. I knew his dark mood had passed, and there was no sting in his hand when he whipped me. He told my folks about the Ford V-8, and everybody had a chuckle despite all the talk about how they had to be stern with me. I suppose I got away with a good bit of naughtiness, but I never gave away the Old Man's fruit any more.

In some areas, the security I felt as a kid gave me a reputation in Monroe for bravery. For example, both my brother and I were unafraid of "haints," which sent a shudder up the spines of most of the local population. Haints were ghosts, and there was a whole folk mythology about the powers, habits and origins of these spirits. In those days people were involved in the lore no less than they are in television today. If a haint appeared to old Mrs. James while she was rocking on her porch one night, the news of the event would occupy the town for days. Everybody wanted to know exactly what the haint had said and done, and they'd swap theories on the meaning of its appearance. I think the world of haints was a special kind of emotional communion over woes, questions and severed ties going all the way back to Africa, but Charlie and I saw them as a source of practical jokes.

Both my mother and father were ambivalent about ghosts. They expressed doubts about their existence, but they spent as much time discussing the latest haint tale as anyone. One peg-legged man and his fat wife used to visit us all the time and stay up late discussing haint legends. One night Charlie and I sneaked out of bed and ambushed them on their way home with sheets over our heads, yelling "Whoooooo!" like haints. The enormous old lady shrieked and took off like a scared horse, but as fast as she flew she could barely keep up with her peglegged husband as he thump-thumped off into the night. Charlie and I laughed about that one for months. Our folks said we were too young and ornery to have proper respect for old people's dealings with haints.

My mother's father, Grandpa King, was supposed to have special connections to the world of spirits. He was a strange old character, as flighty and mysterious as Mister Charlie's father was solid. One day he got up whistling and just whistled his way out of town. It was said that the haints would tell him where treasure was hidden, and the old man would wander off after it. Once, before I was born, he and a bunch of the strongest haint believers lured Mister Charlie to an old deserted house out in the middle of nowhere, where they spent all night digging for a satchel of money. Everybody dug except Grandpa King, who spent his time spinning tales about how the haints had assured him the money was there. When this effort failed, he left town again to follow the haints' directions to treasure elsewhere.

All through my childhood our family communicated with my maternal grandfather mainly through rumor and guesswork. Once he did show up out of nowhere and spent the night at our house. I'll never forget how, after staying up late with the grown ups, he came to the bed where Charlie and I were sleeping and snuggled in between us. The next morning he was sopping from head to toe because I'd wet the bed. As I was lying there cringing at the thought of the humiliation I'd have to endure when he woke up, he bolted up straight out of a sound sleep and landed on the floor. Without a word he commenced a lively dance, spinning around and around. I couldn't believe my eyes. He didn't even seem to notice that he was wet as he danced up a sweat to welcome the morning. Then he turned suddenly to me and said, "The next time you see me, you'll be too big to wear my clothes." That's all he said, and that day he whistled on out of town again. I only saw him once more.

Grandpa King left six daughters behind, my mother and five "aunties." It was said that one of the things that made him a little touched in the head was his inability to have a son. Five times in a row he considered himself burdened with girls, and when the sixth also turned out to be a girl, he snapped. No matter how many times he was told that his last baby was a daughter, he insisted that he had finally fathered a son.

At any rate, this was the explanation offered for why my fifth auntie came to be the way she was. Kammie was the scandal of the King family because all her life she dressed and acted like a man. It was our family's biggest secret from outsiders, especially from white people; everybody knew back in the late years of the Depression in the rural South that it wouldn't be healthy for Kammie to be known as the lesbian Negro. Some of the local white people found out, of course, but they pretended not to know, and Kammie fooled strangers and even some who knew her for years. Once she got arrested for shooting dice, and the sheriff's deputies put her in the men's cell. She pulled it off until she had to use the bathroom.

Kammie may have been a scandal to some people, but I thought she was by far the most entertaining auntie I had. She was a live wire, always telling stories about forbidden places like poolrooms and juke joints. The other adults would frown about those evil subjects, but Kammie had a gleam in her eye; her wild stories were always funny, and she never took herself too seriously. I always liked her and remember being disappointed that she never seemed to stay around long. The only time she ever spent a full day with our family was also the only time I ever saw her wearing a dress, and I was told it was the first time she had worn one in many years. She didn't look like the same person; she seemed uncomfortable, and a lot of her zip was missing. Wearing a dress must have been as nerve-racking for her as it would have been for me, and it was a measure of her love for my mother that she agreed to do it. Mother had forbidden Kammie to stay with us in men's clothes.

Kammie was about the only relative I knew who didn't go to church regularly, which may have been another reason I liked her. Church really took it out of me when I was little. It was an all-day affair; we'd have Sunday School, and afterward a long morning service that lasted well into the afternoon. Then, after a break for lunch we'd have an afternoon Sunday School called B.Y.P.U., and finally an evening service long into the night. The music was lively, but our choir wasn't very good. Apart from the music I thought church was dull, especially when I was five or six years old. I could understand enough to tell whether the preacher was going to lecture or to shout fire and brimstone. If he was shouting, I'd look around to see who was going to shout with him, but this never kept me occupied for long. Charlie and I managed to channel our excess energy into sleep, but every time we drifted off, retribution would come. Thummmmp! One of the old people behind us would lean forward and flick us on our bare skulls. Thummmmp, thummmmp! Our heads were bare, because for some reason our mother shaved off all our hair except for a little patch on the forehead, and this made the flicks hurt even more. The old people delivered them with their thumb and middle finger, the way you might flick lint off your clothes, and they got a lot of power into those thumps. Worst of all, you couldn't cry out at all. It seemed so malicious that I decided that old people felt self-righteous about waking me up for the Lord. I tried all kinds of maneuvers to avoid sitting in front of the hardest thumpers, but somehow they were always just behind me.

Outside of church the old people were all right. In fact, they were the center of attention at a lot of family gatherings, which we had on weekends, and at the all-week revival meetings. The traveling family gatherings were the best. Every summer we used to visit cousins in Downsville, Louisiana, where they had a watermelon farm. The watermelon there was some of the sweetest in the world, and I used to eat it all day and pee all night. I ate so much that I'd go to sleep at the supper table, where mercifully there was no thumping. Later I'd wake up and cry myself back to sleep because somebody had eaten my dessert.

There would always be some moment, usually just after supper, when the grownups' conversation would turn into a storytelling session, and that's when the older people would be on stage. We must have had some high-quality storytellers to keep me there listening when I was free to run off and play. I heard stories about relatives who had gone to Europe in World War I, about great hurricanes and feats in logrolling, which always brought out a round of complimentary stories about Grandpa Russell. And I heard stories about the longevity of our family. One of my great-great-grandmothers lived to be one hundred and fifteen. She smoked a clay pipe, lived by herself and was clear-headed until she died.

I don't remember hearing any stories about Africa, or even about anything African. I do remember an ancient great-grand-mother, then in her nineties, telling of making sacks of food for two slave boys and sending them North. I think they were her nephews or cousins; anyway, she was raising them. The old lady would say over and over that she'd never heard another word about those two boys, and even I, as young as I was, was pierced by how desperate a feeling it must have been to send young children you loved off into the unknown.

The old people steered clear of subjects like Africa and slavery; their talk about race was much more immediate. There were stories about the Kingfish, Huey Long, and what he might have done for the Negro in Louisiana had he not been assassinated. There were also stories about FDR, who was a source of hope, and every now and then there'd be a story about lynching. I'm sure the adults talked about this a great deal among themselves, but in the family sessions the topic was delicate. Usually the tale would take the indirect form of a discussion about some black man who had disappeared. Someone might suggest that he could have run out on his wife, and someone might say that it was the haints, but then someone else would mention that the white people might have gotten him. Most of the blacks who were lynched in those days were not killed in a way that made the papers. They simply disappeared, and the local blacks would be too afraid to mention it, let alone to raise a fuss.

I remember only two family stories about local lynching mobs during the nine years I lived in Monroe, so I suppose you could say it was done in moderation. One involved an old black deputy sheriff—actually, more of a sheriff's helper, since black deputies had no authority over white citizens and very little over black ones. Anyway, he got into a quarrel with a white deputy, which led to a shoot-out. The white wound up dead, and the black was gravely wounded. Despite his condition and his claim of self-defense, the surviving deputy was charged with murder and taken to jail. A doctor attended him there. When an angry lynch mob gathered outside the jail, the sheriff faced them and said he would shoot the first man who stepped forward, and as many as he could after that. He stared them down, just like in the movies. That's the way the story sounded at our family gatherings—though of course none of the local blacks had been anywhere near that jail. To us the sheriff was a hero, and it was felt that he stood up so strongly because he was fond of the old deputy. Of course everyone wondered why on earth the deputy let himself get in a gunfight with a white man. Nevertheless, as we all expected, the local jury threw out the black deputy's claim of self-defense and sentenced him to the gallows. He died of complications from the gunshot wound before the execution.

Stories about such incidents were generally positive and hopeful. At least there had been no lynching in Monroe, which was more than could be said for the tiny town of Ruston, not far down the road. There a black man was accused of insulting a white woman and was strung up by a mob. The next day his body was found still hanging. Ruston, it was agreed, was not as progressive a town as Monroe.

Most of the racial tales I heard in those days had to do with how various kinfolk had handled scrapes with white people, such as the one about how Grandpa Russell had fought off the Klan in 1917. This was when he still lived out in the country, before moving to Monroe. He was a sort of free-lance farmer, with numerous plots under cultivation here and there under various arrangements. Once he did some work "on the halves" with a white man, and when the crop was ready the white fellow told the Old Man to gather the fodder and divide it.

The Old Man said, "Sir, you can have all the fodder. I don't need it. I ain't got no mule to eat it right now, and I ain't gonna do no farming next year."

The white fellow got all steamed up. "Nigger," he said, "don't you tell me what you ain't gonna do. I'll *make* you do it."

That set the Old Man off. "Sir," he said, "you and who else?"

As I listened to this family classic being retold years later, laughter would always break out at this point. Somebody would repeat, "You and who else?" in a voice filled with admiration, and somebody else would chime in, "That's right." Then somebody else might point out how the Old Man had said "Sir" even when he was getting ready to whip a white man's ass. We all knew the Old Man had broken the code of behavior at the crucial moment when he was supposed to back down, even if he had to take a beating to do it.

Then the story went on about how the white fellow made a lunge at the Old Man, which was a mistake. He ran that white fellow right off his own land. But as the white man ran off, he yelled back, "We're gonna come git you tonight!"

So the Old Man went home to move his family out of danger before nightfall. If Mister Charlie weren't telling the story himself, he'd break in at this point to tell about how his father had come home, loaded the family into the wagon and driven them to a friend's farm eight or nine miles away. From the look on the Old Man's face they knew there was bad trouble, and they knew even better when he took them to stay the night with people who weren't relatives; he wanted the family hidden where no one would think to look for them. Mister Charlie told all this with great pride; he had been only five years old at the time, and it was his earliest memory of his father.

After dropping the family off, the Old Man returned to his house and waited there alone, with only his dog to bark a warning. Late that night the Klan people drove up in several cars. They cut the engines, and the Old Man heard a lot of doors slamming, some muffled talk, and then silence. Finally they yelled at him to come on out and get taught how to treat a white man.

The Old Man said, "Sir, you're gonna have to come in this house and get me."

So they yelled back and forth in a stalemate until somebody fired a shot, probably up in the air to frighten the Old Man. Which was another mistake. The Old Man opened up with his shotgun and started pumping shells out into the darkness. He kept blasting and reloading until he heard the cars drive off. After that, nothing happened. Evidently the Klansmen decided that this kind of fighting was not what they had in mind.

There was always a feeling of release when this story ended. Mister Charlie would say that nobody knew if somebody had been wounded that night, but that the Old Man had sure hit some trees. The next day everybody saw limbs on the ground. Then somebody else might talk about how those Klansmen must have worried that the Old Man would use his rifle. (Everybody around Monroe knew that the Old Man had a Winchester, which he usually carried under the seat of his buckboard.) If someone really pressed him, the Old Man himself might clarify a detail or two; otherwise he just sat there. We all knew he was proud of that story, but you couldn't tell it from his face.

Mister Charlie always said that everyone has to draw a line inside himself somewhere, and that the Old Man had drawn his at getting whipped. He was more courteous to white people than Mister Charlie was, more deferential in the manner of the "good ol' Negro." He had bent with these ways for so long that they didn't touch a vital spot, but he had never bent about getting whipped.

Mister Charlie had stories of his own. Once, not long after he got married, he was working for a construction company. A grizzled, mean black dude who also worked there had the reputation for cutting up people with his knife on Saturday nights. He drove a three-mule team for the company, but had a habit of showing up for work late or not at all. He was late once too often for the white boss, who said one morning that apologies weren't good enough any more, and who proceeded to slap and beat the tough guy in front of the other black employees. The tough dude didn't lift a hand, and when it was over, Mister Charlie started laughing. Startled, the boss turned on him and demanded to know what was so funny.

"Well, I thought that fellow was *baad,*" laughed Mister Charlie. "I've heard about him cutting people and whipping two or three at a time, but he just stood there and let you whip him. That don't make sense."

"What would you do if you was him?" asked the boss.

"I'd either run or I'd fight you, but I wouldn't just stand there."

The boss was getting mad; Mister Charlie was ruining his little demonstration. "Yes you would, nigger," he said. "And you can do it right now, 'cause I'm gonna whip *you!*"

"Naaaw, Mr. George," said Mister Charlie, like he was giving advice to his best friend. "I don't think so. If you do whip me, you'll be the best man and I'll shake your hand afterwards. But I'm gonna try my hand, and I don't think you can do it."

The boss came right at Mister Charlie, testing him, and Mister Charlie stood up to him. When they were right in each other's faces the boss backed off, laughing, and said he didn't need to whip Mister Charlie because he was never late.

"I didn't believe you could let the man think that he could whip you at work," Mister Charlie would tell us when this story came up. "He could fire me if he wanted to, but what good would it do me to let him beat me bloody to make me make my own living?" And he would repeat it: *to make me make my own living.*" He would intone the words with outrage in that voice of his that sounded like a kettle drum and carried easily over a dozen other conversations.

Not long before I was born, Mister Charlie had a job with a Mom-and-Pop trucking company. The Mom really mistrusted people, especially blacks, and was so obsessed by the fear that one of her drivers would use some of her gas to go off on a lark that she measured out the gas for each trip with a measuring cup. But occasionally she would miscalculate. One night Mister Charlie ran out of gas about twenty miles from home, and he had to walk. He was mad. And while he was walking, two drunk fellows in a car pulled up to him and asked, "Hey, boy, can you run?"

It was all Mister Charlie could do to ignore them and keep on walking.

Then one of them waved a gun out the window and yelled, "Hey, lemme see you run."

Mister Charlie broke into a trot, but the gun went off. Bang! Whine! A bullet sailed by, and Mister Charlie went into a full gallop. Bang! Whine! He swerved off the road and ran down into a culvert filled with water and trash. He yelled out, "Snakes, you'll have to move over tonight, 'cause Charlie's gonna stay here with you!"

When this line came we'd all laugh; there was nothing else we could do. But back at the company Mom hadn't laughed; she didn't buy Mister Charlie's explanation that there was something wrong with her measuring cup. Her theory was that Mister Charlie and all his fellow nigras showed no respect for her truck, and that if they ran out of gas it was because they had been catting about. They *deserved* to walk home alone at night, she felt. So Mister Charlie lost both the argument and his job.

Mister Charlie had a way of seeing the funny side of tense situations, and the tension wasn't always over white people. Once he was in an all-black juke joint, a place where minor vices were indulged and kids were not allowed. One guy put a nickel in the juke box, and another one started patting his foot to the music. When the first one, mad as a wet hen, said, "Hey, nigga, don't be pattin' your foot on *my* nickel!" a fight started. Mister Charlie would describe how he'd turned over a table in the corner and crouched down behind it. When we asked him why he didn't join the fight and show everybody how strong he was, he'd laugh and say the dumbest thing a man could do was to let himself fight over something as stupid as another man's nickel. The only thing worse than not picking your own fights, he said, was to think you could serve some useful purpose or have some fun in another guy's fight. That wisdom must have sunk in; years later, I'd always remember the juke-joint fight as I watched countless scuffles among basketball players from my usual position on the bench—sitting there, resting alone, with a towel around my neck.

Sound as it was, Mister Charlie's strategy had to be modified on that particular night because the fist fight turned into a shooting match. When guns started going off he bolted from behind his table, ran over a fat guy in the doorway and made a long, flying leap to his truck. "I hit the running board, the starter and the ignition all at once," he'd say.

Mister Charlie was proud of that old truck, but sometimes it got him into trouble when he drove around to jobs. In those days it was unusual for a black man to own his own truck. One day when he was driving through a town, a deputy sheriff pulled him over and began harassing him about driving too fast.

"Boy, whose truck is this, anyway?" demanded the deputy after he had yelled awhile.

"Mister Charlie Russell's."

"Well, you tell Mister Charlie Russell to keep his nigger from driving through here so fast!"

"I sure will," said Mister Charlie. "I'll tell him just as soon as I get home."

We'd always laugh at that one. Mister Charlie always seemed to find a way to laugh when he was the victim himself, but his temper would get loose when it was somebody else. That's what happened in two incidents that permanently changed the direction of our family. One Saturday afternoon—the day my mother went to town for groceries—she came home early, crying. I was about seven at the time, and I couldn't stand it. The only other time I had seen her cry was at my grandmother's funeral. I couldn't imagine anything big or evil enough to make my mother cry, and her sobs shook my whole world. It was as if all my senses had been shut off, so that I couldn't see or hear or anything, and the same big hurt that had grabbed her shook me so hard that I had to cry too.

Mother said that one of the policemen in Monroe had grabbed her and cussed her for dressing like a white woman. He spoke real rough to her, and told her he'd put her in jail if she didn't get out of town. She'd been wearing an outfit more special to her than the one she wore on Sundays. It was a suit, modeled after the horse-riding clothes popular among fancy white women, and she looked fancier in it than they did. Everything about it was just right, and she walked with an extra spring in that white blouse with a pin at her throat and a trim suitcoat and pants. Maybe the pants gave her a touch of Auntie Kammie's independent spirit.

Mister Charlie was there, but he didn't say anything; he just walked around mumbling to himself. I wanted to ask him what was wrong with my mother, but something told me not to say anything.

The other incident happened not long afterward, on a Saturday afternoon in the first spring after Pearl Harbor. We were on our way home from an afternoon of visits and stopped to buy gas and a block of ice. The man at the station was pumping gas for a white guy, and when he finished he stood there talking to the man about this and that, passing the time of day. Mister Charlie was standing outside our car, and he kept waiting while the conversation rambled on and my brother and I jumped up and down in the back seat, eager to get home. After about ten minutes I could tell that Mister Charlie was starting to burn, but he didn't say anything. He was shifting his weight back and forth from one foot to the other. I'm sure the man who ran the station was letting him wait there on purpose, just to show that Mister Charlie could do nothing about it. Then another white guy drove up, and the man waited on him quickly—pumped the gas, took his money and waved good-bye. Then he just ambled back to the first customer and resumed his bull session. My brother and I became absolutely still because we could feel the anger in the air. Finally, Mister Charlie couldn't take it any more; he jumped back in our car and cranked it up to drive off. Just then the first customer left, and the station attendant looked mean at Mister Charlie. He was standing in the door of his station, and just inside was a big rifle. He stormed over to our car and said, "Boy, don't you *ever* do what you just started to do!" Then he cussed Mister Charlie about his manners, spitting out the words. I'd never heard anybody talk to my father like that, and my cheeks stung as if they'd been slapped.

The next thing I knew, I saw Mister Charlie walking toward that white man with a tire iron in his hand. The man got an empty look in his eyes, as if he didn't believe what he was seeing, and his cussing petered out as Mister Charlie walked slowly around the car toward him. He looked too frozen to go after his rifle; he just stood there until Mister Charlie got within a step or two, and then took off running, past the gas pumps and through the parking lot out onto the road. When he broke out running, Mister Charlie let out a loud grunt and chased him up the road with that tire iron in his hand. Then I saw him stop, and his whole back heaving with big heavy breaths as he watched the man go.

By then, my brother and I were about to burst with pride. We were so full of energy that we started punching each other lightly, and we would have cheered out loud except that our mother had on a look that said not to. Still, when Mister Charlie got back into the car we couldn't resist chirping about how scared that man was and how funny he looked running off, until Mister Charlie told us sharply to hush up. There wasn't anything to be happy about, he said gruffly, which stunned and confused me.

Mister Charlie was so worried about what had happened that he took it right up with the Old Man, and they talked it over. "Do you think something's coming on behind this?" the Old Man asked. Mister Charlie said no, but he was worried that something like it might happen again.

It was many years before I understood why Mister Charlie was so upset about something that I'd thought magnificent. "I didn't have hold of myself," he'd say. "I know deep down that I'da hit that man with that iron if he hadn't run off. I'd have ended his life and ruined mine, plus my kids' and my wife's, just 'cause some fool was using me as a boy in front of my family. I let him take full possession of me, a grown man. I don't even like to think about it."

Mister Charlie related this incident to one of his sayings. "When you come across a fool who can't help himself," he'd say, "always remember that he's a fool. Don't bother with him. On up the road he's liable to run into another fool, and one of them will destroy the other." I took all this in, but it never erased the nice feeling I still get from the memory of that guy hightailing it out of the station.

Not long after that, Mister Charlie broke the news that we were going to move out of Monroe. We were pulling up stakes, and maybe we'd become like those families who return every summer to visit from the North, driving long cars, wearing shiny clothes and making people uncomfortable. The whole idea of moving was a shock to my brother and me. We weren't well-traveled; New York, Chicago and Los Angeles were huge fairylands to us—even bigger than New Orleans, somewhere over the Louisiana line.

Even then my young instincts told me that our leaving had something to do with the policeman who'd yelled at my mother and the gas-station attendant, and I was puzzled. I couldn't understand why we had to leave because a white man had gotten scared of Mister Charlie; it didn't make sense. But then nothing about the world of white people made much sense to me. I'd scarcely had contact with any; there were none in my school, of course, and the white kids I did see usually threw rocks at my friends and me when we walked into town. On lucky days they'd just call us a few names. As for white neighbors, there was only one white family that lived anywhere near us, and they were strange. The husband kept to himself and screamed all through the night—such long, horrible screams that everybody talked about how the haints must have gotten him. My mother told me that the man was shell-shocked from World War I, but that didn't explain it to me. I didn't know what shell-shocked meant.

Then there were white strangers, people we'd meet in stores and gas stations. They could be rude to my parents and then pat me on the head without a second thought. It all added up to a mystery, which was one reason I listened to the stories the grown-ups told at the family gatherings. One steady theme was the nature of white people, and I was still looking for the answers.

No one else seemed to wonder as much as I did why we were leaving. Mister Charlie was busy huddling with the men he knew, talking about places up North. Soon there was a big send-off for him when he went off by himself on the train to find us a new home in Detroit. Weeks went by. Finally we got a letter saying that he'd found a job at the Ford Motor plant making war machinery, followed by another letter saying he'd gotten so sick from riding the bus to work in the cold that the doctor said he'd die if he stayed in Detroit. Mister Charlie didn't like the cold anyway, so he took off straight for California. One day he sent for us; he was ready for us to move.

The hardest good-bye for me was the one I said to a girl. Her nickname was "Too Little," which she'd gotten stuck with because she was always saying she wasn't too little to do this or that. She was nine, like me, black as charcoal, and so cute that I wanted to squeal with delight whenever I saw her—though I'd have died before letting anybody know that. I promised Too Little that I'd come back for her just as soon as the family returned home to visit Grandpa Russell.

I sat next to my mother in the colored section of the train all the way to St. Louis, and then, for the first time in our lives, we could sit anywhere.

At first the Old Man did not approve of our migration. He said he was too old and set in his ways even to think of moving himself. I think he doubted Mister Charlie's prospects outside Louisiana and he hated to see him go, but in the end he came to believe that it was for the best. He and Mister Charlie would talk it over between them. One thing was for sure, they'd say: moving would help my brother and me get a better education. All three of my family idols were devoted to the idea of school. Education was a great shining stepladder for black families in those days, though you couldn't point to many who had climbed on it a long way. Still, it was the brightest hope we had as long as there was only one Joe Louis.

The Old Man, who couldn't read or write, was always singing the praises of education. To him, being educated meant being able to think for yourself, and he joked that he never needed schooling to do that. Then he would turn serious and say that he'd gone as far in school as he could for a boy who grew up in the old days with no father, and he'd tell in great detail how he had worked to push Mister Charlie through school.

It had been a hard road for Mister Charlie. During the national outbreak of meanness that followed World War I (one seems to follow all wars), some of the local diehards burned the black schoolhouse to the ground just as he'd started to go there. Citing a temporary shortage of funds, the county government announced that the schoolhouse could not be rebuilt right away. Furthermore, since there was no colored schoolhouse, there seemed to be no sense in paying teachers any more than three months a year. This situation lasted all the way through Mister Charlie's grammar-school years, so he went to school in a church. A bunch of the local black parents risked reprisal from the diehard whites and hired their own teacher at the rate of a dollar a month per head. The Old Man was the ringleader of the group that hired the teacher, and he used to say that Mister Charlie had gotten "a dollar-a-month education."

My father would talk about getting whipped in that church,

and about what a joy it had been to show off his reading for the Old Man. When he was in a dark mood he'd talk about how the white kids would ride by in their school bus and throw tomatoes and rotten eggs at the black kids on foot. Fifty years later, when the country got all stirred up about busing, Mister Charlie would joke that he always thought busing was only for white kids.

The Old Man had one simple rule for Mister Charlie about school: he could drop out any time he wanted, but when he did he couldn't live under his father's roof. It was stay in school or leave home, and the Old Man laid down this law with his usual economy of words. We always heard that Mister Charlie advanced as far as the Negro could go in his time, just like his father in "the old days."

What both of them kept secret from me until long after I was grown and had kids of my own was that this rule had once torn them apart. It was in 1927, the year Babe Ruth had such a great season up in New York. It wasn't such a good year for Mister Charlie. He was fifteen years old and tired of walking eight miles every day to Monroe Colored High School. By the hard, practical reasoning he'd learned from the Old Man himself, it didn't make sense to him. That summer he'd gotten a job driving a tractor for thirty cents an hour, which worked out to about sixty dollars a month. At the time, black teachers were paid only thirty dollars a month—when they were working—and they held down about the only jobs for "educated Negroes." A few preachers, doctors and morticians were allowed "to treat their own kind," but these jobs didn't appeal to Mister Charlie, and for all practical purposes it seemed that he was going to school in order to become a schoolteacher. As the summer drew to an end, it chafed him to think about giving up his tractor job and all the money it paid just so he could go back to school and qualify to be like the parents of some of the kids he knew, who in their prime were earning about half what he was already making as a fifteen-year-old boy. Besides, he liked running that big tractor outdoors better—a lot better—than he liked sitting in that classroom with a bunch of prissy girls who put on airs. He pointed all this out to his father with more and more urgency, finally begging to be allowed to drop school, but the Old Man would not budge. They butted heads, and Mister Charlie said that on many evenings the angry words from supper would still be bouncing off the walls late at night.

So one night Mister Charlie ran away like a hobo, jumping on a train as it went by. All he had with him was his anger, plus all the food he could carry—and about half his wits, since he was all torn up inside about leaving everything and everyone he'd ever known. All night he prayed for guidance, but by the next morning he found he'd already made a horrible mistake. Instead of catching the train north toward St. Louis, as planned, he'd gone east to Vicksburg across the big river and was headed through Mississippi! It took him three months to get out of that state. He had bad luck with the trains, partly because the railroad men were more vigilant, and he had worse luck with the jobs they were supposed to be giving out on the flood levees. After many missed meals and nights out under the stars, his tired feet finally brought him back home to Monroe like the prodigal son. The Old Man said he was too glad to see him to whip him. Many black people ran away from Mississippi in the twenties, some fleeing for their lives, but my father must be one of the few who ever ran away *to* Mississippi.

Mister Charlie didn't tell me about this disaster, because he didn't want to undermine his own rule about staying in school, which was identical to the Old Man's. The only person more zealous about education than Mister Charlie was my mother. She gave me the middle name Felton, after Felton Clark, who was then president of Southern University, and she inspired Mister Charlie to take out two $2,500 insurance policies that would mature into college funds for my brother and me. He started making payments on July 8, 1935, when I was a year old, and he always kept them up. She also agreed with Mister Charlie to limit the size of our family, which was rare in those days. They did this so that their kids would have a better chance of being educated. "We didn't want a house full of half-hungry children," Mister Charlie would say later when we asked him why we didn't have more brothers and sisters. "You can't run hungry. You can't learn nothing hungry. You can't even *think good* hungry."

I went through the first three grades of school in a one-room Louisiana building that was so dilapidated they had to prop up the structure with poles in the winter when the wind blew. Oakland was a different world. We had real desks and teachers for each grade, and all kinds of studies and activities that so excited my mother that she'd make me tell her everything when I came home every day. She'd go through lessons with me and answer my questions and stand up for me whenever I needed it. That warm feeling survived the long jump to California. Every morning I felt I was going out to slay a big dragon for her, and I'd come home from school to tell her how it hadn't stood a chance, just like we'd figured.

School was just beginning in the fall of 1946 when I came home one day to find that my mother had gone into the hospital. It was flu, they said, nothing serious. For the next two weeks whenever we went to visit her she'd laugh and talk about how she had the doctors all confused. After one of those visits Mister Charlie woke us out of a sound sleep a few hours later and said, "Your mother died tonight."

The doctors said it was unexpected, but they didn't even know what that word meant as far as I was concerned. I was twelve. Mother was thirty-two, and she was gone.

The next thing I knew we were on a train back to Louisiana, with the casket in the baggage car just ahead of us. I was in a daze. I remember being cheerful for long stretches of the trip because I was so sure that Mother would come back. For months I'd have dreams of her rocking me awake in the morning, or of her walking into my classroom at school, or appearing out of the tall grass back in Monroe, always hugging me and laughing at the idea that she'd ever leave me. On the train, these visions were much more real than the clacking of the tracks or the eerie silence that enveloped Mister Charlie. Every few hours he'd lead us up to the baggage car; we'd just stand there near the casket for a minute or two and then return to our seats.

All I remember about the funeral was that when they asked me if I wanted to look at my mother's face I refused. After all the crying it was not long before I realized that my future was being discussed in the family councils. Our Louisiana relatives thought Mister Charlie could never raise two young boys by himself out there in California, and they wanted him to move back to Monroe, where he had kinfolk to pitch in and help. When he refused it was assumed that he'd go back to Oakland alone and leave Charlie and me there to be parceled out among our aunties —or at least among the four married ones other than the foot-loose Auntie Kammie. She didn't take part in the discussions, and neither did her father, who had whistled into town for the funeral of his daughter and then whistled on out again before life returned to normal. I would never see him again.

By tradition, Mister Charlie could leave us kids there in Louisiana with absolute assurance that we would be "raised," even if no one ever heard from him again. He could send for us at any time —when he remarried, for instance—or he might never send for us. The extended family would always be there, like a safety net beneath all the children stranded by the hardships of the great black migration out of the South. Over many generations, all the way back to slavery, black families had developed customs for the sheltering and releasing of stray children. There seemed to be intricate rules about which relative would take what child under every circumstance. The taking in was to be done in the closest possible imitation of a natural family, and the giving up was to be done quickly with stoic smiles and a chorus of farewells that it was all for the best.

Years later, sitting in a nightclub somewhere in New York, I was startled at comedian Lenny Bruce's knowledge of black families. Over the course of several evenings he pumped me to find out such things as what it feels like to know that your cousin or aunt can suddenly be transformed into your mother. Bruce admired black families. He thought it would be nice to know that you could go off and get your ass kicked by the world for twenty years and then come back to your kinfolk and be taken in. At the same time he seemed to understand my point that the family would be supporting you only at periods when you were so low that you probably wouldn't appreciate it. "Yeah, but it's still a refuge," he'd say in his harsh accent. Like all the comedians I've known, he seemed serious to the point of being morose when offstage. He'd remark sarcastically that his main family experience had been with the "big family," the Catholic Church, which had enormous political power in all the cities where Bruce performed, and which in his mind was responsible for most of the legal harassment he suffered.

Back then, of course, Lenny Bruce was worlds away from me. At the time, while the adults huddled with each other over my future, I occupied myself by going to see my old friends. This brought another blow; my girl friend Too Little had died the year before, at the age of eleven. It wasn't a romantic loss—I had been stewing over what to tell her about the city girls in Oakland—but it shook me that someone my own age could also die.

The first thing that brought me out of my numbness was Mister Charlie's announcement that he was taking us back to Oakland with him, no matter what the family said. He told everybody that we could make it ourselves, but they seemed doubtful. Our send-off was very emotional; the sadness of the funeral was still heavy, and mingled with the sadness, love and admiration for Mister Charlie as the family's stubborn ambassador to the outside world, I sensed some disapproval.

Mister Charlie was a different man on the trip back to California. Instead of sitting lost in his own thoughts, he talked for almost the whole way just to us, like there was nobody else in the world. He told us that most boys become men when they're old enough to leave their parents but that we'd have to be men early because our mother had left us. He said he had promised our mother before she died that he would send us to college somehow, and he was going to keep that promise. This was why he had to take us with him to California; the opportunities for Negroes were so much greater there than in Louisiana. Besides, he said, nobody could do for his children what he could. But we had to pull together, and being men, we couldn't afford to feel sorry for ourselves. He talked about all the things we'd have to learn to do for ourselves. "We gonna cook," he said. "We gonna wash dishes. We gonna get along. And remember, I've got to work. When I come home I'm gonna be half hot anyway, and I don't want to be raising hell with you about nothing. We gonna wash our clothes. We gonna keep our bed clean. We gonna live like *people*. And you two are gonna get an education." He'd stop for a while, then think of something else and be off again. He kept it up for almost two thousand miles of railroad track. It was an inspired pep talk, probably as much for his own benefit as for ours.

That dose of Mister Charlie's intensity lasted for a long time. We worked like squirrels around the house. I'll admit there were some atrocious meals prepared at our little place in the project, though even today I'm sensitive about the quality of cooking and housework. I think we did fairly well in our own peculiar style, and whenever my brother and I came near to surrendering as the frustrations piled up and the fun passed by, Mister Charlie pushed us on. At the time I had no idea how large a sacrifice he was making for us. He had to give up his hauling business in Oakland because it required too much travel, and he took a lower-paying job doing the hardest kind of work there is: pouring molten iron in a foundry. Still, he was never too tired to laugh and cuff us around when he came home. When my brother became a star athlete in high school and started bragging about how he could run the hundred-yard dash in 10.4 seconds, Mister Charlie listened for as long as he could and then challenged him to a race. As the two of them lined up out on the street with Mister Charlie still wearing his heavy, steel-toed work boots, I thought he might have taken on more than he could handle at his age, but he raced my brother to a dead heat. At least that's the way I called it.

Mister Charlie was long on self-reliance and encouragement but short on sympathy—even shorter than he had been before. He'd always say we couldn't afford that emotion. One day when he was scolding me for something, I stammered around for an excuse until a big wave of self-pity made me blurt out, "Aw, Daddy, I ain't got no mama!"

That set him off. Pain and anger jumped into his face. "Don't give me none of that, boy," he thundered. "I ain't either!"

I could never really tell how much grief Mister Charlie was carrying around about my mother, but everybody could tell about me. It was no secret that I wasn't quite the same person, and people said so. I wasn't reckless any more; in fact, I became a loner and an introvert at about the time all my peers started through such manhood rites as smoking, serious fights and sex. My brother Charlie blossomed into an even more spectacular teen-age success than he had been, but I was held back by serious doubts that I could ever become anything without my mother. The way I saw it, I was paying dearly for having been her favorite. If she had given me a chip on my shoulder, there were a lot of people who were going out of their way to knock it off now. It wasn't so much the neighborhood toughs—though there was some of that—as it was people simply being mean for no reason. A nearby mother would go to my father, for instance, and accuse me of having insulted her. I had no idea why she did it, but Mister Charlie had been in the foundry all day and it was hard for him to believe that she was making something up. He'd wonder about me a little, and so the mother would succeed in sticking a pin in the trust between us. There were countless little malicious incidents like that. The boys I knew could sense that I didn't feel I was the life of the party anymore, and they'd jump on me for it. Or Mister Charlie would start courting a woman, and she'd expect me to baby-sit for her little kid while they went out. Then she'd blame me if anything went wrong at home, or with her and Mister Charlie.

The feeling I had about my mother was a strange kind of emptiness in my chest. It was as if I'd built up a lot of muscles there from lifting weights, and then suddenly the weights were gone. The muscle was flexing for something to attach itself to, but there was nothing except air. Sometimes I'd ache because of the muscle wanting to be used, and at other times I'd feel nauseated because it was in a vacuum.

For months I could think of nothing except all the things I missed about Katie Russell. But one day it occurred to me that I was paying too much for the love she'd given me, and I started thinking that I had been set up—fattened, softened, tenderized and then thrown on the grill. I wondered how she could have done that to me. I felt abandoned, and such thoughts kept creeping up on me no matter how hard I tried to push them away.

As these fears slowly grew numb over the years, I found myself relying more on Mister Charlie. He'd come home talking about how we were going to make it, laughing and telling tales, but he refused to put up with any sentimental nonsense, and gradually I became sure he'd never crack.

Other than Mister Charlie, I relied on books. During this time of withdrawal in junior high I had my own private world, and my most prized possession was my library card from the Oakland Public Library. I went there almost every day, and it was not long after my thirteenth birthday when I read two passages that focused the grief I felt over my mother's death into forces that I've had to contend with ever since. The first passage was in a book on early American history. I was breezing along through a chapter on the American Revolution when I did a double take on one sentence. It was as if somebody had stuck a foot out there on the page and tripped my mind as it went by. I looked again, and this sentence jumped out at me: *Despite the hardships they suffered, most slaves enjoyed a higher standard of living and a better life in America than they had in their primitive African homeland.*

I had to get up and walk out of the library. For weeks afterward I went around in a fog. The sentence stunned me. There it was, written plainly, that people were better off here as slaves than they had been as free people at home. I couldn't believe anyone had the nerve to say something like that, especially in a history book. My brother and I had always had a special reverence for history books; if something was written down in one, we believed it meant you could rely on it without question. History was the final referee of what was true. We had one in the house, and we used to settle arguments by saying, "Let's look it up in the book." And now, here in a history book was an attack on my very essence as a person.

That day in the library is still vivid to me. I remember that I was sitting at a long table, with my right forearm across the top of the open book and my left forefinger running down the page, the way I used to read. I remember being so taken aback by the sentence that I couldn't swallow. I thought of "darkest Africa" pretty much the way young white boys must have thought of it, as a place where Tarzan ran around among animals and witch doctors. I didn't know or care what slavery or Africa was really like, but I was repulsed by the idea that life could be better without freedom. To me, being a slave meant you had to buckle under.

As far as I can remember, this was the first time I was ever enraged. I had been scared before, like once when a white man chased me across a field in Louisiana threatening to "hang" me for throwing a pebble at his car. I also had been afraid and hurt when my mother died. But I hadn't been angry, because such occasions were too big and I was too small. They were simply things I discovered as the world revealed itself to me—no different from discovering comic books, schoolrooms or crocodiles, except that they hurt. But there in the library, with another hurt, it was as if I could say *no*. For the first time I felt grounded in anger, and it would last for years to come.

It was in the Oakland library that I discovered one of my favorite books, Richard Halliburton's *Complete Marvels of the World*. I loved to browse through his stories about the pyramids, the Hanging Gardens of Babylon, the Taj Mahal and the other marvels he had visited around the world. One day I came upon the chapter on Christophe's Citadel. Halliburton called Christophe "the most masterful Negro in history," describing how the man had joined a bloody slave revolt against the French and had gone on to become emperor of Haiti. As a slave, Christophe was a dishwasher, but as emperor he fought and defeated the armies of Napoleon himself, and then built a magnificent though brutal kingdom, topped off by the construction of his Citadel on the crest of a 3,000-foot peak near the Caribbean. The Citadel, I learned, was the greatest monument in the Western world built by black people, and Haiti became the first free black country in our hemisphere.

Christophe sent chills up and down my spine. I read everything I could find about him, and every new story made him bigger in my eyes. He was shrewd. In his war against Napoleon he made a convenient alliance with another of Napoleon's enemies, England, but he didn't trust the British. "As soon as we get rid of

Napoleon," he said, "they'll turn on us and try to conquer Haiti for themselves." So he tried to keep the British wary of him. According to one story, he once held a council of war strategy at the Citadel, during which a British general boasted that England had the most tightly disciplined army in the world.

"No, it doesn't," said Christophe. "*I* do." An argument broke out, and Christophe finally took the British generals to the outer walls of his fortress to offer proof. The Citadel's walls were so wide that the soldiers used them for a parade ground. Christophe walked to within earshot of a company of his own soldiers marching along the wall. "Column left!" he shouted, and the soldiers promptly turned left and stepped off the wall to their deaths in perfect order. They went off steadily and silently, row by row, so afraid of Christophe that not one of them made the slightest sound of protest. The soldiers didn't cry out, but the British generals did; they begged Christophe to stop the slaughter, shouting that he had made his point. But Christophe stood there without a word and let the whole company plunge to its death. Later he said that in fact his action had saved lives, since the British seemed to lose interest in attacking Haiti after this episode.

Christophe was a monster, but he lived with such grandiose flair that I couldn't help being awed. He built lavish palaces for himself and his queen; he practiced an odd mixture of voodoo and Buddhism, which he celebrated according to his own deadly whims; and he created a whole Haitian royal family in mockery of the European masters he had driven from his land. As I recall, there was a Duke of Marmalade and a Countess of Lemonade. As his madness grew he enslaved his own people, and drove three thousand workers mercilessly for ten years to build his Citadel. He ordered the women slaves to carry eight ten-pound bricks up the mountain each trip, and soldiers had to drag cannons up with ropes. Once a soldier objected when Christophe assigned twenty-man squads to bring each piece of heavy artillery up to the construction site. Twenty men, he protested to the emperor, were not enough; it would take at least fifty. Christophe had the soldier shot, along with the four soldiers nearest him when he protested.

Then he said he'd bet that the fifteen men left in the squad could get the cannon up the mountain themselves. They did.

Like the pyramids in Egypt, the Citadel remains an architectural miracle because of its technological mysteries and the unbelieveable feats of human labor it required. The colossal structure perched atop a cone-shaped mountain has puzzled engineers, who calculate that with no foundation support it cannot stand the way Christophe built it. But it has lasted a century and a half. One off-season when I was with the Celtics, I made a trip to Haiti just to climb that endless footpath and see the Citadel's ruins. The view over the surrounding valley is spectacular, but what really took my breath away was a sense of Christophe's presence in this huge pile of stone and brick. I saw a quicklime pit in the center of one courtyard, in which brass buttons from Christophe's uniform were found, along with the bullet he killed himself with, rather than be tortured to death by his mutinous army. When the aged and insane emperor fell sick, partially paralyzed by a stroke, the army finally revolted, and his spell was broken. Christophe's family, so the story goes, dumped his body into the vat of quicklime so that the rampaging soldiers could not mutilate it.

As a thirteen-year-old kid in the Oakland Public Library, I never dreamed, of course, that I would ever see the Citadel. But at a time in my life when I was meek and shy, I would thrill every time I read about how Christophe outfoxed another general, or how he drove people to accomplish the impossible. Part of me identified with him even after I grew old enough to be revolted by his cruelty and tyranny over his own people. I know better than to admire him, but part of me still does so.

Henri Christophe was my first hero after my mother. To me, he was just the opposite of a slave: *he would not be one.* He was indomitable. I think his life brought home to me for the first time that being black was not just a limiting feeling. Christophe could not be held back by anything, and his power reminded me of my mother. She too believed that anyone could command any stage; all that was required was the right style and strength. My father and the Old Man had their own kind of strength; it was wise and deep, and it endured. But it didn't have the same kind of romance or sparkle that I had gotten from my mother.

Mister Charlie was so tough over the years that I sometimes thought I was the only one who never saw his big, generous, amiable side. He always carried more than his load for me and always encouraged me to keep working, but he went out of his way not to indulge me. As a father, he was like one of those hawks that will fight any enemy for its young but that always kicks the little one out of the nest for a trial flight just when it wants to get warm. He expected my brother and me to get along in school without any worry on his part. Charlie and I even signed each other's report cards all the way through school; Mister Charlie said that they were for us, not for him, because failure in school would hurt us more than him. He'd give us the opportunity; we had to do the rest.

When I turned sixteen I asked Mister Charlie to take me down to get my driver's license like all the other kids. His reaction was typical. "What do you want a license for?" he asked. "You ain't got no car."

"Well," I said, "I thought maybe you'd let me borrow your car every now and then."

He looked at me as if I were crazy and said he wasn't about to pour extra iron at the foundry to buy extra gas and insurance so that I could goof off for my own pleasure. I could get a license as soon as I could afford a car, he said. I thought he might as well have locked me away in a dungeon, but though he would break his back for my food and education, he didn't believe in lifting a finger for my pleasures or vices. Never, even after I was in college, did he offer to buy me a beer. "If anybody's gonna get drunk off my money," he'd say, "it's gonna be *me*."

Once Mister Charlie caught me red-handed smoking a cigarette. I had been taking great pains to keep my habit secret for at least three years, and I was mortified. "Don't look so scared, son," he laughed. "I know you been smoking all these years. You been stinking up the closet almost every night. Who did you think you were fooling?"

He was laughing at me. I was embarrassed, and angry that he'd let me stuff myself in that closet all that time. "How come you didn't tell me you knew?" I asked.

"Because as long as you were hiding it," he said, "I knew you wouldn't be bothering me for money to buy those things."

Mister Charlie showed me only two soft emotions: laughter and pride. He was democratic about humor and would laugh even if the joke was on him. And he would glow whenever I did something well—which was not often during my early teens. There was a flip side to the pride, however, and this was the old Russell stubbornness, the peacock feathers. We both had it. Once we had an argument over a little money I'd saved for a rainy day. I wanted some new clothes to wear when I began college, so of course I felt it was pouring right then. Mister Charlie said it wasn't raining hard enough. The feud went on for my entire freshman year. He came to every basketball game I played in, but we didn't speak. We were each sure we were right. I knew Christophe wouldn't have backed down, and Mister Charlie knew the Old Man wouldn't have either.

The war of silence went on for nearly nine months before my brother finally interceded. First he went to Mister Charlie and said, "William is really sorry. He wants to talk to you, but he's too stubborn to apologize." Then he came to me and said the same thing. By repeating these identical stories over and over, he finally managed to get Mister Charlie and me together. We both mumbled what passed for apologies, and the stalemate ended.

In the summer of 1953, after my freshman year in college, I drove down to Louisiana to visit the Old Man. By then he was over seventy and retired, but he hadn't changed much and was still the center of attention. He still had fruit in his house all the time, and three cats with three little doors for them to enter and leave his house. When I asked him why he had three doors when one would do, he smiled and gave me the same answer he always had: "When I say scat, boy, I mean scat!" It always made me laugh.

The Old Man was still a drayman, except that he didn't do it for money any longer, and about all he carried were old people. His job was "taking care of the old people." Many of them were younger than he was, but he would never have referred to himself as old. His role was a combination of minister, chauffeur, father, listener, deliveryman and overall spirit-lifter—and he filled the job because he loved it and because no one else had the energy or the respect required. He was on the move constantly, making his rounds, making sure people had a way to get to church, to the doctor or to the store, or delivering mail, a message or some fresh fruit. I still don't know how he came up with all that fresh fruit. Every day of my visit that summer I tagged along the way I had as a boy. By now I was a strapping young athlete, but I could barely keep up with the Old Man, and my tongue would be dragging when he finally headed home.

I had grown nearly two feet taller since leaving Monroe and had developed arms as long as shovels. I was very aware of my new size and athletic prowess that summer, jumping around and peering down at things I had once looked up at, but nobody else in Monroe cared about my sports reputation. To them I was still old Mr. Russell's grandbaby.

Things were a little different on my next visit, in 1955. That season, our University of San Francisco basketball team had lost only one game and had won the national championship. I was an All-American and living the college athlete's dream. To top it off, Mister Charlie and I drove all the way across the country to have dinner with President Eisenhower at the White House. This really knocked people out in West Oakland—a Negro getting invited to supper with the Main Man. Actually I was a little swell-headed at the time and made sure people knew that the President couldn't shake *me* up, no matter how many D-Days he'd launched.

On the way back, Mister Charlie and I drove by way of Louisiana. In Mississippi, Mister Charlie got into another scrape with a gas-station attendant. It all started when he walked into the station's restroom instead of the "Colored" outhouse in the back. The man pumping our gas instantly lost control, yanked the nozzle out of the tank and slammed it back in the pump. Sitting there in the car, I had a sinking feeling that the only way he was going to feel better was if he and a few friends got to beat somebody up. The feeling grew stronger when Mister Charlie came out of the restroom and answered the man's hostile questions with simple yeses and noes and a lack of deference that will drive your average nigger-hating cracker up the wall.

This fellow was definitely up the wall, but he was also suspicious about something. "Boy, what do you do, anyway?" he asked Mister Charlie.

"We're, er, ah, United States, Federal," said Mister Charlie. "That's who we're with."

I couldn't believe it; Mister Charlie was pulling a number on this guy. When I yanked my head around to look at them out the back window, I saw the white man staring intently at our University of San Francisco window sticker—U.S.F. I could barely contain myself.

"I *thought* you was some of them big fellers," said the attendant, shaking his head like he was on to something. "Where y'all coming from?"

"We just finished some business up in Washington," Mister Charlie said confidently.

"That's what I figured," sighed the attendant. He had us wired as Feds, and it took all the starch out of him. "You fellers stop in any time, you hear?" he said, real friendly.

Mister Charlie took off, beaming. About a hundred yards down the road I exploded in laughter, and I kept laughing for at least twenty miles.

"Boy, this world will make you tell some tales," laughed Mister Charlie. When we cruised on into Monroe, tales of my success and the story of Mister Charlie and the U.S.F. sticker went round the town.

The Old Man was just the same, making his rounds and receiving visitors. That summer I saw how he could bring out Mister Charlie's soft side, and I figured he was the only man alive who could do it. There was a huge old oak tree in front of the house in Monroe, which the Old Man himself had planted as a boy. In the late afternoon, between visitors, the two of them would sit under it and have some time to themselves, the Old Man in his chair and Mister Charlie next to him on the ground. The Old Man would put his hand on Mister Charlie's head and rub it while they talked for hours, and I would stand off and watch from a respectful distance.

I visited Monroe again in 1962, after six seasons of professional basketball. The Celtics had won championships in five of those six years, building a sports dynasty, and I was just coming off my third season as Most Valuable Player in the league. I had all the trimmings of a professional star, including a new steel-gray Lincoln convertible. When I pulled up into the Old Man's front yard, it looked like a spaceship, and black people came from all over town to gawk at it.

I had brought my two young sons, Buddha and Jacob, to see the Old Man, and I was steaming because it had been so difficult to feed them while driving through the South. There I was, a sports star with at least two thousand dollars in cash in my pocket, driving a big fancy car and looking way too big for ordinary men to mess with; yet people turned me away at restaurant after restaurant. My sons kept complaining of hunger and asking those penetrating child's questions, and for the first time I appreciated what Mister Charlie must have gone through as a father nearly twenty years earlier. I couldn't find a decent hotel that would let us spend the night, either, so I put the top up on the Lincoln and we napped by the side of the road.

So on arriving in Monroe I was in no mood to indulge my assembled aunties (other than Auntie Kammie) as they jumped around holding a piece of paper with a phone number on it. "This white man called you," they said excitedly. "He's from the newspaper!" It was a big event for them, so they were shocked when I said I had no intention of putting myself through an interview. My aunties looked at me as if I were Nat Turner.

The Old Man ignored all the fuss around his house and went off to take care of the old people. He was about eighty then—we were never sure of his exact age—but seemed spry as ever. My sons became the third generation of Russells to tag along behind him.

I had lost track of Auntie Kammie by the time I was old enough to understand much about her, and Mister Charlie had told me almost everything I knew. On one of his trips back to Monroe while I was playing pro basketball, Mister Charlie happened by the old juke joint for a drink and some conversation. While he was sitting there with the old gang, a little man with a large straw hat on his head came over to his table and whispered that he had to meet him outside right away. That juke joint could be a fairly rough place, and the little man had spoken in a menacing voice, like a conspirator, so Mister Charlie was wary. But he figured he could still handle such a small fellow if he had to, so he pushed his way through the crowd and walked outside to where the little guy was waiting.

The conversation was awkward. When Mister Charlie asked what was going on, the little man took his hat off and stood there. Finally he said, "Don't you know me? It's Sammy."

Auntie Kammie always called herself Sammy. Mister Charlie couldn't believe it. Fifteen years or more had passed since he'd last seen her, and she had a touch of gray on her head. He grabbed his sister-in-law around the shoulders and swung her around him several times like a dancer. It was an emotional moment for both of them. Auntie Kammie was apparently worried about whether she could trust Mister Charlie after all these years, and he was embarrassed about not recognizing her. "Sure I was gonna hug her," he said. "She's my family. Beside, God may want her to be like that, for all I know." He and Auntie Kammie went back in the juke joint and had drinks just like any two other guys. He even claimed to have actually bought her a drink or two, which is a rare honor by him.

During my own visits to Louisiana one thing I did not hear much about was basketball. Neither the Old Man nor my aunties cared about the game; it was foreign to them. It must have seemed strange to them that this young man of their family, who could not even eat in Monroe's restaurants, could be toasted and paid astronomical amounts of money to play with a ball in front of white audiences. It made even less sense to them than the idea that I was simply chosen for these honors by some magical force, like my mother's blessing or God's mysterious will. And how could I argue with them?

The Old Man and I never had a single conversation about the sport. We always talked about the same subjects. He was interested in my career only as it affected my dignity and values. Was I away from home too much to be a good father to my kids? Did I understand money? Was I at peace with myself? He saw only one basketball game in his life, and what he noticed about it had nothing to do with the scoreboard. It was in 1967, my next-to-last season with the Celtics, and I was the player-coach. We were playing an exhibition game against the St. Louis (now Atlanta) Hawks in Alexandria, Louisiana, and Mister Charlie drove all the way from California to take the Old Man to see me play.

It was a big day for all three of us. As Mister Charlie drove into the parking lot at the arena it became clear that the Old Man was absorbed with worries about the color line, which just then was breaking. Anxiously, seeing no colored section, as there still was in the local courthouses, he asked where they would sit at the game, and Mister Charlie told him they'd sit wherever their tickets said to. The Old Man took that in and bided his time. Before the game started Mister Charlie introduced him to Bob Petit, one of the best players ever and my old rival from the Hawks. By then Petit was retired and living in Louisiana. Mister Charlie was so conscious of the Old Man's nervousness that he introduced Bob as "Mr. Petit" and threw out so many "Yes, sir's" and "No, sir's" that finally Bob interrupted him. "What's got into you, Mister Charlie?" he asked with a laugh. "When did you start calling me Mister?" The two of them had known each other for more than ten years. Mister Charlie apologized and after that talked the way he usually did. The Old Man took this in, too.

At half time the Old Man looked for the colored restroom, and his son marched him right in to piss with the white folks.

During the game Mister Charlie got all wound up trying to explain basketball strategy to his father, telling him about presses, fast breaks, rookies, the foul situation and everything else he could think of that might be on the coach's mind. The Old Man listened hard, but asked only one question: "Do them white boys really have to do what William tells them to do?"

When Mister Charlie said yes, the Old Man just shook his head.

Down on the court I was preoccupied with basketball and only heard about all this after the game. Mister Charlie came into the dressing room with the Old Man, his buttons busting over the Old Man's adventures that day. As he started telling me about it, Grandpa wandered off. After a few minutes we saw him standing not far away. Panic shot through both of us: the Old Man was crying. I thought he was having a heart attack; I had never seen him cry. We rushed over, feeling the awful choke of helplessness. Then, we both saw that he was not in pain. He was staring as if stunned, transfixed by the sight of Sam Jones and John Havlicek in the shower nearby. My two teammates were busily lathering up and talking, oblivious to the Old Man's emotion.

"What's the matter, Papa?" Mister Charlie asked anxiously.

The Old Man looked up at us and made a slow pronouncement. "I never thought I'd live to see the day when the water would run off a white man onto a black man," he said, "and the water would run off a black man onto a white man." He kept shaking his head. "I've been to church all of my days, but I never thought I'd see anything like this. You know, I can tell those two men *like* each other."

The Old Man really got to me that day. Right there, in the midst of postgame clatter, locker-room talk, reporters, and towels being thrown around, he froze time for an instant to articulate what he would take home with him from his first and only basketball game.

According to Mister Charlie, the Old Man had come to grips with the experience by the time they got back to Monroe that night. He'd talk to himself about the water running from black to white, and with every telling he gained confidence. Pretty soon he was laughing as he told people what he'd seen. He told everybody. People would come over to his house just to hear him repeat the story again. Mister Charlie said the Old Man must have told the story once for each drop of water he'd seen in the shower.

•   •   •

My grandfather was overwhelmed by what he'd seen and what it meant, my father was grateful for it, and I, the young ornery one, was looking way past the showers to the dark corners where I saw bigotry still hiding. But I think we all had a gritty, independent framework; they were different, but somehow the same. The Old Man wouldn't leave Monroe, see foreign lands or develop the slightest interest in certain aspects of modern life, but he could judge by the standards he had chosen for himself, and he chose them with his usual strong grip. He was the kind of man who could decide to stay where he was and yet convince you that he knew what he was sacrificing. That's the feeling he gave when he stayed behind in Monroe.

It's also the feeling Mister Charlie aroused when he decided to stay on in the foundry after I offered to fix it so that he'd never have to work again. In 1965, when I signed a contract to play basketball for well over $100,000 a year, I called him and told him that now I had enough money to pay him a full salary *not* to pour that molten iron any more. I almost begged him to quit, but he turned me down without hesitation. "Of *course* I'm gonna stay here and work," he said. "I've given this place eighteen of the best years out of my life, and now I'm gonna give them a few of the bad ones." That made me laugh myself dry. Later he said that he could never be dependent on another man to provide his own living, and that in any case he wouldn't know what to do without working.

In 1969 Mister Charlie called me to say that the Old Man was sick in bed. Since it was a matter of record in our family that he had never spent a single day of his life in bed, we both knew that Grandpa was dying. He went quickly, and I flew home for my first Louisiana funeral since my mother's.

I was numb, and feeling guilty that all the love I felt for the Old Man wouldn't erupt in tears. At the time my own life was torn apart by so many things—the least of which was the end of my basketball career—that my attention kept wandering. I was furious with myself for being so distracted. It was as if my mind was being attacked by a swarm of bees. Never had I felt so cut off from what made me. It was not until two years later that I

really felt the impact of the Old Man's death. I was visiting
Mister Charlie in Oakland, where he was still going strong in the
foundry, and suddenly he got real serious on me. "You know, I
watched you in college, winning those championships," he said.
"And I used to go on all the trips. And I watched you be so good
in the pros and make so much of yourself. I even went to Boston
a few times. But the proudest I've ever been of you is when I saw
you get off the plane to come to my father's funeral."

That's when I first realized that the Old Man was really gone.
Mister Charlie has said many times that my grandfather plowed
deep in the heart.

It was also several years after the funeral that I realized
something else: that I had not gone with the rest of the family to my mother's grave to pay respect to her memory. I went
out of my way to avoid it, as I had on every trip to Louisiana
since 1946. In my usual fashion, I didn't even acknowledge to
myself for more than a decade that this was peculiar. I kept
telling myself that visiting graves was morbid, not my style.
But a few years ago I could no longer avoid the notion that
there was something else to it. The idea jumped out at me
from one of the sayings I use all the time. If I'm angry with
someone, I'll say, "He'll let you down if he has to die to do
it." And if I'm talking about a close friend, I'll say, "He'd
have to die before he'd let you down." For years I had been
accustomed to thinking of these remarks as jokes. That happens to me a lot; I get used to thinking of something as a
joke, and it never occurs to me that there's another meaning
underneath. But I think I must have known all along that I
was talking about my mother, and it was just too painful to
admit it. To do so, I would have had to admit that I was
being selfish in feeling that she died for no other reason than
to abandon me. I had to see that I still blamed her, and that
my anger had poisoned my feelings toward all women. Every
time I started getting close to someone, I'd pull back and protect myself. I had never really let her die. It was one of those
longstanding Russell grudges, and it was one that hurt me and
a lot of people around me.

Even now, more than thirty years after her death, I have never visited my mother's grave. But I will soon, on my next visit to Louisiana, because I am making peace with the one in the family who first believed that I was special.

2

Magic

During my junior year in high school, in 1950, I had a mystical revelation. One day while I was walking down the hall from one class to another, by myself as usual, it suddenly dawned on me that it was all right to be who I was. The thought just came to me: "Hey, you're all right. Everything is all right." The idea was hardly earthshaking, but I was a different person by the time I reached the end of the hall. Had I been methodical I would have immediately written down my thoughts. Over and over again I received the idea that everything was all right about me—so vividly that the thought seemed to have colors on it. I remember looking around in class to make sure the other kids didn't think I was acting strange.

Those moments in the hall are the closest I've come to a religious experience. For all I know, it may have actually been one. A warm feeling fell on me out of nowhere. I wondered why the idea hadn't occurred to me before; everything seemed to fall into place, the way it does for a kid when he first understands simple multiplication.

Everybody remembers the "Aha!" sensation when a good idea hits you. I remember sitting in a logic class at the University of San Francisco, puzzling over something the priest had been ex-

plaining to us for the previous few days. Then it came to me. Bells
went off; the mental pleasure was so great that I jumped as if
someone had pinched me and yelled "Hey!"

The priest said, "Congratulations, Mr. Russell. You have just
had your first real and complete thought. How does it feel?" He
was patronizing me, but I didn't care because he had just given
me a new way of seeing things.

What I saw in the hallway at high school that day was more
than just an idea; it was a way out of self-rejection. In the four
years since my mother had died, everybody I encountered felt that
there was something wrong with me. Worse, I *agreed* with them.
I was clumsy at everything. When I opened a soup can, it felt as
if I was trying to take apart a watch with a sledgehammer. I was
insulted all the time. At my first and only football practice the
coach lined up players to run over me all afternoon, and then
complained to the team that he'd gotten the "bum of the family"
instead of my brother, who was a star football player at a rival high
school. I dropped football, swallowed my pride and went out for
the cheerleading team. I didn't even make that. I was the classic
ninety-pound weakling—except that nobody would have dreamed
of using my picture in an advertisement.

The white cops in Oakland stopped me on the streets all the
time, grilled me and routinely called me "nigger." Whenever they
said it, it put me in such a state that I would shrivel up inside and
think, "Oh, God. They're right." I gave everybody the benefit of
the doubt—friends who ignored me, strangers who were mean—
because I thought they were probably justified.

All this changed after that trip down the hall. I finished classes
that day and went home feeling as if some golden bird had landed
on my shoulder. Every time I checked to see if it was still there,
I half expected it to be gone. Maybe it would leave just as mysteri-
ously as it had come, and then I'd turn back into my old self. I
remember going to bed that night thinking that sleep would be
the real test. If I still had the warm feeling the next morning, I
told myself, I'd accept the change as permanent; otherwise it
would be just another of life's mysteries. I was so eager to find out
whether I could keep this new gift that it took me hours to doze
off.

I woke up the next morning and checked my mind to see what thoughts were in it. "Hey, you're all right," my mind told me, and I realized the feeling was still there. I jumped out of bed so happy that I embarrassed myself; you could have made moonbeams out of my smile. I decided I was a man.

From that day on, whenever I've felt hostility from someone, I've assumed that it was their problem rather than mine. It was just the opposite from the way I had been before. The teachers at McClymonds High School seemed different to me, for example. I knew that nearly all the teachers did not like their students, and since I had always looked up to these teachers as adults and authority figures, I'd assumed they must be right; there must be something wrong with all of us. But after my revelation I decided that there was nothing wrong with me, or with most of the other kids, so it must be the teachers.

There *was* something wrong with them. They were stuck in a ghetto school at low pay, trapped there just as firmly as their pupils. None of the kids really expected to go to college, and very few of the faculty expected to go anywhere either. It was not a school that inspired high hopes for anybody, and most of the teachers were bitter about it. They ran kids through "job-training" classes that consisted mainly of personal errands. They prepared kids for the harsh realities of the outside world by deflating their dreams with cynical comments. Once I almost told a teacher that I wanted to be an architect, but I stopped myself; I knew what she would say.

Hostility and failure were still all around me, but I no longer accepted responsibility for them. Now people had a hard time making me feel guilty, and those who called me "nigger" saw me raise my hackles instead of tucking in my tail. I kept telling myself that it was all right to be who I was, and if I was all right, then anybody who insulted me when I was minding my own business deserved to be pushed back into his own territory. That's what I tried to do. I had a lot of fights in my late teens, and I was big enough to win most of them. My cowering look turned into a glowering one. The adults in my neighborhood, who seemed to notice every inch I grew as I pushed up past them, said I was growing up.

The process of growing up was anything but routine. In fact, I don't think I even *would* have if it hadn't been for that revelation which shook me out of self-hatred. It gave me a sense of confidence. At that time, no reasonable person could have looked at me or the circumstances of my life and predicted that I would accomplish anything. I was trapped and basically untalented; I had a way of gnawing on my failures as if they were leftovers from yesterday's lunch; and even after that day in the hall, I had no great sense of purpose. There were no thoughts of being a president or a star. I was still aimless, but one crucial factor had changed: whatever happened to me, I realized, I would still know that I was not fundamentally flawed. And if *I* knew that, what other people thought didn't matter. Most of them were probably attacking me because of some failing that they saw in themselves. I was basically sound, everything looked brighter to me, and I had a new sense of wonder. It was like waking up.

I knew at the time that this was a significant event in my life, but I didn't realize just how important it was. I was only sixteen, after all, and so every little change would look big. I kept waiting for something to come along and top the experience, something just as startling but more mature that I couldn't even imagine. But many experiences have come and gone in the decades since, and I'm still waiting for something to have a greater impact on me. Kids think that their really important life will begin when they're an adult, but many adults realize later that the important things in their lives happened when they were kids.

Magic interested me a lot in those days. I wondered if there was magic in the universe. If not, how could I explain my revelation? As far as I could tell, it came for no reason. Magic had preoccupied me for a long time, going back to the days of the haints in Louisiana and to my mother's stories about how I was charmed, but it was not something I thought about seriously until high school. I could see both sides. On magic's behalf I could easily accept the idea, for instance, that the earth could lie as barren as the moon for thirty-five thousand years after a nuclear holocaust, without a single weed growing, and that then, suddenly everything could start growing again. Poof, like magic. I still believe that most of what people really care about comes from the realm of magic—sex, religion, art, the spark in someone's personality.

But I also see so much logic in nature that I'm inclined to believe the scientists' theory that there is a logical explanation for everything, including how the universe got there. We just don't know enough yet. Scientists are fascinated by magic, probably more so than astrologers or mystics, but they want to evaporate all magical happenings with the heat of their intelligence. That can be very boring.

I have gone around and around in my internal debate about magic. To deny it completely would be to set myself against the special moments I've experienced. Of course I could relate to them by denying the very quality that made them special—their magic. I could claim that the magic I have known was a product of ignorance on my part, that it was only an unsolved problem. But I can't do that. I have to allow a place in my world for magic. Still, how big a place? Everything I've seen in my travels tells me that if you let magic get its foot in the door, pretty soon that foot will be on your neck. Once you allow for magic's existence, you'll soon be explaining all sorts of unknowns and taboos with rules and formulas based on magic—and from there it's a short jump to superstition and bigotry. My guess is that racism, most wars, and all religious dogmas originated as innocent bits of magic. Somewhere back in dim history, somebody saw something go poof, and he felt warm and awed. His experience itself was a mystery, and magic was the answer. Everybody who heard about the experience got the same feeling, and they all wanted answers. Eventually the magic would become the source of power, interpretations, rules, punishments and heartache.

The compromise I've worked out for myself is designed to keep magic in its place. I believe in magic's first seed, that first marvelous moment of awe when the feeling seems to glow like a lightning bug. It's the kind of rush you get when you discover how amazing nature is while climbing around in the Rocky Mountains or chugging down the Congo River. That flash of awe is the heart of religion; it's more of a question than an answer. Or maybe it's just an intense appreciation for feeling able to ask such big questions. Whatever it is, it's very personal. I don't try to communicate my thoughts on the sources or implications of magic because I think the very process of explaining ruins it. Ask me a thousand different questions about religion and I'll say only that I believe there's something going on out there that fills me with joy and wonder.

It's one thing to have your vision in some romantic place like the peak of Mount Kilimanjaro; it's quite another to have it at McClymonds High School in West Oakland. It was so unexpected that I didn't know what to do with it. But though there was no outlet for the new optimism, I didn't really care at the time. Then I gradually woke up to basketball, which was well suited to my new confidence. In fact, I developed more assurance in just about everything except women. Over the years I've decided that the magic of women comes from an entirely different department in the store.

I showed an ineptitude for romance with the very first three girl friends in my life. In my dreams I made sweet music, but when I was awake it sounded as if I were plucking a harp with a garden rake. When my new strength appeared I had trouble sorting out the good aspects of being confident from the bad ones.

First there was Phyllis. I met her in 1950, when I was a junior in high school. It all started when a boy named Johnny Rivers and I started shoving each other in class, and after the teacher broke it up we agreed to meet after school and fight it out. Fortunately, we had the good sense not to tell anybody where the fight would be, so nobody came to egg us on. Both of us showed up in a mood to negotiate, and when it got right down to it we decided not to fight; in fact, we decided to be friends. We started having lunch together, and that's where I met Phyllis. I fell madly in love with her at first sight. She had skin the color of a new penny, and the blackest hair I'd ever seen. I used to study her face so much I'd lose all track of our conversation. I'd be looking at her, and suddenly my eyes would zoom in on a tiny part of her and blow it up big in my mind's eye, and that's all I would see. Bells clanged

and whistles blew, like the pipes under a merry-go-round. I figured
I was in love.

Johnny was a musician who played drum gigs on the weekends,
and Phyllis wanted to be a dancer; so they talked about music a
lot. But there was nothing else between them. By my standards
then, they both seemed to have a lot of money, and every day they
would go to a restaurant at the corner of 12th and Market for
lunch. Going outside school for lunch was pretty fancy. My father
was struggling to earn money in the foundry and could only give
me a quarter for the standard fare at the school cafeteria. I was
desperate to see Phyllis, so every day during lunch I would wander
over to the restaurant, trying to look as if I'd just eaten, and ask
Phyllis and Johnny if I could join them for dessert. Pie à la mode
cost a quarter, and that's what I'd have. I'd try not to look hungry
when it was gone.

I went through this ordeal every day for months. We'd sit there
for about thirty minutes, and Phyllis made me forget my stomach.
I almost never spoke but that was all right; I'd sit there and
fantasize about rescuing her, marrying her and winning duels for
her. But finally it started to bother me that I was just an extra
presence there, and I made up my mind to tell her how I felt.

One day the two of us were walking back from lunch, and I
took a whole bunch of deep breaths. "Hey, there's something I
want to talk to you about," I said—which was probably as many
words as I had ever said to her in one spurt.

She said, "Okay," and waited for me to say something.

I decided I wasn't quite ready. "Let's wait till we get back to
school," I said.

We kept walking. My palms were sweating, but my whole body
was a goose-pimple farm. I stalled for as long as I could. Just
outside the school she stopped, and I asked her to wait until we
got to the top of the stairs. Finally I'd run out of time, and she
asked, "All right, what is it?"

"Well, I really like you," I said.

"That's nice, because I like you, too."

I was not prepared for her answer, and figured there was a
misunderstanding. "No, no, no," I said. "You don't really know

what I mean. There are two ways a guy can like a girl. He can either like her as a friend, or he can like her the way a guy likes a girl. I like you the way a guy likes a girl."

"Well, that's the way I like you, too." She gave me a smile of encouragement and waited for me to make the next move.

I was stunned. I'd start to smile and then my head would cloud up with worry. Something wasn't right, but I had no idea what it was. I couldn't believe this was happening. Phyllis began to look puzzled by my confusion, so I managed a smile. Finally, without a word, I gave her a very significant nod and walked off as nonchalantly as I could. I hoped she'd think it was a normal way to end our first intimate conversation.

I did not speak to Phyllis again for six years. Not one word. I quit going to the restaurant for pie à la mode, and I didn't even say hello to her in the halls for the rest of the way through high school. Whenever I saw her walking down the street I'd walk three blocks out of my way. Way to go, Russell, I kept telling myself; the girl of your dreams is waiting, and you're frozen up like a water pipe. She was as beautiful as ever to me, but I kept avoiding her.

Years later Phyllis and I had coffee when I was with the Celtics and after she'd joined the Air Force. We laughed about our strange romance and decided it was sheer panic.

In the eleventh grade I went after Betty. She was plain and insecure, just the opposite of Phyllis. I made a point of walking home from school beside her, and every day another kid would appear out of nowhere and walk the last bit of the way with us. He was her boyfriend, I learned, but it didn't seem to bother them that I was there. Betty would wait for me and act hurt if I was late. I knew she'd be waiting, so I always showed up; I didn't know how to get out of it. When I finally got up the nerve to ask her to go out with me, she said she didn't have an available night for three weeks. I thought she was trying to brush me off, but I agreed to wait. I think she was impressed with my determination. We made a date to go to the movies. To save enough money for a real evening I started skipping lunch again. Every night for three weeks I hid my unused quarter in my little corner in our place in the housing project. Apparently you had to starve to get anywhere with girls, and the pain was almost unbearable. Even in those days I ate the way a buzz saw cuts through wood. I was already six foot five and about one hundred and forty pounds, with a physique like a nail. My arms and legs were out of control, and I moved like a newborn colt. Food was my great joy, but it was worth not eating if it would help me with Betty.

When I showed up for the big night, Betty wasn't ready. I was prepared for this and waited on the sofa downstairs, trying to make small talk with her parents. While I was waiting, her boyfriend waltzed through the door and said he had come to take Betty out. I gaped at him, and the parents were embarrassed. Nobody knew what to do. When Betty appeared, her mother bluntly asked her which one of us she was going out with. Betty pointed to me, and I heaved a sigh of relief. Then she pointed to the other guy. Back and forth; she couldn't make up her mind. Finally all three of us took off for the movies. The boyfriend must have had plenty of money, because he insisted on paying for Betty. I guess he had a job.

When we got home from the show, the three of us stood around awkwardly. Then suddenly the other kid said, "Excuse me," and started kissing Betty. Before I could blink he had her locked in an embrace. Betty gave me a sympathetic look over his shoulder, but kept right on kissing him. I couldn't believe it; it was the first time I had ever seen people kissing passionately in real life. There seemed nothing to do but walk away.

The next year, as a senior, I started watching a girl I used to call Nitro (as in nitroglycerine) because I could never tell when she would explode on me. In fact, I could never tell when she was going to do *anything*. All I knew was that she was tall, already had a kid, and teased the sharpest boys in school. Naturally, I decided she was my type, so I started studying her from a safe distance. After several weeks I got up the nerve to say something to her. She gave me the kind of cold, final hello that could float across a room and bolt the doors shut.

After a few more weeks I concluded that my best approach would be to call her. This seemed foolproof, so I stopped her in the hall one day and asked if I could.

"I don't want to talk to you," she said sassily, the way she usually talked to the boys. Then a look of genuine puzzlement came across her face, and she scrunched up her nose. "What would I want to talk to *you* for?"

That question pretty well finished me off, and I didn't chase any more girls in high school. Whenever I was around one, I felt the way I had before my revelation: my confidence would vanish so fast that I couldn't believe I'd ever had any.

Having two personalities, both of them real, threw me off balance. I would misjudge a situation in one role and then over-compensate with the other. Can you imagine the trouble a juggler would have if half his oranges weighed an ounce and the other half weighed ten pounds? That's the trouble I had.

It was only by the sheerest luck that I developed an outlet for my confidence. There is a gray area between magic and luck, and my basketball career started off somewhere in the gray area. Looking back, I can see a whole string of unlikely events that had to occur. I can also remember moments when new skills seemed to drop down out of the sky, and I felt as if I had a new eye or had tapped a new compartment in my brain.

First there was George Powles. The white teachers at McClymonds tended to be the most bitter of a bitter lot, stuck there in an all-black school. Powles was white, and he was also stuck with the junior varsity basketball team. At our first practice he told us he didn't know the first thing about basketball. The principal of the school had just stopped him in the hall a few days earlier and informed him that he was the new coach of our team. Powles was a baseball coach by trade, but he said that he would learn with us and try to be fair. He did both.

Among the teachers, Powles was generally unpopular for his pro-student attitude. He had the kind of idealism that could cause trouble if it infected students, and he was criticized as one who curried favor with kids by doing things they liked. That's exactly what he did for me, and I'll always be grateful to him.

At the end of our tryout period I was clearly the worst of the candidates for the Jayvee team. I could run and jump, all right, but if there was a basketball within twenty feet of me, I went to pieces. There were sixteen of us. Powles was provided with fifteen game uniforms, but he told us he didn't want to cut anybody else. As the sixteenth man on the team, I was to share the last uniform with a boy named Roland Campbell. When he wore the uniform, I sat up in the stands. Every game we switched. Powles couldn't have been kinder to me. He even gave me two dollars to join the local Boys Club so I could gain some experience, and I burned up enough energy on those courts to light the city of Oakland.

Powles knew less about basketball strategy than I knew about Emily Post, but he had a keen sense of psychology that helped us win. He used to pace up and down in front of us to lecture us on the race question. "We might as well face it, boys," he would say gravely. "You are a Negro team playing against a lot of white teams. If you fight in a game, they'll call it a 'riot.' If the white team fights, they'll call it a 'scuffle.' That's all there is to it. We can't help it. So I won't have any fighting on this team. If you want to beat somebody up, just beat them with the basketball."

That's what we did. Powles was honest and straightforward, and he made sense. Nobody on our team forgot what he said, and we never fought. Often our white opponents started shoving hard if they fell behind, hoping to provoke a fight, but we'd just whip them harder on the court. One of us might say to a white player, "Hey, man, we can't have no rioting out here!" and then we'd all laugh. The coach taught us that in order to do anything well, you have to be something of a gentleman, and since we were black, he'd say, we had to be *perfect* gentlemen.

Coach Powles moved up to the varsity for my last two years at McClymonds, and so did I. Our team was excellent, but I was mediocre at best. I was the kind of player who tried so hard that everybody wanted to give me the "most improved" award— except that I didn't improve much. I was an easily forgettable high-school player. McClymonds was part of the Oakland Athletic League, which had only six teams. At the end of the season the newspapers published a First All-League Team, a Second All-League Team, a Third All-League Team, and a long list of Honorable Mentions that included just about everybody, except for me. I never made any of those lists.

When I finished at McClymonds, luck struck again, in the form of the California High School All-Stars. For the previous four years or so, a local basketball lover had gathered together a team of players and taken them on a tour of the Pacific Northwest, challenging local teams. The Oakland Jaycees and the Mohawk Athletic Club, of which I'd never heard, put up money so the team could go barnstorming off to the North for about a month.

Circumstances conspired to put me on this team, even though I was not of all-star quality right there in Oakland, much less in all of California. First of all, the tour took place in January, right in the middle of both the basketball season and the normal scholastic year. It was designed exclusively for graduating "splitters" —students whose school year ran from January to January. This factor alone ruled out most of the good players. Secondly, the man who ran the tour was trying to build up his program, and he badly wanted to have a player from McClymonds, which had had the best team in Northern California that year.

I was the only graduating splitter on the McClymonds team, so I was picked. My more talented teammates at McClymonds kidded "All-Star Russell" about being selected as their representative, but I didn't care; I was happier than if I'd found a thousand dollars under my pillow. The tour would give me the three wishes I would have put to any genie who came along: a chance to play basketball every day, a trip out of Oakland, and a way to avoid the burden of facing the real world and looking for a job. So in January of 1952 I said good-bye to Mister Charlie and took off for the bus station. Getting to go on the tour was luck. What would happen along the way was magic.

By modern standards the California All-Star tour was anything but elegant. We traveled by regularly scheduled Greyhound bus. When we finished a game in one town the team would tramp down to the bus station to buy tickets to the next. We would sit in the station for hours if necessary, because we always left when the bus was ready. That's the way we traveled for thousands of miles—up through Oregon to Seattle, on up into British Columbia through towns like Victoria, Nanaimo, Blaine, New Westminster, Birnaby, Penticton and Trail, and then back down through Spokane to Idaho. Mostly we played against high-school teams, but also there were Western Washington College in Bellingham, Washington, and the University of British Columbia. Sometimes we would get farmed out to host families in a city so that we could stay two or three days and get in some practice, but usually we'd go right from the bus station to the basketball court to a restaurant and back to the station. I remember being stunned by sights like the Cascade Mountains and my first glimpse of a Canadian Mountie. Of course there was a lot of horseplay on the bus, and I got so little sleep that my eyes swelled up as big as tires. I loved every minute of it.

The coach was a man named Brick Swegle, who had invented the tour. He took his wife along, and they ran the show in tandem. I remember them as a pair. They'd both stand up in the front of the bus. He'd say one sentence and she the next, alternating like actors in rehearsal. Then the two of them would sit down up front and start passing a bottle back and forth, probably hoping that a snort or two would help drown out all our noise. But after a few drinks the Swegles would start making their own noise in loud arguments. We would quiet down in the back so that we could hear what they were saying, and when they simmered down, our volume would swell back to normal. The ordinary bus passengers in the middle rows got quite a show.

In Canada, rebounds were called "caroms," and in many of the towns the game was played on a "casaba court." The very philosophy of the game in those days would be unrecognizable to most people now. The idea was never to leave your feet except when jumping for a rebound. If you had the ball on offense, the idea was to dribble, fake and move past the man guarding you so that you had a clear path to the basket for a moment. Then you would try to drive in for a lay-up. If your path was blocked, you would shoot a set shot if you had time; if not, you would pass. The jump shot—which has become the staple of modern basketball—was relatively new then, and many coaches were dedicated to stamping it out; they thought it was a "hot dog" move that should be confined to the playgrounds where it originated. Once you went up, said the coaches, you were helpless, because if anything hampered your shot in the air, more than likely you would come down with the ball and have to turn it over to the other team. The standard line in coaching was: "If you have to jump to shoot, you didn't have a shot in the first place." Some coaches would bench a player automatically for taking a jump shot, and I witnessed a couple of strict disciplinarians who actually threw players off their teams for this offense.

On defense it was considered even worse to leave your feet. Nine times out of ten, coaches would say, when you went up for a fake the guy with the ball would just run around you for a lay-up. The idea was for the defensive player to keep himself between his man and the basket at all times. Prevent lay-ups, keep control, stay on your feet. By jumping you were simply telegraphing to your opponent that you could be faked into the air. Defenses had not begun to adjust to the jump shot.

According to the classical style of basketball back then, the game was built around the lay-up and the set shot. At McClymonds we preferred free-form "playground basketball," including the jump shot. We never jumped on defense, but we loved to go up in the air on offense. It was more fun—and it worked. Our success caused great anguish among conservative coaches, who feared that the lazy and undisciplined aspects of "Negro basketball" would bring nothing but evil to the game.

Like George Powles at McClymonds, Brick Swegle was not the average coach. He was a maverick. I never knew what he did every year other than run the All-Star tour, but my hunch is that he had a lot of fun at whatever it was. On the tour he allowed us to do just about anything we wanted on the court. He'd make substitutions, call time-outs and encourage us, and together with his wife he'd handle the logistics of travel, but out on the floor we were pretty much on our own.

So we played "Negro basketball," though there were only two black players on the team. It was a holiday for our white players, who loved jump shots like everybody else but had been anchored to the floor by their coaches. We ran and jumped on that tour, and we wore out most teams. In some cities the opposing coaches told Mr. Swegle that our tactics were "not cricket." He'd always shrug his shoulders and say that his boys were having fun. We were also winning. In one game the opposing coach got cocky when he saw us open up with jump shots. "Let 'em have that shot!" he yelled at his players. He shared the established view that the jump shot could not work because it was performed off balance, whereas the set shot was sturdy, balanced and repeatable, like a free throw. Sooner or later, he figured, this awkward new shot would ruin us. His players were also under orders not to jump on defense, so we shot short jump shots all day, while our opponents just stood there. All through the game the coach defiantly told his players to let us have the jump shot, and we won 144 to 41.

I was like a sponge on the whole trip, soaking up whatever I could learn from the other players. For the first time the game obsessed me. Whenever I was on the sidelines, in practice or in a game, I studied the moves of my teammates. Bill Treu in particular fascinated me. He was a Mormon, clean-scrubbed, honest, friendly, and our best player. In one game he scored fifty-three points. Treu was the first player I'd ever seen who relied on ball handling. Most of the kids I'd known at McClymonds would take the ball and race at breakneck speed directly to the point at which they'd take their jump shot or pass. Treu hardly ever went anywhere in a straight line; he was always cutting and weaving. His head and his eyes would scissor back and forth in a constant fake as he hesitated, switched hands and changed direction in order to get open. He was the first player I'd ever seen who could spin repeatedly while dribbling and still control the ball—the way Earl Monroe would later play in the pros. On the bus I would talk with Treu for hours on end about how he'd developed each fake and spin. He loved talking about his moves, which were his proudest possessions. I looked for Treu to become a great player later at Brigham Young University, but I understand that the Mormon Church sent him on a two-year mission overseas, after which he stayed out of competitive sports.

Eural McKelvey, the only black player on the team other than myself, tried to make a science out of rebounding. He was the first player I ever heard talk about such refinements as which way the ball was likely to bounce from shots taken at certain spots on the court. He wanted to know everything, and he was always thinking. Also, he ran swiftly and gracefully, and threw up an accurate jump shot. Like Bill Treu, McKelvey talked to me endlessly about basketball. I kept peppering him with questions, and from the questions and from the way I was playing he knew that I was learning from him. Some players hoard their ideas like trade secrets, but Treu and McKelvey seemed to like helping other players. In Coach Swegle's bubbly atmosphere their unselfishness spread to the whole team.

McKelvey has remained a friend ever since. When Mister Charlie retired from the foundry at the age of sixty-five, he started working in a fruit-canning plant a few weeks every summer "just to keep in shape." McKelvey, who is the foreman of the plant, kids Mister Charlie about pulling his share of the load, but he looks after him as if he were his own father.

Within a week after the All-Star tour began, something happened that opened my eyes and chilled my spine. I was sitting on the bench, watching Treu and McKelvey the way I always did. Every time one of them would make one of the moves I liked, I'd close my eyes just afterward and try to see the play in my mind. In other words, I'd try to create an instant replay on the inside of my eyelids. Usually I'd catch only part of a particular move the first time I tried this; I'd miss the head work or the way the ball was carried or maybe the sequence of steps. But the next time I saw the move I'd catch a little more of it, so that soon I could call up a complete picture of, say, Bill Treu's spinning right-handed lay-up from the left side of the basket.

On this particular night I was working on replays of many plays, including McKelvey's way of taking an offensive rebound and moving quickly to the hoop. It's a fairly simple play for any big man in basketball, but I didn't execute it well and McKelvey did. Since I had an accurate version of his technique in my head, I started playing with the image right there on the bench, running back the picture several times and each time inserting a part of me for McKelvey. Finally I saw myself making the whole move, and I ran this over and over, too. When I went into the game, I grabbed an offensive rebound and put it in the basket just the way McKelvey did. It seemed natural, almost as if I were just stepping into a film and following the signs. When the imitation worked and the ball went in, I could barely contain myself. I was so elated I thought I'd float right out of the gym. Every time I'd tried to copy moves in the past, I'd dribbled the ball off my arm or committed some other goof. Now for the first time I had transferred something from my head to my body. It seemed so easy. My first dose of athletic confidence was coming to me when I was eighteen years old.

The technique itself was not new to me. When I had spent so much of my free time in the Oakland Public Library, after my mother died, I'd check out reproductions of paintings and take them home with me—prints of Da Vinci and Michelangelo rolled up in a scroll and tucked under my arm to keep other kids from seeing what they were. I got enough kidding just for going to the library; if the guys in my neighborhood had discovered what was under my arm, they'd have teased me into the San Francisco Bay. Safely at home, I would unroll the prints and study them. Almost always I selected paintings of faces and scenes. I don't know where I'd gotten the idea, but I also thought if I could memorize paintings of magnificent buildings, it would help me become an architect. I wanted to conceive of a building in my mind and then make it reality.

Those paintings held me spellbound. I would study a Michelangelo for hours, trying to memorize each little detail, working on one section of the painting at a time. It took me weeks before I was satisfied that I could close my eyes and re-create anything resembling what I saw in the reproduction. Then I would psyche myself up for the acid test: drawing the painting from memory.

I'd put the print away and start sketching, but the result always frustrated me. When I'd finished, the outline and general shapes would resemble the painting closely, but the details would be cockeyed and jarring. It always looked as if Michelangelo had sent his work into the nursery for completion. Finally I decided I had no gift. This failure—plus the fact that not a single student at McClymonds expected to go to college—sent my dream of being an architect into limbo.

On the All-Star tour through the Northwest, I suddenly knew that I could do on the basketball court what I had not been able to do with painting. I got the details right, and repeatedly they fell into place. Whenever I pulled off one of McKelvey's moves I'd try to review what I'd done while running back up the court. I could see the play I'd just made, and if there were an extra jerk in my arm or a faulty twist in my body, I'd try to correct it the next time. The important thing was that I could see what was wrong and what was right, and that my body responded to what I saw.

For the rest of the trip I was nearly possessed by basketball. I was having so much fun that I was sorry to see each day end, and I wanted the nights to race by so that the next day could start. The long rides on the bus never bothered me. I talked basketball incessantly, and when I wasn't talking I was sitting there with my eyes closed, watching plays in my head. I was in my own private basketball laboratory, making mental blueprints for myself. It was effortless; the movies I saw in my head seemed to have their own projector, and whenever I closed my eyes it would run. I had fantasies too, of course, such as visions of soaring high enough to dunk the ball with my feet, but most of what I saw was within the realm of possibility. With only a little mental discipline I could keep myself focused on plays I had actually seen, and so many of them were new that I never felt bored. If I had a play in my mind but muffed it on the court, I'd go over it repeatedly in my head, searching for details I'd missed. I'd goofed because I'd overlooked a critical detail in my mind, so I'd go back to check my model. If this didn't work, I'd have to wait until I saw McKelvey or one of the other players make the move again, and then compare what I saw with the model in my head. It was like working a phony jig-saw puzzle: one piece in the completed picture was slightly imperfect, and I had to find out which one it was. Many a night on the Greyhound I dozed off right in the middle of my detective work.

Whenever I did find myself running out onto the court, it was like the movies, except that the sounds were so much brighter: the squeaking shoes, the thumping rhythm of basketballs bouncing, the breathing, shouts and grunts of the players, the whistles of the officials. Once I got used to these sounds I could concentrate on my movies. Usually I'd have two or three new moves in mind to try out each day, and I'd want to make adjustments in several of the old ones. I'd practice them during the warm-ups. Most players spend warm-ups limbering up with their favorite shot. I spent mine working on moves, one at a time. It was always exciting to try one for the first time. In a split second, while walking away from the bucket with a practice ball, I'd think of a move and run it through my mind. Then I'd try it—once, twice, three times. Usually I'd make adjustments after each try, but occasionally I'd get it right on the first go, and to me that was like being able to slap a Michelangelo right on the canvas. I'd say to myself, "I've got it! That's another one." Then I'd try another. During warm-ups I seemed aloof from my teammates, but I was really paying tribute to them by practicing their techniques.

Although Bill Treu played forward, he handled the ball like a guard, and it didn't take me long to figure out that some of his moves were not suited to a player my size. I couldn't dribble through crowds the way he did, or twist my way to the bucket at high speeds. I was too tall for so much dribbling; the ball would be stolen or I'd throw it away.

On the bus at night I'd still watch Treu go through his paces in my mind, but it was fruitless for me to insert myself in his place. It was frustrating to think that some of the images I had assembled were useless, so finally, more or less as a lark, I started imagining myself in plays *with* Treu. He'd be spinning in for a lay-up, and I'd be shadowing him on defense. Since I knew his move so well, I'd imagine myself as his mirror image; I'd take a step backward for every step he took forward, and so forth. It was as if we were dancing, with Treu leading. When I saw him go up to lay the ball in the basket, I'd see myself go up and block the shot. I enjoyed the two-man show in my mind, so I expanded it. I sketched out scenes of Treu and me fast-breaking together, pirouetting together, hanging in the air together. Any way he bent, I'd bend with him.

The first time I pulled one of these defensive moves on Treu in practice, I was ecstatic. Not because I liked to match Treu's standard of play, nor because I had a premonition that defense would become my calling card in basketball. I was happy because those defensive moves were the first that I'd invented on my own and then made real. I didn't copy them; I invented them. They grew out of my imagination, and so I saw them as my own.

The very idea that I could innovate in basketball thrilled me. It came so soon after I discovered that I could copy offensive moves and thereby make progress. A few weeks earlier I had not even been able to walk on the floor smoothly. Actually, I hadn't really wanted the ball to be passed to me because I didn't know what to do with it. What I'd really liked about the game were running, jumping, grabbing rebounds—just being out there. Now, as our tour rolled through the snow to a string of small cities in Canada, I was not only learning the game but was also adding to it. Every day turned into an adventure, and I wondered why the game had only started coming to me *now,* when I had only a few weeks left in competitive basketball.

I blocked a lot of shots on that tour, mainly because it was fun to carry out some of the designs I had made up to use against Bill Treu. Nobody, including myself, thought of the blocked shot as much of a defensive weapon; in fact, nobody thought much about defense at all. We were in a different era of basketball, when people thought of defense as a time to rest when you didn't have the ball. A blocked shot provoked only yawns or criticism. There had been a time when blocked shots were a potent weapon, and the early seven-footers in the game camped under the basket to bat shots away from the rim. But this had brought on the goal-tending rule against touching a shot in its downward flight. After that, players tended to forget about blocking shots because they didn't want to give the opposing team an automatic two points. It was too risky. Players who tried to block had to leave their feet, and were likely to foul or be left behind as the shooter scooted around them. For all this risk the blocker could hope only to knock the ball out of bounds. The idea of blocking a shot *and* keeping the ball in bounds was unheard of, as was the more difficult move of tipping the blocked shot directly to a defensive teammate. In our minds a blocked shot had about the same impact as calling time-out: it stopped the clock and gave the ball out of bounds to the team that already had possession.

Like the jump shot and defense in general, blocked shots would take some time to work their way into favor with basketball coaches. But even in those days they were fun to watch and to do, and on the Northwest tour we were playing for fun. An acrobatic block might draw an "ooh" or an "aah" or even a handshake from your teammates. (This was before the palm slap. Black players never slapped each other on the ass back then, and we were shocked when we saw the white ones doing it.) I blocked so many shots after a couple of weeks on the tour that my teammates began referring to them as "Russell moves," which pleased me. They were acknowledging that I had a trademark they admired, and this was the first sign that my basketball personality would be built around defense.

In time, I also conjured up some offensive moves of my own, but most of my innovations were defensive. The other players on the team showed me more than enough tricks to keep me busy copying them. On offense I was catching up and had a long way to go; on defense I was breaking new ground. This encouraged me to figure out new ways to block shots.

Hindsight is the land of opportunity for boasting, and it would be nice to claim that I concentrated on defense because of some extraordinary insight, but it was nothing like that. Defense came to me more or less accidentally. It fit well into the peculiar way I studied the game on that trip. I was the only left-handed player on our team. When I imagined myself guarding a player on the court it was easy for me to see my left hand working against his right one. I'd see one of my teammates go up to take his favorite shot right-handed, and I'd go up on the mirror foot to block the shot with my mirror hand; the symmetry was clear. It was more difficult for me to copy the same right-handed shot offensively because I had to flip every movement around so that I could see myself doing it left-handed.

Being "other-handed" always favors the defense in basketball because your stronger and surer hand is opposite the shooting hand of the player your're guarding. My natural left-handedness was one of several factors that pushed me toward defense. Of course I didn't care about any of this at the time; just playing the game kept me busy and happy. Beyond that, I was awed by the mental camera I'd discovered. I was like a movie director who discovers the miracle of film editing and then stays in the splicing room until exhaustion finally stops the fun. As our tour went farther north into Canada, the roads stretched for hundreds of miles between stops, which sometimes gave me twelve straight hours of mental basketball on the Greyhound. When we got off the bus I couldn't wait to get on the court, and after a game I couldn't wait to get back to the Greyhound so that I could review, compare, expand and dream up new material. The tour was one of those rare times in one's life when fantasy and reality are so close together that they feed each other.

One other strange thing happened before our team returned to California. During a game a teammate leaned over to me and said, "Hey, you can jump." What he meant, of course, was that I could *really* jump. I'd begun to notice the same thing. Whenever a clump of the taller players went up off the floor for a "carom," there'd be an instant when I found myself up there alone. And if I didn't get the ball, there'd also be an instant when I was left there after all the other players had taken off up the court. I can remember being up in the air, watching an opponent land and take his first step away from me, thinking to myself, "Hurry up, floor. Come back to me." In cartoons the Roadrunner can spin his legs like an eggbeater and take off while still in the air, but it doesn't work that way for basketball players. You have to wait until you land, which is the only frustration that comes with jumping high. Otherwise it is one of the purest pleasures I know for an athlete.

People in all kinds of cultures are known to "jump for joy" in moments of supreme happiness. Jumping is an internationally recognized expression of joy, and basketball is a sport organized around jumping. Most of the time people jump spontaneously after something makes them happy. They turn their pleasure into energy and burn that energy by leaving the earth for a second or two. In basketball, the jumping comes first. It's possible for a player to jump because he's happy, but it's more likely that he's happy because he's jumping. I have heard players complain about almost every detail of the game—the rules, the size or color of the ball, the shape or temperature of the dressing room—but I've never heard anybody complain about the fact that the game requires jumping. Naturally, some of the enthusiasm drains as the player becomes older and tired. You learn to economize by not jumping unnecessarily and not jumping unnecessarily high; you appreciate easy rebounds. But there is always some of the original joy of soaring off the floor, even for an old pro who may feel it only once a game when he grabs a rebound as high in the air as he can go.

On that tour I was in the first glow both of jumping and of discovering new moves. They reinforced each other: I jumped higher because the moves in my mind were beginning to work on the court, and some of the moves worked better because I was jumping so high. I was learning to jump with a purpose, but I still jumped for the fun of it, the way I had ever since I was a kid. Belatedly, I was going through the frisky period of most high-school players. They jump when they don't need to, to show off, elaborate jumps, with their elbows flared out like wings. They may see a rebound coming to them chest-high while they are flat-footed, but they jump as high as they can anyway. On their way back to the floor after a particularly high leap, they bend their legs more than they need to, just to prolong the sensation. They slap the floor with their shoes when they land, making as much noise as possible, because a loud slap is a sign of a long trip in the air.

Two slaps sound louder than one, so they land one foot at a time. The high jumpers talk with their feet.

I made a double-slap landing when I got back to California after the trip. At home with Mister Charlie, I piled so many stories on him that he had to slow me down. He could tell there'd been a big change. "I can play now," I told him, and he understood what I meant. Mister Charlie was even more enthusiastic about my report than I thought he would be. He was especially happy because he knew something I didn't, and when I found out what it was, the news felt as good as the second foot smacking the floor loudly. He told me that a stranger had been calling while I was off on the tour, and that he wanted to talk to me about going to college. It was the most exciting thing I could have hoped to hear. Both Mister Charlie and I had given up on the idea of college because of the expense, and now, for no apparent reason, the dream was lighting up again. We each got carried away for a few minutes, until Mister Charlie said we had to be realistic. We weren't even sure the stranger would call again, much less that it would all work out. All we could do was hope and wait, and in the meantime we had to pretend nothing had happened. I knew he was right, but it was all I could do not to spend all my time daydreaming about college.

A few days later I applied for a job as an apprentice sheet-metal worker at the San Francisco Naval Shipyards. I don't know why I chose sheet metal, except that all the other job categories on the Civil Service application sounded even drearier. Soon I was hauling heavy objects around the shipyard, waiting for that stranger to call.

Hal DeJulio was the classic alumni booster, the kind of man who stays close to his alma mater throughout his life and who gets together with his fellow alumni to protest effectively against coaches who don't win. He was in the insurance business, but he liked to spend most of his spare time around young athletes. As a former basketball player for the University of San Francisco, he knew many of the old athletes around California, and they kept in touch. DeJulio loved to watch basketball games; he'd show up unnoticed in the stands at various high-school games, scanning the floor for someone who might help USF. When he found a prospect he'd report back to the college coach, hoping to discover and sponsor a player who would become a star. Even then, all universities had networks of volunteer alumni scouts, and USF had a tiny network, so DeJulio tried to make up for it by working extra hard.

It was a miracle that DeJulio had ever noticed me. Shortly before I left McClymonds we had a big game against Oakland High, led by an All-Star player named Truman Bruce. DeJulio came to watch Bruce, and also to take a look at the three All-Stars on our team. I was not one of them. No one was aware of the scout's presence at the game, least of all me. As it turned out, I played my best game for McClymonds that night, scoring fourteen points. This was hardly a spectacular point production, but it was the most I ever scored in high school. Later, DeJulio told me he was impressed that I'd scored eight points in a row at the end of the first half and six points at the end of the game. He thought I was a game winner, and he liked the way I played defense against Truman Bruce. I jumped higher than he did and ran down the court faster. DeJulio approved of the way I hustled. Like most alumni scouts, he had the temperament of a rooster. He liked scrappers, and I was one.

DeJulio didn't tell Mister Charlie his name or what school he represented, so when he finally did call I had no idea who he was. He asked me whether I was interested in going to USF. "What's USF?" I asked.

"The University," he said. He seemed irritated that I didn't know what USF was, even though it was just across the Bay from Oakland. I had never heard of USF.

"You mean San Francisco State?" I asked.

"No," he said. "The University of San Francisco."

"Oh," I said.

After that awkward beginning we had a comic conversation, though it didn't seem funny at the time. DeJulio kept trying to pump me up by telling me what a great game I'd played against Oakland High a couple of months earlier. While he was chattering away about it, I was trying to interrupt him to say that he hadn't seen anything. I wanted to tell him about what had happened to me on the tour, but I didn't even know how to begin. Finally he said that he thought he could arrange for me to work out with the USF basketball team and show my stuff to the coach, Phil Woolpert. I said I'd be glad to come. A few days later I had what amounted to a college audition. I was nervous. On top of that, I couldn't find the practice gym in San Francisco for hours, which made me late. In fact, I couldn't even find the University. (At that time, USF didn't have a gym of its own, so the team practiced in a nearby high school.) When I finally got there, I was in a daze from frustration and nervousness. Which was probably good, because it numbed me. I don't remember anything about that workout except that I ran and jumped without the ball a lot. By the time it was over, I'd gotten up a good sweat and worn away my frustration. Coach Woolpert thanked me for coming over and said I'd be hearing from him soon. He was noncommittal. As I was leaving he told me to take the entrance examinations just in case he could arrange a scholarship for me.

Every day I carried steel at the shipyard, every night I played playground basketball for several hours, and day and night I waited.

In March my old team at McClymonds was preparing for the postseason tournament in northern California. Traditionally the team played a tune-up game against a rag-tag team of McClymonds alumni. That year I was the youngest member of the alumni team, only two months out of high school. I remember the game vividly. It was the first time I'd played before a crowd since the Northwest tour, and it was also the first time since the possibility of going to college had entered my life. My moves were elementary to basketball buffs, but they were there that night the way they'd been on the tour. I was showing off— scoring, rebounding, blocking shots. Then, just before half time, something so good happened that it scared me. I got the ball near the basket on offense, went up as high as I could to take a short jump shot, and suddenly realized that I was looking *down* into the basket. For an instant I was looking over the front edge of the rim to the back, and the basket itself looked like a skinny oval from that perspective. The sight was so strange that I missed the shot by a couple of feet. My first thought when I landed was that I could hurt myself jumping so high. It was the first time I really became conscious of altitude on the basketball court. Previously I'd thought of jumping only as a matter of time—the time you enjoyed in the air, going up, hanging there, and then coming down. Now I thought of jumping as the distance I had to fall. I had to be at least four feet off the ground in order to have my eye level rise above the rim of a standard ten-foot basket, and I was stunned at the idea that every time I jumped my system had a shock similar to jumping off a four-foot ledge.

But the fear wore off quickly. I was hypnotized by what I'd seen at the top of my jump, and in the second half I did it again. For months later I was mesmerized by those short glimpses down into the basket. I'd stand by myself in an empty gym and jump over and over, looking for that sliver of light. I got so practiced at it that I trained my eye to see the back edge of the rim as it appeared to rise toward the level of the front edge during my jump. As I slowed down near the top of the jump, the back edge would disappear behind the front when my eye level was even with the rim, and then, for one instant, the back edge would rise above the front edge and I'd see down into the basket.

Leaping high had hooked me. Two years later, during the off-season at USF, some friends and I tested how high I could reach from a running start. I left chalk dust from my fingertips at a point fourteen feet above the floor—four feet above the basket and a foot above the top of the backboard. I loved jumping. It would have been easy for me to dunk the ball even in a twelve-foot basket, and a lot of the tall players in pro basketball wouldn't have any trouble either, so the proposals that are circulated from time to time to help the shorter players by raising the basket to twelve feet are silly. If you want to help shorter players, put the basket nearer the floor. If it's more like a hockey goal, the height advantage will diminish. As long as the basket is above our reach, height and leaping will be rewarded. The game is designed to make its players reach into the air.

The good news finally came by mail, in a letter informing me that I had been granted a scholarship. It probably moved Mister Charlie even more than it did me, for it meant that he could fulfill his promise to my mother to send me to college. We were stunned. Neither one of us could really believe that all the talk from Hal DeJulio was turning out to be true. We thought there must be some sort of magic or blessing behind that letter. After all, I was not even a star high-school player, and here I was being selected at a time when blacks were simply not given scholarships to prestigious four-year colleges. This was 1952; Harry Truman was still in the White House, and Jim Crow still ran the court-houses. The most progressive of the big Western universities, UCLA, may have had black athletes on scholarship in those days, but most of these had to prove their character at a junior college before getting a chance at a university. I was getting a straight pass. It did not occur to me that it happened because I was so good a prospect. Basketball was play; college was serious. USF didn't even have a gym, and college athletics weren't the business they have since become. I thought of college ball the same way I thought of high school—as an extracurricular activity—so I didn't draw as strong a correlation between my athletic skills and my college opportunity as I would now. For me, the benefit of the scholarship was entirely the chance to be in college. I would have played basketball wherever I was, including the shipyard, and I thought the reason I was going to college was one of those myster-ies—a mixture of changing times and smiling fortune.

My string of luck on the court kept running at USF, and I had a continual sense of discovery. It had taken many lucky develop-ments in a row for me to be there at all—from George Powles's decision to let me share the fifteenth uniform to Hal DeJulio's decision to scout the only high-school game in which I'd scored more than ten points. My whole career turned out that way, though at the time I often thought the deck was stacked against me. I often felt it was a curse to be left-handed, for instance, but by the time I reached the pros I realized it was an enormous advantage; by making me appreciate defense, left-handedness helped me to be innovative. For years I also worried about my lack of "natural" basketball talent, the kind of skill that some future stars have when they're six years old and have hand-eye coordination that is the envy of every kid in the neighborhood. I didn't have that, but by the time I became a pro I realized that players who rely only on instinctive talents are fragile. They are the kind who can be stars one year but retired the next because they've "lost it." They don't work at the game because they've never had to. More important, they have no history of learning how to compensate for lack of physical skill. Old pros must have this ability to be competitive after they've lost spring and speed, and eventually I was grateful for all the time I'd spent with my chin in my hand trying to figure out how to make up for the fact that natural players could do things I couldn't.

In the early years I faced no pressure and made no crucial decisions. The All-Star tour had come to me as a gift; I didn't have to compete for it. As for college, I didn't have to choose from among fifty or a hundred schools drooling over my services. I didn't have to evaluate my future by weighing my prospects at various schools under different coaches. I didn't even have to decide how to go about evaluating my future. Only one school was interested in me, so I went there; it was that simple. Often these days we read about young black kids calculating every angle to find a way of using sports "to get out of the ghetto." That whole idea would have been foreign to me. First of all, I didn't think of where I lived as a ghetto, though I suppose that's what it would be called by today's standards. To me, where I lived was simply where I lived. But even if I had been itching to escape from home, I wouldn't have thought of pro basketball as the way to do it. The league only had eight teams back then, none on the West Coast. Pro basketball was not a visible profession, not something kids thought about much, any more than today's kids are likely to consider a professional career in softball.

To those of us in West Oakland, San Francisco was an exotic land. The Bay Bridge spanned a cultural gap so wide that the two sides had a language barrier; I used to joke that I never knew the word "mother" could be used by itself until I got to San Francisco. Suddenly my life had veered off course because somebody thought I was potentially a basketball player, and instantly I found myself in a sea of white people. Jesuit priests in stiff collars lectured me about Thomist theology, and students spent a lot of time earnestly discussing subjects like Chinese brainwashing techniques. I never knew what to expect. If they'd taken me out of class one day and fired me into space as the first astronaut, I'd have taken it in stride.

Back at McClymonds I told the kids that college was no big deal, but for the first time they treated me as if I *was* a big deal. The flattery hit me in places that had never been touched before, and I liked it so much that I went back to Oakland for a McClymonds football game. As I was standing on the sidelines I sensed someone next to me. It was Nitro. We started talking, which in itself was an achievement for me, and wound up sitting together on the bus after the game, kissing and groping all the way home. When we said good night she gave me her phone number and asked me to call her the next day. I was stepping high.

The next day when I called Nitro she lit into me. "What did you call me for?" she demanded. "I don't want to go out with you."

"Wait a minute," I said. "What's going on?"

She stammered a bit and then said quickly, "Well, I know your brother Charlie, and I think I'm going to go out with him." And she hung up. I idolized my older brother, who excelled in both sports and women. When he talked about girls it was a foreign language to me.

I didn't hear anything more from Nitro until the next spring, when I went out for the track team and highjumped six feet eight inches at my first meet. At the time the world record was six eleven; everybody was shocked by my jump, including me. The newspapers were full of stories. Not long afterward the president of the University summoned me to his office, pointed to a newspaper on his desk and said, "Mr. Russell, that's good. I want you to jump a few inches higher and get a world record. It will be good for the University." Then he dismissed me. It was as if he'd ordered up a world record from Sears. I thought he was weird and that he probably hadn't ever learned how to talk to real people.

In the midst of all this publicity, Nitro sent word over the boy-girl grapevine that she'd like to go out again, and we started dating steadily. Things were going so well by the end of the summer that I came up with a brilliant idea: I bought a ring and asked her to marry me.

"Marry you?" She winced as if I'd asked her to count the wings on a cockroach. "I'm going out with two other guys, and I like *both* of them better than I like you."

I was crushed. I remember thinking that it was as if there were a big parade going by but I couldn't hear the music. Maybe Nitro didn't see me; maybe I was invisible. It was the only time I ever flirted with the idea of suicide; the pain was so intense. I worked up a plan that seemed flashy and artistic. I had a blue 1941 Packard, an old classic, and I planned to drive it into the San Francisco Bay at high speed. I had a vision of a headline: BASKET-BALL PLAYER DIES IN BAY LOVE CRASH—and of Nitro lying on the rug, her heart struck by a sledge-hammer's blow of remorse. The vision was good, though I didn't like the idea of my demise being reported on the sports page. But after picking out my spot down at the Bay and mulling over a few phrases for my farewell note, I decided the hell with it.

The first piece of luck I ran into at the University was Ross Guidice, the freshman coach. He had something you can't buy from the coaches' catalogue; in fact you rarely even hear about it. Guidice always supported a player's love of the game, and he did so with a generosity and good spirit that I've never seen since. If a player wanted to spend three hours being drilled after prac-tice, Guidice would stay; all the player had to do was ask. I took him up on the offer. On many occasions we worked four hours at a stretch, just the two of us, alone in the gym—on Saturdays, holidays, at night. As many hours as I'd put in, he'd put in. He'd talk, demonstrate and sweat, always with great patience, and I never sensed a complaint about the sacrifice he was making. My antennae were sensitive to hostility and irritation even then, but all I ever felt from Guidice was enthusiasm. He was excited over every bit of progress I made. He was the same way with other players, so I knew that he hadn't taken me on as a charity case; he simply loved to help people who wanted to be helped. For many years after Guidice left basketball and went into business, I used to think that if a kid were to walk into his office and ask for coaching help, Guidice would go right down to the gym. I'd have bet that he'd walk right out on the customers in his store in his street shoes, just to teach basketball. He was that unselfish.

It was a good thing for me that he was, because I didn't know much. Despite all the breakthroughs I'd made on the tour, I was still playing elementary playground basketball. Guidice taught me quickly but gently how ignorant I was. I knew many ways to get off a short jump shot, but I knew little about screens or passes. When I graduated from high school I didn't even know what a hook shot was. This astounded Guidice, but he taught me how to shoot one. Without him it would have taken me years to catch up with what other players knew about basketball.

K.C. Jones took up where Guidice left off. When I was assigned a room with him in a USF dormitory, I had no way of knowing that we'd become lifelong friends. At first I didn't think we'd be friendly at all, because K.C. didn't speak a word to me for a solid month. Not a *word.* He'd slap my bunk on the way out of the room in the mornings, and he'd nod at the salt or sugar during the silent meals we ate in the school cafeteria. That was the extent of our communication, until one day when he suddenly started talking like a normal person. Nothing in particular had happened; he just started talking. It was as if somebody had forgotten to plug him in before then. To my relief, I found that he'd just been shy, even more than I was. Once he got used to me we became inseparable. At a Jesuit university, we were in an alien world, so we leaned on each other. At first I did most of the leaning; K.C. was a year older and had a slightly better scholarship, so he looked after me. He seemed to spend his money more freely on me than he did on himself. He bought me shoes, meals, movie tickets and books.

K.C. was usually silent except when basketball was being discussed. The barest mention of the game would throw him into a Socratic dialogue that would go on for as long as anyone would carry his half of the conversation. Since I was always around, the conversations would ramble on for hours. We decided that basketball is basically a game of geometry—of lines, points and distances—and that the horizontal distances are more important than the vertical ones. If I were playing against someone a foot shorter, the vertical distances could be important, but in competitive basketball most of the critical distances are horizontal, along the floor or at eye level. Height is not as important as it may seem, even in rebounding. Early in my career at USF, watching rebounds closely, I was surprised to discover that three quarters of them were grabbed at or below the level of the basket—a height all college players can reach easily. (This is also true in the pro game.) Generally, the determining distances in those rebounds were horizontal ones.

K.C. and I spent hours exploring the geometry of basketball, often losing track of the time. Neither of us needed a blackboard to see the play the other was describing. Every hypothetical seemed real. It was as if I was back on the Greyhound, assembling pictures of moves in my mind, except that K.C. liked to talk about what combinations of players could do. I had been daydreaming about solo moves, but he liked to work out strategies. K.C. has an original basketball mind, and he taught me how to scheme to make things happen on the court, particularly on defense. In those days almost every player and coach thought of defense as pure reaction: that is, you reacted to the player you were guarding. If he moved to the left, you moved with him, shadowing him. Whatever he did, you reacted to guard the basket. K.C. thought differently. He tried to figure out ways to take the ball away from the opponent. He was always figuring out ways to make the opponent take the shot *he* wanted him to take when *he* wanted him to take it, from the place *he* wanted the man to shoot. Often during games he would pretend to stumble into my man while letting the player he was guarding have a free drive to the basket with the ball, knowing that I could block the shot and take the ball away. Or he'd let a man have an outside shot from just beyond the perimeter of his effectiveness, and instead of harassing the player would take off down the court, figuring that I'd get the rebound and throw him a long pass for an easy basket. He and I dreamed up dozens of plays like these and fed into our equations what we knew about the weaknesses of our opponents. On both offense and defense, our plans included two or three alternatives if the primary strategy failed to work. We liked to think ahead, and before long K.C.'s way of thinking erased my solo images. Whenever I got the ball near the basket, I tried to have two or three moves in mind in advance. They didn't always work, but at least they were there. I found that such planning cut down on my mental hesitation on the floor and generally reduced the number of times I messed up teamwork. I began to daydream about sequences of moves instead of individual ones.

Gradually, K.C. and I created a little basketball world of our own. Other players were lost in our conversations because we used so much shorthand that no one could follow what we were saying. Most of the players weren't interested in strategy anyway. Basketball talk was mostly an ego exercise in which they flapped the breeze and pumped themselves up over their last performance or in preparation for the next one. The prevailing strategy was that you went out, took your shots and waited to see what happened. It was not considered a game for thinkers. K.C. and I were thought to be freaks because of our dialogues on strategy, which were fun for us but dull to everyone else. I used to get a kick out of a remark by Einstein, who said that his most difficult thinking was enjoyable, like a daydream. We were inspired, rocket scientists in sneakers.

After a game, only K.C. and I would appreciate certain things that had happened out on the court—at least that's the way it felt. We shared an extra fascination for the game because of the mental tinkering we did with it in our bull sessions. For example, K.C. was instantly aware of what I thought was the best single play I ever made in college. We were playing Stanford in the San Francisco Cow Palace, and one of their players stole the ball at half court for a breakaway lay-up. He was so far ahead of us that nobody on our team bothered to chase him except me. As he went loping down the right side of the court, I left the center position near our basket and ran after him as fast as I could. The guy's lead was so big that he wasn't hurrying. When I reached half court I was flying, but I took one long stride off to the left to change my angle, then went straight for the bucket. When the guy went up for his lay-up in the lane, I too went up from the top of the key. I was flying. He lofted the ball up so lazily that I was able to slap it into the backboard before it started down. The ball bounced back to K.C., trailing the play.

Probably nobody in that Cow Palace crowd knew anything about how that play developed. They didn't see where I came from, and they saw only the end of the play. But to K.C. and me, the sweetness of the play was the giant step I took to the left as I was building up speed. Without that step the play would have failed, because I'd have fouled the guy by landing on him after the shot. The step to the left gave me just enough angle coming across to miss him and land to the right of him without a foul. K.C. was the only guy in the Cow Palace who noticed that step and knew what it meant. I noticed similar things about his game, and they were the starting points of our daydreams.

There always seemed to be new lessons to make the game more interesting. In my sophomore year Coach Woolpert gave us a lecture on peripheral vision. People have a line of focus on whatever they're trying to see, and objects outside that line are blurry. In fact, they lose sight of the objects *within* their peripheral vision unless they train their eyes to pick them up. K.C. and I became fascinated with this and practiced for hours. We stood near each other day after day, focusing straight ahead at different distances while trying to keep track of each other peripherally. Eventually we discovered that under certain conditions you can hide on a basketball court. With no one on the floor but ten players and two referees, you can still position yourself so that a player facing you will not see you. It's possible because everyone has a blind spot in each eye, about fifteen or twenty degrees on either side of straight ahead. Most people are not aware of this.

K.C. had such a bad case of appendicitis that year that he could not play, but he could talk and experiment with me. I'd stand still a few feet away, and he'd rotate slowly until part of me faded into his blind spot. Once we convinced ourselves that it really existed, our experiments began. We discovered that the blind spots seem larger when the eyes are tilted. A player who dribbles with his head down, adjusting with the tilt of his eyes, will tend to have a larger blind spot. Also, a dribbler will have more of a blind spot on the side where the ball is. He won't lose sight of you completely, but his impression may be so dimmed that he won't react the way he should. This was our theory, anyway, and it had some practical effects. I found that if I positioned myself in a player's blind spot as he drove toward the basket, he'd be more likely to charge right into me or to take a shot easily within my blocking range. When K.C. could play again he found that he was more likely to succeed in a steal if he tried to make his move through a player's blind spot.

K.C. and I also talked a lot about jumping. If an opponent goes up for a jump shot and you're trying to block it or just harass him, you have to come as close as possible to the arc the ball makes between the opponent's hand and the basket. Since the ball usually climbs rapidly after it leaves the shooter's hand, your hand must intercept it as it travels through the first one or two feet of that arc—the earlier the better. Therefore your hand must be close to the plane of the shooter's body. In other words, you've got to be close to a jump shooter in the air to have a chance of blocking his shot. That's why there are so many fouls called in the act of shooting.

K.C. and I noticed that most defensive players got close to a shooter by jumping toward him and then reaching up for the ball. We figured out that you wouldn't lose as much reach toward the arc of the ball if you jumped straight up and reached out instead, so we tried not to jump toward our opponents, for often you commit a foul with your body. It's also the way you get hurt, because your body is unstable when it's leaning in the air. The vertical technique—jumping straight up and reaching out with your arm—puts a premium on long arms and high jumps; it was made for people built the way I am. After I worked on it I could get rebounds even when I was screened, because I could jump straight up and reach out over the screener for the ball. I could also block shots that could not be stopped with any lateral motion in the jump. In one game against Marquette University, for instance, I found myself standing right behind a player as he went up for a jump shot facing the basket. He was already in the air when I went up behind him, reached over his shoulder and batted the ball in the direction it was already going. The shot missed, the ball bouncing off the backboard. Blocking shots this way made jumping even more fun.

K.C. and I were to keep our dialogues going for many years with the Boston Celtics, as my lucky streak continued. I can think of no coach other than Red Auerbach who could have made me feel as comfortable or work as hard as I did, and I was lucky to play with teammates who had such compatible ideas about how to have fun and win.

Despite all this good fortune, though, I remember that the game lost some of its magical qualities for me once I thought seriously about playing for a living. This first happened in 1955, in my junior year, after USF won the NCAA national championship. As a result, all through my senior year at USF I played with the idea of turning professional, and things began to change. Whenever I walked on the court I began to calculate how this particular game might affect my future. Thoughts of money and prestige crept into my head. Over the years the professional game would turn more and more into a business. When you play for money you're concerned with using the old skills you can count on, instead of the new ones that might light on your shoulder that night. You concentrate on the hard, proven coinage that you've minted in the past and begin to lose the sense of discovery and fun that first attracted you to the game.

In other words, the child inside you is growing up, and it is a painful process. Also, I don't think many professional players ever completely lose their young fantasies; I know I didn't. On the Celtics there was a lot of exuberance and horseplay even in the later years. We played like children and quarreled like men—

instead of the other way around—and it helped us win. Even old pros can't win unless they're having a little fun. When you see a long row of grim faces on a team bench, you can bet that these players who seem quite adult will squabble like kids in the locker room. In sports, as in a lot of other professions, you have to be childlike without being childish, and there's a world of difference.

Throughout my career, every now and then some event would come along to remind me of the pure joy basketball had been when I first felt the magic. These events always occurred around kids. In 1959, after my third season with the Celtics, the State Department asked me to go on a good-will tour overseas. Back then such requests went to athletes and entertainers who had made a name for themselves, and I felt honored by the invitation. Since I had already been to Latin America on a State Department tour of the USF team and to Australia with the Olympic team in 1956, I asked if I could go to Africa. Carrying only some Celtic films and a planeload of basketballs, I was soon off to Africa, courtesy of our government.

It would have been hard for me to have been more naïve about international politics than I was then, and I had no idea what propaganda purposes the State Department had in mind for me. Had I known what they were, I was so true blue that I probably would have agreed anyway—until shortly after I got to Africa, that is. The State Department representatives who greeted me were seedy, alcoholic types who started calling me "boy" before I reached the last step of the exit ramp from the plane, and they spoke of their African hosts with contempt. One after another, they seemed to be arrogant louts, almost competitively eager to be racist. I was stunned; I had expected to find our least bigoted diplomats in black Africa. Instead they were the worst, or at least far less capable than the American diplomats I'd met in Latin America. After a while I became angry and hard to get along with; I didn't want to be around those people, which seemed to suit them just as well. I wound up on my own for most of the trip, without dinners, press conferences or American diplomats.

Being largely on my own turned out to be a good thing, for I saw more—and there was a lot to see. My trip took place at an exciting period in Africa; the fever for independence was everywhere. Except for Portugal, the European nations were preparing to grant nominal independence to their colonies, and wherever independence was not assured it was being agitated about and fought for. In Khartoum, the capital of the Sudan, black liberation groups from all over the continent had gathered to conspire with and against each other, and the city was full of spies and intrigue. Future presidents, then still outlaws, lived there, and issued militant statements about their homelands. Most of the excitement seemed to center around the huge Continental Hotel, which sat in the fork where the White Nile joins the Blue Nile. I stayed in Khartoum several extra days just to hang around that hotel and watch. Of course people watched me too, because I was a giant.

I found Liberia the most Americanized of the black nations—hardly a surprise since the country had been built by black settlers from America who had subdued the native blacks in pretty much the same way as the white colonialists had elsewhere. Still, the country was African, and the mixture of African sights and American culture did strange things to me. I felt both close to home and very far away. In the schoolroom of a small Liberian town, one kid asked me why I had come to Africa, and I found myself answering that I was here because somewhere in Africa was my ancestral home and I wanted to feel it. The kids cheered, probably because it was so rare for an American black to speak kindly about Africa. They were so happy that I got all choked up and had to cut short my speech. I realized that I was telling those children something that I hadn't even told myself, and somehow it seemed appropriate.

The kids moved me on several other occasions in Africa—in Ethiopia, the Ivory Coast and other parts of Liberia. In cities in those countries I gave the same kind of basketball clinics as I did elsewhere, but I also made excursions out into the countryside. A local man would accompany me as interpreter, and we'd take off in a Land Rover until we ran out of road. Then we walked. Often the walk lasted a full day—just the interpreter and me and my basketball, traveling by path to a village in the middle of nowhere.

Usually people came from several surrounding villages to see me, and I was told that this kind of gathering was rare. (I believed it, because once or twice the people from different villages didn't get along with one another at all.) Word of my appearance had spread, I don't know how. The interpreters told me that I had been billed as a giant black man from America who could do tricks. The word used for me also meant magician.

In such villages, several hundred Africans would be clustered around in a semi-circle when I arrived—adults at the edges and kids in the middle. I'd smile and bow politely to the men who greeted me, but I couldn't really talk to them so I'd plunge right in. Every face always had looks of curiosity; probably they had never seen anyone my size. They'd never seen a basketball either, or a light bulb or faucet. "I play basketball," I'd say. "That's what I do. Now I know it's unusual for a grown man to say he plays basketball, but I'm going to explain to you what it is. The game is played on a court, with a wooden floor and a basket at each end, and you try to put this ball through the basket."

I'd wait for the interpreter to catch up with me, one sentence at a time, and I'd hold the basketball up and palm it and spin it on a finger. The kids seemed to be as curious about the ball as they were about me. "You can only touch the ball with your hands," I said. "You can't kick it. The reason I'm trying to tell you about the game is that I've had so much fun with it that if I show you how to do it, maybe you can have fun with it, too."

That's all I ever said in the beginning. Then I'd motion for the kids to stand up and throw the ball to one of them. That always produced the first laugh. Some of the kids would drop back, but no one left. I taught them to throw passes, and we'd do that for a while. Usually the interpreter wasn't needed much, because the passes and gestures explained themselves. I showed the kids how to put spin on the ball to make a pass bounce in odd directions, and if the ground were hard enough, I'd show them how to dribble and then play keep-away with the most agile kid. Soon we were running drills, with passing lines and jump balls, and then I'd hold my arms in front of me in a circle so that they could have shooting practice, using me for the basket. By the end, the kids would be laughing, crawling all over me and bubbling with far more energy than I had. It's impossible to convey what a good time I had. After sleeping in the village, I'd leave the next morning for the long walk back to the Land Rover, always a little sad but with a memory full of happy kids' faces. As long as my supply of two hundred basketballs lasted, and as long as my bicycle pump worked, every village got a present. There was a trail of inflated basketballs behind me all through Africa.

I was twenty-five years old on that trip and had played basketball almost constantly, up to eight hours a day, for ten years. I would do so for ten more. That's a lot of effort to invest in a game. But I felt renewed by the notion that I could go out under the sky in a foreign land, with nothing but a hundred words and a basketball, and communicate so well with kids that within a half hour I'd see the same looks of joy that I'd felt with my first high leap. The experience made me feel like a magician.

There were many moments during that African trip that helped me to hang on to the child inside me. Even in my last year with the Celtics, when I was gruff, cynical and so tired that I often felt like an eighty-year-old man, I'd sometimes stop during a time-out and realize that everything was all right. I felt relieved, lucky and a little awed, just as I had years earlier in that high-school hallway.

3

Sports

I used to have fits of worry every now and then about the usefulness of basketball. In fact, I doubted the worth of *any* sport. "It's only a game," I kept saying to myself, and there were a lot of people who felt the same. How can anything as playful and childish as a game be important? When I was a basketball star, a carpenter or a doctor would fawn all over me, and I'd be embarrassed because I thought what *they* were doing was real. But then I read a book by an English writer who said that war is only a game. Some people think love is only a game. On Wall Street they have a game called the Stock Exchange. Almost anything looks like a game from a certain angle, so maybe sports aren't so frivolous after all. If Shakespeare can compare all of life to a stage, maybe it's not odd to believe that part of the play can take place on a basketball court.

Some athletes try to figure out what role sports fulfills in the world, where it fits, and how we should think about it. I used to talk with Bob Cousy on the subject and compare thoughts with football players like Jim Brown and Bernie Casey. If we're professional athletes, we'd say to ourselves, just what is our "profession" all about? It's not an easy question. If a kid goes into any other field, from fireman to statesman, he'll learn why it is necessary and find a lot of literature on the subject, but he won't find much clear thinking about sports or athletes. There is no philosophy of sports worth mentioning.

It's natural for people to be curious about their work, especially those of us who stumbled on sports on our way to an ordinary career. Think of it: you're rolling along through life, heading for the office or the shipyard, and all of a sudden you wake up and find yourself about to run out on the floor of the Boston Garden for a championship game on national television. You've already vomited in the dressing room, and your teammates have a dazed look in their eyes, as if they realize they're about to be run over by a car but can't do anything about it. Even Red Auerbach is quiet; that's how tense it is. While you're waiting there, shivering in your own sweat, you can literally feel the energy being released by the fans in the stands. Perfectly respectable people are yelling and screaming, behaving as they never would anywhere else. I used to joke that if you could bottle all the emotion let loose in a basketball game, you'd have enough hate to fight a war and enough joy to prevent one. As a player, you're about to run your guts out in five or six miles of short, frantic springs. The President of the United States has expressed interest in the outcome of the game, and bookmakers have covered their margins on millions of dollars' worth of bets. And while you're trying to rest there in your own private cocoon before the action starts, there's generally a moment when you find yourself wondering how it all came together.

As I see it, the world of sports is in very fine company, with a fine heritage. It is one of the Big Four. Only four kinds of events —politics, religion, the arts and sports—have been able to draw consistently large crowds of paying customers throughout history. That must mean something. From the early Greek Olympics, the gladiators in the Roman Coliseum and the tribal games of Africa, sports has appealed to something deep in people. Sports may have been neglected by historians, but it has been popular for as long as there have been players and spectators around, and unlike the other three fields it draws people to its events mostly on the basis of enthusiasm. At any concert, church service or political event, you'll find a lot of people showing up out of duty.

In all Big Four events, rules are crucial. In politics we have criminal rules, tax rules, international rules and the rules of war. In religion there is everything from rules on food and sex to rules of worship. In art there are prevailing conventions of poetry, music, literature or film-making. These rules serve vastly different purposes in each field. In politics rules are what you fight over, and a new government is elected to change or defend them. A revolution produces a whole new rulebook that even changes the *way* you fight over rules. In religion the rules are what you fail to live up to. In art, rules can be what you ignore or break to create something fresh and unique.

In sports the rules make everything fair. Everyone accepts the goals of the game as defined by the rules, and the way the game is played. Only when all questions of ends and means are answered do you really have a game. Sports *must be* fair; justice is always swift and exact, according to the rules, which answer all necessary questions and not a single extra one. At least that's what the referees say.

There are occasional disputes, however. That's why we get pictures of baseball managers kicking umpires in the shins, and that's why I spent years watching Red Auerbach yell at referees with the veins on his neck standing out as thick as ropes. Kids will become so angry and indignant that they can't have a game; one of them will pick up his ball and go home, or one player will have a fight with another. In sports there is a fine line between order and anarchy. Arguments about justice, while vehement, tend to be simple, with a lot of cussing and name-calling. They may lead to a rhubarb, but they are soon over. Even with millions of dollars of prize money at stake, disputes over an interpretation of the rules almost never threaten a sport itself. Fans may yell, "We wuz robbed!" but eventually everyone accepts the outcome of the game as it was declared.

Rules open doors in the sports world. They are boundaries, starting points, frames of reference. They solve several of the most difficult problems of ordinary life by determining what's fair and real. Everything that is out of bounds is not real, and you don't have to pay any attention to it. The rules control all space and motion within the game, and in many sports the time as well. You can call time-out and stop the clock, but when time-out is over, you step into the real world where the rules apply and everything else vanishes. You lose yourself in the spirit of the game, whether you are playing or watching. If it is a rhythmical sport like basketball, Ping-Pong or tennis, you soon absorb the rhythm of the game. Back and forth across the net or up and down off the floor bounces the ball. Sometimes it's slow and lazy enough to hypnotize you. Then all of a sudden the rhythm changes to blinding speed and there's a long instant of tension. Will he make it? Then the answer, and the rhythm changes again.

Whatever the game, each one has its own personality. The rules make its character. You can see how sports fits into the grand scheme of things by comparing its unique approach to rules with those of politics, religion and art. Sports may have the time-out, but war has the truce and art has the intermission. The basic difference between the four is how big a chunk of time each one tries to handle. Religion bites off the biggest bite you can imagine —eternity—and claims it. Time is endemic to all religions; they're always considering the long run. Art is similar in its approach; the artist may not speak of it, but he is searching for immortality and "eternal truths." Even in politics one is dealing with lengthy periods. How long will the principles of the Constitution last? A long time.

Sports has the shortest view. Nothing lasts much longer than a season, and the basic unit of time is the moment. Sports fans and players appreciate each instant; a relic from sports is a "great moment." The only sports people who indulge in long-range thinking are statisticians and record freaks; they try to make each moment in sports bigger by comparing it with every other moment in as many ways as possible. Thus we hear about "The Most Rebounds in One Quarter of a Championship Series Game in the NBA—19, by Bill Russell, Boston Celtics vs. Los Angeles Lakers, April 19, 1962," or about the "Most Consecutive Strike-Outs by a Left-Handed Batter in World Series Play." Such records give a little immortality to nearly every contest, where time is diced up into thousands of tiny pieces, so that almost every moment can have a record attached to it. But whenever a record is broken you can expect it to be followed by the next broken record. Records march on, pretty much like time itself.

Sports not only claims smaller bits of time, it also claims smaller bits of truth. Artists or professors of literature say quite seriously that "Art is truth." They don't mean a fleeting bit of the truth: they mean *The* truth. Religious leaders say the same thing, and so do politicians ("We hold these truths to be self-evident . . ."). Sports has a humble approach; the only truth it claims is the score, which changes all the time. The "final" score lasts only until the next game. Such humility has a liberating effect. Because sports doesn't assert any overarching truth, people can say just about anything they want. Sports is the land of exaggeration, and the bigger the yarn the better people like it. You can have "The Game of the Century" every week or so, and you can say, "There is no tomorrow" in the heat of the finals, and all that happens is that spectators become a little more nervous about the outcome. Think of the reaction if the Pope or the President of the United States announced that there was no tomorrow.

In sports, exaggerations that would otherwise be threatening or enraging seem humorous. "I am the greatest!" shouts Muhammad Ali. People may agree or disagree, but there is a chuckle running underneath it all. Or Babe Ruth can point to the right-field wall before a pitch and then hit a home run there, and the gesture will become part of baseball's mythology. "The King of Swat" could hit the ball "a country mile." On the field, sports figures can swagger and act like children. They can even be a little crazy; in fact, they probably *must* be a little crazy. All of which is fine, because it threatens no one. And the reason it doesn't is because it all takes place in the sports world, where no rigid truth has to be respected.

The athlete or fan can make up any nickname, trademark or eccentricity; the sky's the limit. Sports is so fundamentally unpretentious that the craziest of pretensions appear funny. All sports has an element of humor, perhaps because it's so patently ridiculous to be out there knocking another man down, jumping over a hurdle or trying to knock a little white ball in a hole with a stick. Even some of the players' nicknames seem to jump out and tickle: Earl "The Pearl" Monroe, "Dizzy" Dean, "Too Tall" Jones, "Sugar Ray" Robinson, "Minnesota Fats," "Big Daddy" Lipscomb. You can go on forever. (Only in the Republican sports like golf is there a run of pedestrian names.) Every outlandish name is insurance against pomposity.

I think of all sports as a mixture of art and war. The mixture changes with different sports, but it's always there. The art jumps out at you in a sport like women's gymnastics, a sport of dance and body sculpture, but I can tell you from having seen several Olympiads that those young girls are as competitive as any boxer. They're out there to win, and they'd sharpen their teeth on the balance beam if it would help.

Looking at all sports on a scale between art and war, I've always thought of basketball as being on the artistic side, more of a ballet than a brawl. But of course every athlete tends to emphasize the artistic qualities of his own sport. Still, when we see Julius ("Doctor J.") Erving fly through the air and under the basket, his back arched, his arms stretched, holding the ball like an orange, and see him make an impossible twist at the last instant to stuff the ball backwards through the basket, we say that was a beautiful move. And everybody means that adjective literally. Doctor J.'s moves *are* beautiful in the same way that an ice skater's leap is beautiful—or even in the same way that a painting is beautiful. The form inspires wonder, and the motion has something to say. Among other things it says that Doctor J. is a great basketball player. (The flamboyant moves are pretty, but I feel that the more difficult and artistic move is whatever Dr. J. had to do to get the defensive men out of the way.)

In any sport a spectacular star will be known as an "artist" of the game. Pelé was one in soccer. When he played, photographers focused on him to get shots of him in the air, his feet, his moves. Jim Brown had the same sort of grace in football. I've observed people, who don't like football, watching slow-motion films of him running with the ball, spellbound by the way he did it. If there's an ideal way for the mind to control the body, Brown had it.

On a fast break in basketball, the ball flies between three offensive players running at full speed—zip! zip! zip! zip!—and lastly to the unexpected man cutting under the basket at a rakish angle, who goes up and banks the ball off the glass in a lay-up, while the fully extended body of the defensive player climbs the glass after it within a quarter of an inch of touching it before the ball plops through the net. All this within two seconds. By their speed, eyes, minds and coordination, the three offensive players controlled the ball so that it approaches the net from just one of millions of possible angles and heights; at the same time the defensive player figures all this out instantly and inserts his hand at the only point in all that space where he might intercept the ball if his timing was perfect. The whole play has a collective beauty to it. (My own opinion is that the play would have been even more beautiful if the defensive man had blocked the shot, but I'm prejudiced.)

There is individual and collective beauty in all sports, but much of it is hidden from the unsophisticated viewer. You can't really appreciate the art of a hit-and-run in baseball unless you can recognize one. Many of the most difficult moves in basketball take place away from the ball, where no one sees or understands them. There is even some art to all that growling, gouging and earth-moving that huge linemen do in football, I suppose, though their mothers may be the only people who really appreciate it.

It is possible to change the mixture of art and war in any sport by changing its sacred rules. Let's imagine that in another time and another world, Florence Nightingale suddenly became Commissioner of the NBA. To eliminate all violence from basketball and to reward artistry, she threw out the automatic two-point basket and installed a panel of judges to award points based on the beauty of each particular basket scored. Doctor J. might get ten points for one of his flying whirlygigs, but only a point or two for a "garbage" shot off a rebound. But there was still too much hostility in the game, so Commissioner Nightingale eliminated the scoreboard. All beautiful plays in basketball should be appreciated on their own merits, she decreed, without regard to which team made them. As a result, basketball games became exhibitions of jumping, weaving through people, dribbling, leaping and marksmanship; players were motivated only by their love of the art. With all its warlike elements removed, the sport soon became a form of dance for elongated players with certain peculiar moves. Wilt Chamberlain and I came out of retirement to resume our careers and did a splendid *pas de deux* together. My *arabesque* came together with his *pirouette* in what looked like a hook shot from the old brand of competitive basketball.

Curious fans turned out in droves to see the first few games of Commissioner Nightingales's reformed basketball, featuring the bizarre but serene partnership of Chamberlain and Russell. But after a few performances the crowds began dwindling; attendance was soon way down. It fell even further when Wilt and I quit. He walked out because he wasn't getting paid enough, and I because I didn't like having him step all over my feet. Commissioner Nightingale didn't last long; her basketball had ceased to be a sport at all.

This doesn't mean that basketball should never be modified, only that each sport has its own balance and that it can't be tampered with too much. The competitive aspects of basketball aren't important only because they pack fans into the seats; they are vital because once they are in effect the art will take care of itself. If the players are turned loose within the rules, the game will work automatically; they will keep inventing newer and more glorious moves to counter the inventions of the other players. All that is required to choreograph the action is the ball; just throw it out there and the moves will gather around the ball wherever it goes. This is true of many major sports: the ball provokes the art all by itself. A baseball player like Willie Mays can stand all night out in some deserted pasture called center field, but if nothing is hit near him, he doesn't really deserve watching. Once there's a fly to center field, however, the picture changes instantly. He runs in that pigeon-toed sprint, all concentration, with a hundred thousand eyes in the stadium glued to every step. Those eyes belong to people whose entire days are improved by the sight of what Willie does when he gets to the ball. What a catch!

Ideally, there is a harmony between the art and war of any sport. But when you get into the real sports world of promoters and advertisers, huge television contracts, gamblers, frustrated heroes, Monday-morning quarterbacks, phony amateurs, broken noses and broken dreams, very little is ideal. It's not hard to imagine how a sport could become imbalanced, especially on the warlike side. There is always pressure in that direction. War is serious business, and a sport suffers whenever people get too serious about it. That's when the alumni association puts its foot on the coach's neck, the coach puts his foot on the players, and the fans put their feet on anybody they can find.

When I played professional basketball, fans occasionally yelled at me. When that happened, I always thought they had slipped over the line into war. Fan is short for fanatic, and some fans can become pretty extreme. Whether it's local high-school rivals in basketball or Michigan vs. Ohio State in football, the real fanatic enlarges the battle in his mind until he loves his team and hates the other side. Somehow his own personal values are threatened. He can let out all his hostilities, and afterwards say it was only a game.

That excuse has always irritated me. If a fan is an embarrassment to the human race at the Super Bowl, it's not because he's at the Super Bowl—it's because he's an embarrassment to the human race. Like alcohol, sports doesn't lie. What it reveals about a person under its influence was just hiding. People sometimes use sports as a way to deny responsibility for what they really are. A fan gets out of hand when he wants to hate or love something that has nothing to do with sports. He sees victory for his team as a triumph for almost anything he likes—from bell-bottom pants to the principles of the Democratic party—and as a defeat for anything he hates. The fanatical fan expects his team to be like himself. That's how you get the old athlete's image of the all-around hero who is fair, square and patriotic. The image may have little in common with the player, but it's what the average fan wants to see in him.

Fan identification constantly seduces athletes. During my career, people would come up to me and say, "Great game, Bill. I want my son here to grow up just like you." For a long time I was flattered by such comments. I knew that the fan meant he wanted his kid to be like me *as a person,* so I told myself that I must be the best man around since Abe Lincoln. Then I began to wonder. Those people didn't know a thing about me personally; for all they knew, I might be a child molester. Yet here were parents saying they wanted to model their children after me, instead of after themselves. I began to cringe at those comments; instead of flattering me, they made me sad. Over the years I would learn better than anyone that my basketball skills and my parental ones were very different qualities.

Sports inspires misplaced hopes in fans—or perhaps a misplaced sense of morals. They want athletes to set high standards —not to smoke, not to get divorced, not to use drugs. In fact, they insist on it to the point of refusing to see what's going on. Many professional teams are traveling pharmacies, for instance, with cocaine being the current drug of preference. So much coke is snorted in the NBA that if ten players sneezed at once you could bet that one or two of them was losing money. The league hushes up drug cases because they conflict with what the public wants to believe about athletes. I don't believe off-court athletes are much different than their age peers, except that they are wealthy.

Sports also gives people an outlet for bias—witness our "White Hopes" in the NBA, Bill Bradley and Bill Walton. There are rumbles among fans who would love to see these players become "a credit to their race." The irony is that these particular players are far removed from such thinking. Bradley and Walton haven't the slightest interest in being anybody's racial symbol, but the labels get slapped on them by fans, and occasionally by a sportswriter.

Racism on the part of the audience can still be mean and nasty, but owners and coaches can't afford it if they want to win. Inside sports, racism has become more subtle. It lingers on in the attitudes of certain coaches and managers who have strange ideas about, for example, where a black man should play. In football the position of middle linebacker is usually reserved for whites because it is a "leadership" position. On the few pro teams that have black middle linebackers, the coach usually assigns a white player to call the defensive signals.

As far as I know, there has never been a black offensive center in professional football. There are plenty of huge black guys everywhere else on the line, but none actually hiking the ball. In the coaches' minds, center is a white position because it requires intellect and leadership. The center has to have a certain amount of rapport with the quarterback to cut down on fumbles, has to look at the world upside down without getting dizzy, has to remember the snap count *perfectly,* and is the only offensive lineman who is supposed to touch the ball. He doesn't have to be the strongest or quickest offensive lineman, but he has to be steady and reliable. To coaches, all these qualities suggest a white center. Since nobody ever notices the center, the NAACP will never agitate for a black one.

In the early 1970's a team of Miami researchers made a study of possible bias in television sports broadcasting. They assembled a test group of elderly blind people who knew little about football and asked them to listen to games on television. The blind people tried to guess the race of a player whenever they heard one described on the air, and their guesses turned out to be correct an overwhelming majority of the time. When a receiver was described as having "blazing speed," they said black. When they heard about a man "who knows how to get open," they said white. A player who had "poise" and "a head on his shoulders" was white, whereas a player who was "hot," or "amazing" or "intimidating" tended to be black.

Almost everyone has a peeve about the structure of sports. Some say there is too much controversy surrounding it, others are upset that they don't see the old college try as much as they used to, and still others don't like sports as big business. Recently, most of the complaints have been about money. Ever since the music-and-entertainment executive Sonny Werblin introduced show business to sports by signing Joe Namath for $400,000, people have protested that sports has been drowned in dollars. Free agents are too busy running around with their bankers, lawyers and investment counselors to work up a sweat on the field. The problem with modern sports, you hear, is player greed.

I agree that there is something unhealthy about the trend, but I don't think the root of the problem is money, any more than it is the mass neuroses of the fans. I don't believe professional athletes are much greedier than they used to be. The superstars have always been paid presidential salaries. Over the last decade or so the biggest change in salaries for professional athletes has been the upgrading of those for the average and beginning players. The average basketball player has risen to the income level of the average banker, while football and baseball players have risen to the level of the average lawyer. The average golfer would still do as well selling insurance. Professional athletes now have white-collar status, across a career drastically shorter than most professions. Athletes scramble for money while they can get it, because they know their earning power may not last longer than the next tackle or slide into second. Like most people, athletes are financially insecure, and I don't think their appetites have grown any bigger. But the plate has; there is more money around.

Money in sports serves the same function it always has: it is paid to the professionals and slipped to the amateurs. It's a lightning rod for hypocrisy in sports, just as in every other field. (Nobody,—artist, clergyman or public servant—claims to be motivated by money, and yet those professions are exactly where you'll find the biggest checks being written.) Amateur sports is one of the longest-running continuous scandals in the United States. When I was in college an official of the AAU saw me high jump one day and urged me to compete in the Compton Relays. "Name your price," he said. He was just that blunt. In the very same year the AAU sanctimoniously penalized Wes Santee for accepting excess expense money for an event not sanctioned by it, and he was banned from AAU competition for life.

Corrupt dollars were dangled before me long before honest ones. At college, a major part of an athlete's life was talking to AAU officials about extra money. The organization usually won the arguments because it had all the bargaining power. Once a distance runner I knew showed up for an event and found his envelope $75 short of the money he had been promised, so he pulled up lame about seventy-five yards from the finish line. He made his point, but he didn't win the argument.

About twenty years ago I remember having a kind thought for the organizations in control of amateur sports, but I forget what it was. The NCAA, the AAU and the American Olympic Committee spend the bulk of their time sniping at each other, squabbling over turf, moving money around and making deals with the big businesses involved with sports. They base their existence on the idea that sports are pure only when there's no money around, and yet they all hover around the take. Their reputations are staked on their enforcement of rules prohibiting payment of money to athletes, and yet they don't really enforce those rules. They don't want to—and they couldn't if they did, because under-the-table payments are so widespread. Recruitment violations in college sports are like snow in the Alps—all over the place and so bright that you go snow blind and can't see anything at all.

In 1972 I covered basketball for television at the Olympic Games in Munich. It was lucky that we had the cameras focused on the athletes, because what was going on behind the scenes would have scorched peoples' eyes. Deals were being made almost out in the open. It was well known, for instance, that a certain manufacturer had contributed $50,000 (tax-deductible, of course) to the Olympic Committee in return for its promise that the members of the basketball team would wear the manufacturer's product at all games and practices. As a result, an official of the Committee had to go around making sure that the players wore the product all the time. The players didn't like it for the simple reason that it wasn't the best equipment available. The manufacturer had bought what he could not earn by craftsmanship.

Such dishonesty is rife in amateur sports, and is much more incompatible with the ideals of sport than large salaries are. By their very nature, hypocrisy and dishonesty are incompatible with the kind of fairness that players and spectators alike must believe in if sports is to flourish. An athlete is a craftsman, working out in the open, where you can watch him or her sweat. The performance is no more and no less than what you see. The athlete cannot rest on his last performance or let the team get along by itself for a game or two. He can't coast on his diploma. Sports weeds out the slackers.

The hypocrisy of amateur sports is offensive to anybody who cares. To me, being an amateur is like being a virgin. It is an old idea that has some innocence and charm, celebrated mostly by people to whom it doesn't apply. It doesn't look as good on old people as on young ones. It is impossible to keep partially, though many try to do so. It is associated with deception and pretense. And even if you love the idea, you still can't help being suspicious when you see the pious members of the U.S. Chastity Committee charging the public money to peep at their soiled virgins.

Another aspect of sports guaranteed to produce hypocrisy is gambling. Mention the word to any sports commissioner and he's likely to behave like a man coming out of amnesia: "What? Who? What did you say? Who am I?" The subject unnerves the people who are supposed to protect the integrity of their games. They are right to worry, because gambling offers an incentive for point-shaving and taking dives. They should try to keep gambling and sports apart, but this has nothing to do with the *morality* of gambling. The people who run the major horse-racing tracks also have a huge stake in keeping races pure and unaffected by betting —probably a bigger stake than the sports that don't involve betting—but they don't take the position that gambling is immoral or illegal. For Commissioner Rozelle of the NFL it is a different story. He testifies before Congress that it is a scourge, and everybody in pro football should turn a cold shoulder to it; if they don't, he'll make them suffer. A true sportsman won't even associate with gamblers, Rozelle says, and he made Joe Namath sell a New York restaurant to prove it. Rozelle is against legalized sports betting, taking the classic law-enforcement position that it is corrupting and should be stamped out.

I don't like big-time gamblers myself, and I have nothing against Rozelle's position—except for its hypocrisy. He is trying to create an image of pro football's concerns that simply doesn't match with the reality. Let's leave aside the issue of the *owners* of franchises in pro football, who at one time included former bookmakers. That's a murky area that you could expect the Commissioner of the NFL to avoid. This apart, it's easy to see that the NFL takes great pains to service its constituents as *gamblers,* not just as fans. Take those weekly injury lists, for example. In recent years the lists have grown more elaborate. There are strict rules for classifying players as "questionable," as opposed to "probable." The League imposes fines and penalties on teams that conceal their injuries. You have to report them correctly and on time. There are deadlines throughout the week. All this came about because this information can be vital to bettors. A couple of key injuries could make the Steelers a six-point favorite instead of seven and a half. Millions of dollars of bets can turn on that one-and-a-half-point difference, and it matters whether bettors and bookies learn about the injuries on Tuesday as opposed to Wednesday.

If Americans spend $2 billion every year on tickets to sports events, they spend at least $50 billion in bets on those same games. That represents a lot of fan interest, and Pete Rozelle bends over backwards to keep those people happy. At the same time he denounces them and the vice they love. The newspapers also play it both ways by printing the point spreads, the morning line and the how-to-bet columns. You can read the columnist's account of how he made a bundle on the Lakers yesterday, and then turn to the crusading editorial against gambling.

Only once during my career did a big-time gambler approach me about fixing a game. He talked casually and indirectly about the proposition he had in mind, but I knew what he was getting at. "You can't afford it," I told him.

This man was a heavy heavy, and the remark offended him. "What do you mean I can't afford it?" he asked.

"Look," I said, "I'm making over a hundred thousand dollars a year playing ball. During my career I should make over a million dollars. Now, to mess with you I'd have to risk all that, plus my reputation. That's a lot—it's my whole future. So even if I wanted to accommodate you, I couldn't think about it for less than nine or ten million a game—maybe even more. And that's just for me. To make any money, you'd have to be betting enough to have the whole state after you."

I reported this incident to the NBA Commissioner, and though nothing came of it, it demonstrates something about game-fixing in the modern era: that high salaries are actually a further protection against corruption. A professional athlete would have to be crazy to take bribes today. I've always thought the most likely targets of gamblers would be the referees. They make peanuts, they're highly abused both by the fans and players, and they have more control over a game than anyone else. Moreover, the normal incompetence of NBA referees would be a perfect disguise for a corrupt one. It seems to me that the NBA has gone out of its way to keep its referees poor and incompetent—and I mean clear around-the-barn-out-of-the-way. For years I tried to get the league to hire a black referee and recommended more than a dozen good ones. They always found a way not to hire the ones I recommended, but at the same time officials kept telling me they were looking for "qualified black referees." They always used that adjective: referees were either plain referees or were "qualified Negro referees." Finally, in frustration I sent in the name of a referee who was famous as a bumbling idiot, so the NBA hired him, of course, and he was terrible. He couldn't tell a rule book from a slide rule, and was a walking argument against affirmative action. The protests against him were so universal that I finally got a call asking why I'd recommended him. "I got tired of recommending 'qualified black referees,' " I said, "so I decided to recommend an unqualified one for a change, and that's the one you picked."

Sports have to be free-spirited, but they don't have to be free; they don't even have to be cheap. I've seen some extremely well-paid athletes playing for big money but still having more fun than kids in a candy store; I've also seen young boys in amateur sports drooping like draftees reporting to boot camp.

The notion that greedy players are destroying professional sports is a tricky one. I've noticed that you read a lot more about it in the newspapers than you hear about it on television. The reason for the discrepancy is, as usual, the source of the information. Television announcers make a lot of money; I know because I've been one. You get huge checks for little work, whereas the writers get little checks for little work. At first a television salary is a shock; you begin to believe that your face has turned into some sort of rare diamond. From the perspective of the fortunates in this position, sports stars aren't greedy; they only earn a living wage—a hundred grand or so, give or take a Rolls or two—so you won't often hear a television announcer on the air squawking about outrageous salaries. It wouldn't occur to him. Besides, the way retired athletes are entering television in hordes, the announcer might be insulting one of his future colleagues.

It's different with the newspapers, where money is tight. You won't see Dandy Don Meredith on the sports beat of some newspaper because reporters don't make enough money. They know it too, so certain resentments bubble up from their wallets to their brains and then all the way down to their typing fingers. What the reporter sees is that after thirty years of lugging his typewriter, he's earning the same amount as the average rookie shortstop, or about one fourth what the standard basketball rookie makes—even when he doesn't play. The reporter looks at that rookie, who is twenty-two years old, can't quite remember President Kennedy and doesn't care anyway, chews gum and who carries a silk handkerchief so he can wipe ladies' fingerprints off his brand-new car, and quickly concludes that something is rotten.

In most sports, athletes come along in waves that are much shorter than normal human generations; every six years or so you get a new batch. Durable athletes can last a couple of generations or more, but they have to adapt. What has happened in the last three or four sports generations is that athletics have changed from a newspaper activity to a television one. To the extent that a sport is covered on television, the players tend to be paid on its scale. Television pumps money in, and the sport will naturally change to its standards in everything from pay to dress to the prevailing clichés.

The history of organized sports over these generations has been centered around its television negotiations. When the football commissioner negotiated pro football's first big network contracts, CBS wound up financing the first burst of nationwide popularity. Its ratings were so high during this period that the other two networks might as well have gone dark. They showed re-runs. When the NFL, sitting on a gold mine, refused to expand to other cities, a bunch of rich men started the rival AFL. One year Lamar Hunt's team lost a million dollars, and he is said to have told reporters, "Well, if this keeps up I can only last another sixty or seventy years." But as wealthy as these men were, their league really depended on support from the networks, and NBC was only too happy to help them along. New leagues in other sports rose and fell, depending on how successful they were on television. Only boxing made major gains in popularity after failing on the air, and this was because Muhammad Ali's stature rose above both the medium and his sport.

Television has been by far the biggest influence on sports in my lifetime. But though it has made it richer and vastly more popular, it threatens to destroy some sports and ruin the way we think of others. More than any other factor, television accelerates some very unhealthy trends—and I don't mean money. I'm speaking about the trend toward the control of sports by people who have little or no regard for the art in them, as well as the trend toward more and more organization in sports, to the point that its spontaneity is lost.

Television has no nose and not much of a brain, but it has a magnificent eye that can perform miracles. Since the art for the spectator is visual, television and bodily sports are a perfect match. For a card game, you don't need instant replay, but you thank the gods for it when you're watching the downhill ski races at the winter Olympics. Millions of people have come to appreciate unfamiliar games through television, whose eye is so powerful that it can instantly convey the visual beauty of a new sport. Television people know this, and have spared no expense to exploit it. Many of the recent advances in the medium's technology—instant replay, split screen, stop-action, hand-held cameras, color mixing, slow-motion replays and so on—have come about solely because its practitioners have been seeking better ways for the eye to capture the art in sports.

Its sophisticated eye gives television a head start in selling new sports, and with it executives try to build their audience. Their challenge is how to make a huge national audience identify with an event. How do you persuade the New York fan to care about a game between two teams from the West Coast, or the hardened hockey nut to watch baseball? Television thrashes around trying to give every game a meaning that will appeal to a mass audience. Therefore commentators emphasize the role of the coaches in building a team into which the players must fit. Fans may not be able to identify with players they've never heard of, but they can become interested in simple game strategies and philosophies. For this reason the people off the field have become relatively more important; league officials, owners and even commentators themselves have risen to star status as television helps to advertise what they, too, stand for.

Historians should recognize that the first real superstar in modern professional football was not Jim Brown or Joe Namath, but a coach—Vince Lombardi. He was much more of a celebrity across the country than any of his players—in fact, more than anybody who'd ever played pro football. Lombardi was the military commander, the dictator of the Green Bay Packers, and the players were useful only if they fit into the machine he'd designed. It was a winning one, and he drove his men to the limits of their endurance. Stories circulated about how he scoffed at injuries and expected his players to keep going. He demanded that they eat, drink and sleep football, in complete submission and loyalty to his discipline. When Jim Ringo, the Packer center who had played games for Lombardi with broken bones and boils all over his body, asked for a raise one year, he was promptly traded for insubordination. Lombardi was cold and cruel—until the moment of final victory, when he and his players would melt and say that all the pain was worth it. Winning was worth *anything*. The city of Green Bay agreed, and soon there was a Lombardi Avenue.

After Lombardi, television viewers grew accustomed to the sight of the coach brooding on the sidelines. They were all square-jawed and looked sternly out over the field, each of them with solid, unsporty names and a philosophy that could be tested every week. Coaches became the most important personalities in the league, and television analysts would discuss their thoughts, their upbringing, their system and what they had for breakfast. When teams clashed in championship games, the coaches would be examined as if they were Napoleon and Wellington at Waterloo. Television helped sports like football seem more and more like war—organized from the top down, focused on the generals more than on the lowly cannon fodder who did the actual dirty work.

These days commentators often give the impression that a good player is an extension of the coach's mind. They help the fans pretend that they're coaches too, and they spend the whole game trying to anticipate what will happen, matching the action against theories and game plans. Therefore most athletes get evaluated according to how well they follow instructions. A basketball player may drive the lane for an inspired, artistic lay-up, but the announcer will find a way to reduce this to a part of the coach's strategy: "Yes, fans, 'ol Big Foot sure did execute Coach Careful's strategy of quick penetration, keeping in mind the options of passing off or looking for the high-percentage shot." This kind of advertising of coaching strategy is stifling, and it's partly in rebellion that the sports without overbearing coaches—like tennis, golf and the Olympic Games—have become more popular. Other things being equal, the artistic side of any sport will flourish whenever its players tend to dominate the game. The warlike side of a sport will flourish whenever the coaches and other nonplayers dominate. And the fans go back and forth in what they prefer. During the Lombardi era and the Vietnam war, a violent sport, football, became even more warlike and popular. Since the end of the war, baseball seems to be making a comeback. Baseball is a players' sport, with stars and individual quirks and artistic touches.

The trend in modern sports is toward more organization and "meaning," especially for those people who don't play themselves. Television didn't cause this, but it sure helps it. It's bigger and deeper than the pursuit of money. Take Little League baseball, for example. I remember going to a Little League game in 1964, when my seven-year-old son was thinking about playing. I was horrified by what I saw. Spectators were yelling at the coaches, and the coaches were yelling at the players. Parents were yelling insults at their own kids, and arguing with each other over whose should be playing and whose should be benched. And the *managers!* They each had systems of play; those eight-year-olds all batted and fielded the same way, looked at the manager the same way and even ran out on the field the same way. They had no choice; with all the pressure from the coach and their parents in the stands, conformity was the safest course. The kids were pawns. The real game was going on between the parents and the managers, and the contest didn't have much to do with sports. The players themselves had little chance to be kids; they were so organized, pressurized and regimented by the nonplayers that their imaginations were stunted. They couldn't experiment and innovate, goof off and try new things, or develop a sense of themselves as craftsmen. Outsiders had stolen the show.

My son didn't play Little League baseball, I'm glad to say. Part of my aversion to organization comes from my own childhood experience. When I grew up, there weren't many basketball teams or coaches around, and almost everything about sport was unorganized. There was a lot of play, in the strict sense of the word. We tried on our own to find what was fun and what worked. My own basketball confidence came to me long before I received any serious coaching, and it paid off later when I took up the game as a profession. The accomplishments I'm proudest of are the innovations I helped introduce in the way the game is played today: blocked shots, active rather than passive defense, ideas about the horizontal geometry around the basket. I don't think I'd have come up with such innovations if I'd grown up playing the way Little League baseball is today.

It's the players, not the coaches, owners or commentators, who provide the art in sports. Every good player should think that he may be able to change the game, and he should have the craftsman's pride and joy in what he does. In most professional sports the best players are unorthodox. That's why I enjoyed playing against Wilt Chamberlain so much. We had different approaches to the game, and we both knew it, but the differences came from within, not from our coaches. Of course there are stylists in sports, but nowadays you are more likely to hear about the innovative ideas of coaches.

I played in a time when basketball players thought of themselves as gunfighters, and we all went around challenging each other. K.C. Jones and I would drive down to Los Angeles on weekends just to find a game. Stories about showdowns became legends among players. Once Wilt Chamberlain drove down to Elgin Baylor's home in Washington, D.C., for a game. Elgin got up a team for him, and then his team whipped Wilt's team day and night. When Elgin was asked how he'd done it, he answered, "Well, the newspapers in Philadelphia said that Wilt and four cheerleaders could beat anybody—so I gave him four cheerleaders." Out of pride and cussedness, players in those days would respond to a challenge laid down by anybody—even a newspaper writer.

If you were a basketball gunfighter, you worked on your game the same way you'd work on your draw, and you worried all the time about how to develop new tricks and strategies. You also worried about what the other guy might come up with. Even in a team game, every player had to have a sense of himself as craftsman.

It's no secret that I don't believe there are many craftsmen in modern professional basketball, but this may have something to do with the fact that craftsmen in any profession are hard to find in this country, from automobile mechanics to winemakers. In order to be one, you have to have a sense of extending your craft and of pride in your own creation. Whenever I do come on a true craftsman, I have a feeling that life for them is as sweet as it can be.

Perhaps craftsmanship in sports is becoming obsolete for the same reason that it's out of date everywhere else. Maybe it's better preparation for life if Little Leaguers learn how to get along with and obey their coaches instead of discovering a sport on their own and learning to use their imagination to entertain themselves. But I don't think that's the nature of sports, and I don't believe that television or the Little League contributes very much to what health remains in games.

Recruiting doesn't help. In recent years, as the Little Leagues and pee-wee football leagues have grown into big organizations, coaches are beginning to find the good prospects at younger and younger ages. A college basketball coach will rise or fall on how well he recruits high-school players, a high-school coach will be out scouting junior-high prospects, and the junior-level coaches are out scouting the hot kids in the pee-wee leagues. As a result, a good young player has smoke blown in his face by adults from puberty on. Coaches will tell him that he can have anything he wants. If a young boy can keep his head after becoming a local superstar before his voice changes, he's a rare specimen. In the modern era, players are almost encouraged not to take responsibility for themselves or what they do.

It's hard enough to be a craftsman when circumstances work in your favor, but it's even harder when they work against you. Athletes have their own special obstacle in the form of the owners of modern professional teams. Most owners look at players from a viewpoint that's far removed from the welfare of sports. Their most redeeming quality is that generally they don't claim to know or care much about their game; they simply demand a winner from their coach. A new breed of owner has sprung up, mainly in basketball and baseball: the ego-trip owner. Typically, he's not a rich-as-Croesus type with loads of corporate backing, but a self-made man who has built up a moderately large empire in some business lacking glamour, and who goes into sports ownership for the notoriety it brings. He's quoted in the newspapers and invited to fancy parties; he gets to rub shoulders with jocks, to hang out in the press box, to test his theory that he knows as much about building a winner as any coach.

All of which is a depressing contrast to what existed in the early days of the NBA. Many of the original owners in professional basketball got into the game only because they owned or ran sports arenas and needed another attraction to help fill the seats. My old boss, Walter Brown, ran the Boston Garden, helped found the NBA—and wound up as owner of the Celtics. His friends thought he was crazy. Basketball was not popular then, especially in Boston, and even if it had been, Brown didn't know the first thing about the game. He never really claimed to, but he developed a fever for it that only a sports person could contract. Celtic basketball almost sent him to the poorhouse, but he stuck to it.

I've always felt that Walter Brown had a certain nobility. I didn't know where it came from. He had a bad temper and a wild, competitive streak, but he also had a strong emotional attachment to simple fairness. If he saw injustice, he'd either get furious or go to pieces. One story of his anger first made me believe that he must be somebody. Before I joined the team, the Celtics hired Chuck Cooper as the first black player in the history of the NBA. Abe Saperstein of the Harlem Globetrotters heard about it in advance, and stormed in to see Brown at the Boston Garden. As the Globetrotter's owner, promoter and "coach," Saperstein liked to portray himself as the benefactor of all Negroes in sports. He also believed that he had earned a monopoly on the services of every black athlete in the country. In this spirit he had opposed the admission of Jackie Robinson to major-league baseball on the grounds that it threatened his all-Negro baseball teams. Saperstein told Walter Brown bluntly that if Cooper played for the Celtics, the Globetrotters would never again set foot in Boston Garden. It was a serious threat. The Globetrotters were a big attraction, and at the time Brown needed Saperstein much more than Saperstein needed the Garden. Nevertheless, Brown, in one of his finer moments, told Saperstein that he was right about his Globetrotters' not setting foot in Boston Garden again: they would not be allowed. In fact, he said that he was so offended by the threat that *no* Saperstein team would ever play there again. He was true to his word, and he lost money because he stood up for a principle.

Red Auerbach used to have tantrums because he thought

Brown didn't fight hard enough for the Celtics' interests at NBA meetings. I saw the two of them go at it many a time. Walter would say that he had to make sacrifices "for the good of the game," and Red would roll his eyes and then explode. The worst argument I ever observed was when Walter decided he'd have to vote for ending the NBA's "territorial draft," by which each team used to be allowed to deal with one local college player each year outside the regular draft. The rule favored such big-city teams as Boston, New York and Philadelphia, because they had lots of talented players to choose from in surrounding colleges, and worked against teams from places like Syracuse and Rochester. Red loved the rule, but Walter was the swing vote against it because he felt the league would be more balanced without it. Besides, it led to a lot of hanky-panky, with professional teams trying to influence where young prospects lived or went to college.

Walter Brown started off in the entertainment business at Boston Garden. He booked sports events, car shows, carnivals, auctions, concerts—anything to entertain a crowd. Ironically, it turned out that this man from the entertainment business was more devoted to sports than many owners who showed more interest in entertainment. Saperstein paved the way. His Globetrotters didn't—and still don't—have much to do with sports. They exhibit some basketball moves, but they've always put on more of a minstrel show than a sporting event. Theirs is a combined dance and skit, conveying the consistent message that blacks are funny, happy-go-lucky clowns.

Admittedly, any professional sport has to be in the entertainment business, just as any art that's a business is entertainment, from books to operas. This doesn't mean you have to demean the sport itself, as I believe Saperstein did. Sports have been moving toward show business since Babe Ruth, and since the producers of *Monday Night Football* found that their ratings depended as much on the announcers they used as on the quality of the game on the air. In their search for something to replace "home-team" loyalty, the medium has hit on show-business stars. Fans will identify with athletes if they develop the kind of celebrity status and lifestyle that Hollywood is famous for. Naturally, most professional athletes like the idea of stardom, and so do the owners. The idea has been carried a step further with the invention of the "sports feature" shows, in which all-star casts of celebrities give mediocre performances in sports they know little about. These shows may not be bad entertainment or bad business, but they don't have anything to do with sports.

Many elements seem to conspire against sports today, even at a time when it has swept the country. Unfortunately, the quality of many games will deteriorate under pressure from television's mass audiences, organization and the general drift of the times. If I sound a bit gloomy, it's not because I think the future of all sports is hopeless. After all, sports is one of the Big Four and has a long history of taking care of itself. Even if some games dry up and blow away, others—lively and unformed—will spring up to take their place. Some games will rejuvenate themselves and others will decline, but sports will endure because people will always love the mixture of fun and excellence.

4

Champions

I made up my mind to be a champion basketball player in Provo, Utah, at the beginning of my sophomore season at the University of San Francisco. I was on edge; part of me wanted to knock somebody in the head, and part wanted to crawl into a hole because of the pressure. Everybody, including me, sensed that there might be something special about the way I was developing as a player, but this didn't mean that everybody liked it. One night I was walking down the hall of my dorm when the captain of the basketball team stopped me. "You know, you think you're pretty good," he said in a hostile tone. "But you're not playing with the kids now. You're playing with the men, and I don't think you can cut it." This guy was supposed to be my teammate, our team leader, but he had never said anything to me that wasn't an insult. A lot of it was race, I knew. The Jesuits at the University had very progressive attitudes about racial matters, but not all the students took them to heart, especially on the basketball team.

We were in Provo to play Brigham Young University early in the season. Their center was only about six foot four and, on the first play of the game he got the ball, dribbled around me, and ran to the bucket for an uncontested lay-up. "Hey," I thought, "this little guy's quick," and I took off up the court thinking of ways to keep that from happening again. As I crossed the mid-court line ahead of the ball, our captain ran past me. "Why don't you try playing some defense?" he growled. The game was five seconds old, and he was already cutting me up.

Emotions that had been building up all fall in practice finally spilled over inside me. The way I reacted was to say to myself, "He wants defense? He'll get defense. That center won't get any more points tonight." And he didn't. Whenever he got his hands on the ball, I was inside his jersey and two feet over his head at the same time. At USF you weren't supposed to dance with girls as close as I was playing that guy. I was in a frenzy, and defense was all I wanted to do. I didn't shoot, I didn't want to pass or set picks, and I didn't want to pick up anybody else's man on defense either —especially the captain's man—he could have all the free lay-ups he wanted, as far as I was concerned.

In the locker room at half time I was still burning and stalking around like a wounded animal. The coach, Phil Woolpert, jumped right on me. "What's the matter with you, Russell? You've been reading your press clippings," he said. There was silence in the locker room; that question hurt all the way down to my toenails. Phil didn't even bother to ask what was eating me, even though something was obviously wrong. Over the years, since our basketball careers ended, Phil and I have become good friends, but back then we did not always see eye to eye.

Right there at half time in Provo I decided that I was going to be a great basketball player. Everything inside me poured itself into that decision; all the anger and wonder joined together with one purpose, and energy was coming out my ears. That half time was filled with silence, and then I went out in the second half and whipped most of the Brigham Young team myself. I was smoking and dealing. I scored twenty points, blocked shots almost at will, and was jumping so high that I could have blocked a lot of them with my head. "Screw these guys," I thought. "I don't give a damn what any of them does. I'm just gonna play ball." I felt that way the whole season. I expended tremendous amounts of energy and played inspired basketball, but I couldn't have cared less about the coach or any of the other players. At the end of the season I looked up and saw that we had a mediocre record of 14–7, though we had enough talent to be one of the best teams in the country.

I've never forgotten that sophomore season in all the succeeding years of argument about who the best all-time basketball players have been. It's a big temptation for me to judge a player by the won-lost records of the teams he's played with. It's not hard to see why. My high-school teams lost only three games in the three seasons I played. On our Northwest tour the California All-Stars lost only one game, and that was to a college team. My freshman team at USF had a record of 19–4, and during my last two college seasons we went 57–1, with two NCAA championships. Then I went touring in Latin America with a team that won almost thirty games without losing one. After playing on an undefeated Olympic team, I spent thirteen years in the NBA. In twelve of those thirteen years the Celtics reached the finals of the play-offs, and in eleven of them we won the championship, including eight in a row. Since then no team in the NBA has won even two in a row.

I was the only player who was in all those places, so I suppose I could say, "Well, I'm the reason." But my sophomore year in college showed me otherwise. We had wall-to-wall jerks on that team, and we couldn't win. I played my heart out, but our team was riddled with dissension, and I was part of it. I was not strong enough to change the atmosphere for the better, and the team wasn't strong enough to change me, so we feuded. There was bad feeling among almost all the players, so though everyone played well, we still lost. Sometimes I'm haunted by the thought that my whole career could have been like that one season if certain ingredients hadn't changed. Most of them had to do with the team. My attitude became different when the atmosphere on the team improved, so I can look back and see how important the personal chemistry was among us. That's one reason why I still have strong feelings about individual honors in team sports, especially one like basketball in which it's vital that individual skills mesh together.

One of the major changes in my junior year was that we no

longer had the players I believed were the biggest jerks; they had graduated. Another factor was that K. C. Jones returned. His appendix had ruptured before that game in Provo, and he played only one game in my sophomore season; in fact, he almost died of complications. One day when his condition was at its worst, the whole USF student body was asked to turn out for a special service to pray for his recovery, and hundreds of kids showed up. That touched me, for K.C. was already one of the best friends I will ever have. Aside from that, he was also already a star basketball player, and it showed the next year. The whole team felt better. Winning is even better when you like each other. It becomes infectious. Winning in college had an innocence to it because we were not even out in the world yet. Being champions was great, but it was also fun. Everything was so fresh.

In the pros the game changed drastically for me because there weren't any average players. All-Americans are common; everybody's good. If my analogy that athletes are treated like pretty girls is valid, then professional sports is a kind of Miss America contest. Everybody out there is *beautiful*, and they're all vain enough to show up. In professional team events it's tough to keep everybody pulling together over the long haul.

I decided that professional sports is about winning, and so I made up my mind that I wanted to win every game. That was the goal to pursue, much more than a big salary, a rebounding title or selection to the All-Star team. To a degree, it helped that I came along at a time of great prejudice against blacks, because I was less inclined to go after honors and selections that depended on the judgment of other people. I already knew that you could get burned that way. It also helped that I came into the league without much confidence in myself as a shooter. Many of my detractors said I could never make it in pro ball because I was a bad shot from more than three feet out, and I shared their skepticism more than I ever let on. When I first entered the league, the only shot I felt sure of was my dunk shot (and I'd even missed some of them), so I didn't figure to run off with any scoring honors. But I did think I could help win games, and that's what I tried to concentrate on. Everything else would follow.

The process of trying to figure out what it would take to win every game took me back to the times at USF when K.C. and I would talk for hours about basketball tactics. I had a lot of baggage to get rid of, but K.C. and I had made a start. If you fix your mind on the goal of winning and stay honest with yourself, you'll come to realize that winning isn't about right and wrong, or the good guys and the bad guys, or the pathway to good life and character, or statistics. Winning is about who has the best team, and that's all.

In order to win you have to get yourself past a lot of things that may not be vital to winning but make you feel good, like scoring a lot of points. You have to forgo the pleasure of proving a point, because what somebody else wants you to prove may be inconsistent with the way you should play to win. At first this idea was difficult for me to accept. When I came into the NBA, it was widely believed that any big player had to be able to shoot well from the outside, like Dolph Schayes, Tom Heinsohn, and Bob Petit. If he couldn't, coaches, writers and fans would shake their heads and say, "He can't play." That's what they said about me when they saw that I couldn't make shots from twenty feet, so naturally the one thing I wanted to do was to stand outside and shoot twenty-footers. I missed almost all of them, of course, and when I did people shook their heads and said, "See what I mean? He can't play."

After a few kind words from Red Auerbach, like "Russell, what the hell are you doing shooting from way out there, besides making a fool of yourself?" I realized my stupidity and left those shots for Bill Sharman. That lesson was relatively easy because I couldn't make those shots; it was much harder to learn not to "prove" things that I *could* do, like blocking hook shots. In the NBA back then, a hook shot was considered almost unstoppable. I could block one, but I had to learn that proving it was not the point. Blocking hooks to show that I could do so would be bad strategy on my part. For one thing, I didn't want players to stop taking hook shots, which they might if it became known that I could stop it; for another, I'd already learned that you don't try to block every shot. What you try to do is to intimidate your opponent with the idea that you *might* block any shot. Knowing which shots to go after is one of the most difficult arts in defensive basketball, and it contributes a great deal to winning games. But proving your point about hook shots is not part of the art.

None of the Celtics, least of all myself, eliminated completely all those little personal goals that can interfere with winning. But we didn't have to. For my first few years I looked at the numbers after the game because I wanted to lead the league in rebounding. Cousy wanted to lead the league in assists. Sharman wanted to lead the league in free-throw percentage. Heinsohn wanted to lead the league in field goal attempts, and Red wanted to lead the league in technical fouls and fines. The good thing about it was that no two Celtics had the same goal, and that nobody was trying to play the wrong role.

Professional athletes, being competitive and vain, usually find it difficult to accept limited roles, but the Celtics were wise enough to know how important it is. Sam and K.C. Jones knew for a certainty that neither one of them would ever start as long as Cousy and Sharman played, but they accepted their roles because we were winning. Similarly, Frank Ramsey and John Havlicek were better players than various Celtics who started ahead of them, but neither of them fussed. Instead, they made the "sixth man" part of the language of basketball. They were perfect for the part because they were hybrid players, not pure guard or pure forward. Havlicek was so good and so durable in this role that if I were playing in an imaginary pick-up game among all the players I've ever seen, he's the first one I would choose for my side. I used to worry that he was *too* much of a team player, if that's possible, and that he would overreact to suggestions about what would help the team. For the first part of his rookie season, Havlicek was so unselfish that he would always pass the ball, even when he was wide open. He thought a team player is one who passes all the time, which is not true. A team player is simply one who does all he can to help the team win. This may mean shooting more, rebounding more, sitting on the bench more—anything. The whole team, including Red, urged Havlicek to shoot more, and when the message finally got through, he went out one game and put up forty-two shots! It was some sort of team record at the time, and we teased him about it for weeks. (He was usually on the receiving end of Celtic humor.)

Red would never let things get very far out of focus. He thought about winning more than I thought about eating when I was little. He ached when we didn't win; his whole body would be thrown out of whack when we lost. He didn't care about any player's statistics or reputation in the newspapers; all he thought about was the final score and who had helped put it on the board. He was our gyroscope, programmed solely for winning, and it was difficult for any of us to deviate from the course he set for us.

Red has always been one of the most single-minded men I've known. Suppose, by the 1990's, I were to become the first black President of the United States, had cured cancer, had won the Nobel Peace Prize and had picked up a dozen Oscars in my movie career. If someone were then to ask Red about me, he would say, "Russell? Oh, yeah! He played for me. A great player. I don't care how old he is, he could *still* play better than any of them out there now." Under similar circumstances, I think he'd say the same of Cousy, Heinsohn, Sam Jones or K.C.

But being single-minded about winning didn't mean that Red knew only one road to travel. He was always coming up with a thousand angles. He was open with us about some of them and secretive about others, but that was all right. What really mattered was that we trusted him; we knew his actions were directed solely toward winning and not out of some petty grudge against one of us. We also respected his intelligence. Red is not someone you would wish to have leading a platoon against yours in a war game. He had just enough imagination to discover what he needs to win but not enough to slow him down daydreaming on the way. He'll get there quickly and come up on your blind side.

It was just as important that Red respected our intelligence, too. He was smart enough to know that you can't win without intelligent players, so he acted as if he had what he needed. We didn't harbor any rocket scientists on the Celtics, but we had a lot of players who were smart about the game. I don't believe that a championship-caliber player in any sport can be stupid about the art and war of his game. He may not speak the same language that most professionals do, and he may not have a lot to say to people outside his game, but within his world he will be an advanced student. This has to be true, because physical abilities are relatively equal at the top of professional sports. On the Celtics, we believed that the principal difference between good teams and great ones was mental toughness: how well a team could keep its collective wits under pressure. That's something no coach can give you. In each split second a basketball game changes as fast as ten rapidly moving objects can create new angles and positions on the floor. Your game plan may be wiped out by what happens in the first minute of play. The coach can't be out there; the player has to see what's going on. More, he has to predict where a pattern of action will lead, and then act to change that pattern to the advantage of his team. Teams that can do this under the greatest pressure will win most of the time.

Red gave us credit for understanding that different players had to play different roles in order to win. We couldn't expect to do so if each player took on the identical role of scoring as many points as possible, hoping that ours added up to more than our opponents'. One of the first things he told me when I joined the team was that he was counting on me to get the ball off the backboard and pass it quickly to Cousy or Sharman for the fast break. This, plus defense, was to be my fundamental role on the team, and as long as I performed these functions well he would never pressure me to score more points. He also promised that we would never discuss statistics in salary negotiations.

This one conversation accomplished as much as a whole season's worth of tactical coaching. It showed me that Red knew what he was talking about; he was asking me to do what I did best, and at the same time what the Celtics needed most. In addition, he removed a lot of the pressure I felt about scoring more. All that was to the good. If he'd said to me, "What we need from you is twenty-five points a game," I might have been able to do it, but we wouldn't have won much.

By design and by talent the Celtics were a team of specialists, and like a team of specialists in any field, our performance depended both on individual excellence and on how well we worked together. None of us had to strain to understand that we had to complement each other's specialties; it was simply a fact, and we all tried to figure out ways to make our combination more effective. That kind of togetherness was purely pragmatic, predicated on winning in a team sport, and it didn't have anything to do with the popular image of the Celtics as a team full of "Celtic pride," whose players stuck together on and off the court. People often confuse the two kinds of togetherness or unselfishness, mostly because they are looking to make a game more of a moral testing ground than it really is. Some people may think that a bunch of guys with a cooperative approach to life got together, applied their philosophy to basketball, and suddenly there was Celtic basketball —living proof that it pays to be nice. Others may think that our fierce desire to win etched our strategy of togetherness, as if we'd all decided that since it worked out on the court, this approach would work in life, too, and we'd become living proof that success breeds happiness.

Both notions are exaggerated. The Celtics played together because we all knew that it was the best way to win. Each player was as competitive as Attila the Hun, and if individual combat would have won championships, we'd have been fighting each other. Off the court, most of us were oddballs by society's standards—not the kind of people who blend in with others or who tailor their personalities to match what's expected of them. If somebody had decided to build a "cooperative" basketball team back in the 1950's by observing players in everyday life—looking for those who went to meetings, were polite and followed the will of the group—he certainly wouldn't have picked a Celtic. Basically, I think we liked each other because we liked each other, and we won because we knew how to, but they were two separate things. Occasionally, however, a player would go so far in his devotion to helping the team that it gave you a special glow. This happened to me on my first day of practice in 1956. Arnie Risen, the starting center on the Celtics when I joined the team, came up to me and said, "After practice I have some things to show you." I'd never seen him before in my life. After practice he took me aside and told me what to expect from the different players around the league. Right there on his own time he gave me pointers. It really warmed me, because we both knew that I was getting ready to take his job away. But he knew this was inevitable; he was nearing the end of his career, and he wanted the team to win more than he wanted to hang on. To Arnie it was simply the most sensible way to behave. I doubt that you would find his attitude on most pro teams in the '70's and '80's—and if you did, it would be only on the best teams.

I've always thought that the main source of Celtic "togetherness" was that we were *literally* together for so long. During my thirteen-year career the Celtics made a grand total of one trade: Mel Counts for Bailey Howell. That's all. From time to time Red would pick up an old-timer like Wayne Embry or Willie Naulls, and squeeze another year or two out of him. Otherwise, most of the players were drafted from college and stayed. Many of us— Sam Jones, K.C. Jones, Satch Sanders, Frank Ramsey, Tom Heinsohn, Jim Loscutoff, John Havlicek and myself—never put on another pro uniform in our entire careers. On paper Cousy belonged to a couple of other teams, but he never really played for anyone but the Celtics. We all knew that the game was a business and that we could be traded tomorrow, but Red did a good job of making us believe that we would stay as long as we contributed to winning, and this made us feel secure.

The team's stability was also sound strategy on Red's part. He believed that you don't tamper with a championship team; as much as possible, you keep the combination intact as long as you can. This may seem obvious—the only way to proceed—but many franchises have broken up championship teams in violation of Red's rule. The Golden State Warriors, for instance, traded a key player in the off-season within weeks after winning the 1975 NBA championship, and the team soon lost whatever had held it together.

If you want to win so badly that you sweat and claw and sacrifice to do it, then winning will make you smile. The Celtics smiled a lot, which always helped us overlook a petty feud with a teammate. You don't fight as much when you're winning. That's nice, but in the back of our minds we always knew that our friendliness and team spirit was contingent on winning, which gave it a hard edge. As much as Red cared about the Celtic players, there was a hard edge to his friendship too.

Whatever free spirit we had came originally from Walter Brown; at least I like to think so. Walter loved to win, too, but I believe that he liked us whether we were winning or not. He would make sacrifices that weren't based on even enlightened self-interest, just on pure sentiment. Walter was the kind of guy who would bet only on horses named after his mother. Ninety-nine times out of a hundred, guys like that wind up as hopeless suckers, and everybody will say they prove that you've got to be tougher in the world. That's what people said about him as he poured his money into the Celtics year after year, to the point of bankruptcy. By most standards these cynics were correct, too, because even Walter wasn't convinced that basketball in Boston would ever pay off. It wasn't a calculated risk with him the way it was with Red. Walter simply thought that it *ought* to pay off because he loved the game, and that was enough—just the way somebody might believe that in a fair world you ought not to lose money for betting on a horse named after your mother.

Walter Brown became a character out of a fairy tale when that horse finally won, against all odds and logic, and the Celtics became a success. He was goodness rewarded, like Tiny Tim or Johnny Appleseed. If the Celtics had played basketball the way he ran the team, we would have lost regularly. We knew that, but we loved Walter anyway. We could play in a cutthroat league and still wish the world were fixed so that more people like Walter could prosper. We could agree with Red when he was trying to prod Walter into fighting harder for the team, but at the same time we'd be laughing and shaking our heads at the old guy's sincerity. Walter was the complete father figure, and in that role he was actually better suited to the lean times than the fat ones. When financial success finally came he was bombarded with demands out of the real world, like pension demands and a player's union. He hated these because he couldn't believe that the players would doubt his good intentions.

But though Walter was beloved, he still got his share of ribbing. Everybody did; it was the backbone of the Celtic tradition. Walter was vulnerable because he was the slowest driver in history. Every summer he drove up to Cousy's basketball camp in New Hampshire, about one hundred and twenty-five miles from Boston, and for him it was a three-day trip. I don't think he ever went more than thirty-five miles an hour in his life. We used to play exhibition games in Providence, about fifty miles from Boston, and after the game Walter would come into the locker room, say, "Nice game, fellas," and leave to drive back to Boston. Then we'd have a postgame meeting, talk to the press, shower, and every single one of us would pass him on the way back. We'd go flying past him, and if you looked sharp you could see him cringing behind the wheel. The closest I ever saw him come to terror was just after he let Red take a spin in his new Cadillac. "That's a nice car, Walter," Red said, "but the motor starts skipping when you go over a hundred and five." Certain Celtics were known to bribe cops to stop him for speeding, just to hear about the look on his face.

The players' driving habits were just the opposite of Walter's, of course. We were the scourge of every police force in New England. Frank Ramsey was probably the wildest. One night in the early years, when we were playing an exhibition game in New Hampshire, I asked Frank if he knew the way to the next town. "Yeah," he said, "follow me." He took off, with me following close behind, shot through an intersection and went flying down a little country road out of sight. I tried to catch him—eighty, ninety, a hundred miles an hour—muttering under my breath. But the cops stopped me. "I know it doesn't make any difference, officer," I said to the one writing out the ticket, "but I was only speeding because I was following an outlaw Boston Celtic named Frank Ramsey to a basketball game. He was going too fast for me." The cops looked shocked, and then to my delight said they'd help me catch him. They jumped back into their car, turned on their revolving light and siren, and we roared off after Ramsey just like they do in the movies. I wanted to catch Frank so bad I could taste it, but we never got close; Ramsey was long gone.

Actually, speeding was mild stuff for the Celtics. We may have been old-fashioned gladiators in the pioneer days of pro basketball, but we had a gaudy, high-pressure, show-business life. Pressure builds up, but you can't let it get to you in the game, so you let it out almost everywhere else. Since almost all of us were married, it would be rude to go into detail, but if a bomb had blown up our road hotel on any given night, it's safe to say there'd have been a large number of extra bodies in the wreckage. Whenever the NBA expanded there'd be a rush among the players to scout out women in the new cities. Our life was a lot like that in a war zone. We were young and crazy, and whatever maturity we had was used up on the court.

On the Celtics it was generally a mistake to be discreet about anything, because sooner or later you'd be found out, and when you were, that tender spot was exactly where your teammates would aim their jokes from then on. It was safest to be wide open. Our humor was toughening.

Pro basketball is a high-intensity business, and you can't afford to be worrying about your insecurities when you're playing, so anything the slightest bit offbeat about one of us was bound to be pecked at until the player could laugh at himself. Only people who can laugh at themselves are really confident, and we always laughed at ourselves.

Once we were playing Wilt's team in the semi-finals of the NBA play-offs, and the series came down to the seventh game. As usual, there was so much tension in our dressing room before the game that nobody could talk. I'd already thrown up once, and was thinking about doing it again. While I was sitting there in misery, I looked over and saw one of our players trying to light a cigarette. He went through three or four matches to get that last pregame smoke going, but his hands were shaking so badly that he couldn't manage it. I watched him sitting there shaking like a man with the DTs, and suddenly I started laughing. My laugh is so loud that I've seen people on planes move to the other end just to get away from me. If a giraffe could laugh, it would sound like me. So when my laugh burst out into the fear-stricken silence of that dressing room, half the players jumped a foot and the rest were so scared that they threw towels and shoes at me.

I didn't care; I was laughing, out of control. The guy with the cigarette saw that I was looking at him. "What's the matter?" he asked, looking peeved.

"You better play your ass off tonight, boy!" I shouted. "If you don't, you're in a heap of trouble!"

"What do you mean?"

"Well, if we lose tonight, by this time next week you'll be back home with your wife!"

Now everybody in the locker room was watching this player. We all knew that he had a permanent girl friend on the side during the season, but he had to go home during the off-season, and everybody knew he preferred his girl friend. He tried to look disgusted at me while still attempting to light his cigarette, but he couldn't hold it. His big belly laugh rumbled up and popped out, and he blew the whole unlit cigarette across the room and started hee-hawing as much as I was. The other Celtics all broke out laughing, too—one by one, and then in a rush. We laughed for five solid minutes, and you could almost see the compressed tension oozing out of us like heat waves rising off the desert. Satch Sanders was on the floor with his feet up in the air, and other guys were crying. When that fateful knock came on the dressing room door, we were so loose we were limp. We went out onto that court still chuckling and proceeded to win another series on the way to another championship.

In order to communicate humorously with a teammate in the heat of a game, without words, you have to know him very well. The love of humor on the Celtics helped sharpen our knowledge of each other. I remember once when Bob Cousy threw me a pass under the basket near the end of a game. I was wide open, and all I had to do was dunk the ball. But a number of things instantly went through my mind. The opposing center was Walter Dukes, who loved to hit me in the head after every shot I took. I could count on it; Walter would slap me so hard on the side of my head that I'd shed tears involuntarily. He didn't mind getting caught.

And I thought about how we were ten points ahead with less than a minute to go, and then I decided, "Nope, it's not worth it," so I simply just dribbled the ball out from under the basket. Cousy was out there laughing. He *knew* when he passed me the ball that I wasn't going to take the dunk. He *knew* that Dukes always slapped me on the head, and he *knew* that I'd figure that we had the game well enough put away so that I wouldn't take my beating. He and I laughed so hard that we lost the ball, but not the game. Cousy was always doing crazy things when he figured the pressure was off. He'd bring the ball up the court looking serious and call a nonexistent play—Twenty-two!—and turn his back after passing the ball to Sharman, who'd be dumbfounded.

There were only a few players in the NBA whose humor was so natural that they could play well under pressure while constantly chuckling on the court. Of these, the jolliest one was Walt Bellamy, a center whose career overlapped with mine. He was a childlike bear of a man and was always scowling, grumbling and talking to himself with this little grin underneath that nobody could resist. During games, he referred to himself in the third person, as "Good ol' Walt Bellamy." If a referee called him for being in the lane too long, he would get this exaggerated look of mock pain on his face and keep chattering: "Oh, *why* did they call three seconds on good ol' Walt Bellamy? Mister Russell and Mister Chamberlain—why they can *homestead* in there and they don't get called for it. No, sir. But not good ol' Walt Bellamy. All he's got to do is *look* in there. Just abuse him. Call *anything* on good ol' Walt Bellamy." By this time, he'd be at the other end of the court, laughing to himself.

Sam Jones was a master at laughing while playing his guts out. His humor was always therapy for us, and Red knew it. Sam wasn't a great theoretician of the game, but he was slick. He'd hustle people out on the court all night and have a high time doing it. He always had something going with Wilt, for instance. Against Philadelphia he'd dribble the ball around the top of the key toward the corner, and I'd set a good pick against the man guarding him. When that happened, Wilt was supposed to pick Sam up. Sam would stop about eighteen feet out, and in a falsetto voice would call, "You better *come on* out here, Wilt Chamberlain!" Only Sam could sound that sassy, and he always added Wilt's last name, like a mother scolding her child. Wilt would be near the basket, about a step and a half from blocking Sam's shot, but in the next instant Sam would yell, "Too late!" as he let fly a bank shot—which always went in. He'd do it over and over. Sometimes he'd yell two or three times before shooting, if he were open long enough. Finally Wilt would be irritated enough to come out after him, and the instant Wilt lunged to block the shot, Sam would flip the ball to me and I'd dunk it. Which also irritated Wilt, because he hated to see me dunk.

All the Celtics enjoyed this by-play immensely, but I had mixed feelings. I knew it was good for us to have Sam teasing Wilt, because it's always wise to get your opponent distracted. On the other hand, as a general rule I didn't like Wilt to get riled up, so once I made the supreme mistake of asking Sam to lay off. It was a confession of worry, which was like declaring open hunting season. "What's the matter, Russ?" Sam would ask. "You ain't *afraid* of him, are you?" This got around to the other players, and every chance they got they'd ask me if I were afraid of Wilt. On my bad nights, K.C. would make matters worse. K.C. harassed all the centers in the league. He was a master at it. He'd run by an opposing center while the teams were switching at the end of a quarter and, without a referee or a fan in the whole place noticing it, would step on the guy's foot as he went by. Or he'd grab his jersey—anything to irritate the man. K.C. picked on centers because he thought it was important to distract them, and because they were usually too slow to retaliate. K.C. always seemed to step on Wilt's feet a few extra times whenever I showed the slightest worry about his mood, and then he and Sam would laugh themselves silly at my distress. They were right, of course, because I had no business worrying about Wilt's attitude.

There were some nights when I simply didn't feel like playing. Not many, but a few. A basketball season is an endless line of boneweary nights, and I would be so exhausted after the play-offs that it would take me a month or so just to recover the energy to function normally. I'll admit that I gave in to the fatigue during some games, and be out there just going through the motions. That's when I could count on it. *Whack!* A loud noise, and pain would shoot upward from my kidneys. I'd glower at the other center. A few plays later, *Whack!* It would happen again. After a few more whacks, I'd be beating that other center to death with the basketball, just like my old high-school coach had taught me. I'd forget that I was tired. But once in awhile, if I were lucky, I'd turn around after a whack quickly enough to see that it was not the other center who was hitting me, but sneaky little K.C. Jones, my own teammate! I'd let loose a string of obscenities at him, and K.C. would stare back at me with an innocent smile. "Well, you weren't doing nothing out here," he'd say, "so I had to get your attention." I'd give him another string of obscenities, and then we'd laugh.

We also used laughter as a way of communicating about problems that other teams might sulk about. Once I got a rebound under our basket, and seeing that the other team's defense had broken down somehow so that both Sam and K.C. were standing wide open at the foul line, I deliberately passed the ball to Sam. He was the better shooter; it was that simple. As we ran back up the court, K.C. gave me his impish grin and said, "Didn't think I could make it, eh, Russ?" He laughed about it. He knew I'd done what was best for the team; at the same time, it stung him a little to be reminded that he wasn't the team's best shooter. But K.C. would laugh at that sting until I laughed too, and it went away. It was his way of restoring his own confidence.

But laughter was also simply pure recreation, and we had some purely witty contributors, like Satch Sanders. From the day he first arrived in his big knee pads (which Red took away from him), horn-rimmed glasses held on with a rubber band, and other affectations, Satch interfered with Red's serious intentions. Red would get angry because Satch could make people laugh without saying a word, by just standing there, and nobody could explain why. Satch had a way all his own. Once he got so nervous in a White House receiving line that all he could say as he shook President Kennedy's hand was, "Take it easy, baby." One day he decided that it was time to get married, but when he showed up to pop the question to his sweetheart, she was not at home. Finally, Satch got tired of waiting and went over to another girl friend's house and married *her* instead. (Of course it didn't last.)

Then there was Gene Conley, a marvelous athlete who backed me up at center and also pitched for the Boston Red Sox. Conley had a hostile streak as deep as a well, and used to throw at Mickey Mantle's crippled legs whenever he pitched against the Yankees. Apparently Mantle had once told reporters that Conley didn't have much of a fastball, and Gene never forgot it. "A man with legs like that don't have no business bad-mouthing pitchers," Gene would say, "so I throw at those little stems of his every game. I still hit him every now and then." Conley was the only Celtic who could play with a hangover and without sleep, and he loved to spin yarns about it. He could make everybody laugh, but he had one drawback: he couldn't prevent himself from hurting people physically. Often he'd hurt Celtics shooting warm-ups; he'd be out there in another world and run right over somebody. After a few such injuries, Conley found himself shooting all by himself in a cleared zone that everybody avoided. Finally he managed to hurt himself. He was standing there shooting a simple set shot, when he somehow twisted his back and was laid out on the floor with an injury. "A man with a back like that don't have no business shooting set shots," we told him, as he was carried off the court.

Frank Ramsey was the pluckiest character on the team. He was always talking about money and made shrewd investments. He played championship basketball, but he was put together in an odd way: he was so pigeon-toed that you thought his feet would trip over each other, and when he ran his ass stuck up in the air like the back end of a bootlegger's car. People laughed when they saw him run for the first time. What the bumblebee is to flying, Ramsey was to running: it looked impossible. But he got things done on pure Kentucky grit. I never played with anyone who more relished being in the middle of a scrap. He was only six foot three, but he'd crash right in there, get offensive rebounds, dribble past everybody and lay the ball in, and nobody could ever figure out how. It was because he could jump high, run fast and play hard, but this never seemed to dawn on other players because he didn't look as if he could move.

Frank talked flawlessly all season long, but whenever the play-offs rolled around, he stuttered. You could count on it at the end of the season, and Red used to ride him about it unmercifully. Once Frank was sitting in the locker room before a play-off game, staring at a swollen, jammed finger. We were always getting our fingers jammed, but that didn't stop us from playing, because the trainer put on a small plaster cast to guard against further hyperextension. When the trainer got to Ramsey, Frank held up his wounded finger and said, "Do you think you could fuh-fuh-fuh-fix my fuh-fuh-fuh-fanger?"

Red overheard. "Having trouble with your f's again, eh Frank?" he taunted, and went into his merry, obnoxious laugh.

"Fuck you, Red," said Frank. "How's that?" The whole team cracked up, and we laughed our way all through the play-offs.

Ramsey's exquisite sense of timing never failed him in a joking session, and neither did his determination in a game. The grimmer the situation, the more cocky he'd get. "Are you worried, Rams?" we'd ask in a tight situation. "Naw," he'd drawl, and we'd all laugh and feel better.

In his last season, 1964, Frank was running out of gas when we came up against the San Francisco Warriors in the finals. We had a problem. Ramsey, a swing man who played guard or forward the way John Havlicek later did, was lined up at forward against the Warriors' Nate Thurmond, who was six eleven. Ramsey was eight inches shorter, so there was a clearcut height disadvantage. Unfortunately, the rest of the Celtic front court had one too. I was giving away more than five inches to Wilt, and Heinsohn was giving three to Wayne Hightower. Things also looked tough in the back court as well. It was our first season without Cousy, and K.C. and Sam had to handle two great guards, Al Attles and Guy Rodgers. But Frank wasn't worried—naw—and helped design a foolproof strategy.

Wilt wouldn't ever leave the area right under the bucket; it was a matter of principle with him. Nate Thurmond put his big self near the bucket, too, just on the other side of the three-second lane. So I could stand right between Ramsey and Wilt, touching both of them, and whenever Thurmond tried to post Ramsey and shoot over him, I'd jump out over Frank to block the shot. (Nate wasn't a good passer in those days, so we didn't have to worry about him shuffling the ball off to Wilt.) After having a few shots blocked, Nate decided he'd move a little further out so I couldn't guard both him and Wilt. He was a good shooter, and outside my reach he could shoot an easy jump shot over Ramsey. But as soon as Nate went up to shoot, Frank ran right by him toward the other basket, almost under Nate's feet. As he took off, he'd make some crack like "So long." Now Nate knew that if he missed that shot, I was going to get the rebound and throw the ball to Frank for the dreaded Celtic fast break at the other end. That's exactly what happened the first couple of times, and it began to work on Nate's mind. Frank's grinning didn't help. Soon you could see Nate looking down at Ramsey out of the corner of his eye whenever he went up to shoot, and the look on his face would be puzzled and resigned, the way Wily Coyote looks at the Roadrunner when he knows he's about to fall to the bottom of the canyon and go splat again. Nate kept shooting, but he couldn't make a nickel; whenever he got the ball, he'd be worrying about Ramsey. The Celtics won that championship easily, four games to one.

Like all the Celtics, Ramsey used his laughter as a whip on the other players. If you had any exposed nerve, he'd make you laugh at it and keep going. The first time I ever got one of my teeth knocked out—somebody had hit me in the mouth with an elbow, and a front tooth fell right into my hand—Ramsey came running by and saw me standing there with a stricken look on my face. "Look at that," I pleaded, holding out my hand.

Frank didn't even come to a full stop. "Look at *that,*" he said, as he yanked out his bridge and flashed me a toothless grin. "That ain't nothing," he said. "Put that thing down somewhere and let's go." So we went.

Despite such episodes, I'll have to admit that as a target for physical and psychological abuse, I was among the privileged

Celtics. Tommy Heinsohn was at the other end of the scale. Everybody but the rookies rode him, and Ramsey in particular used to drive him bananas. In practice, Frank would snap at Heinsohn, pull his pants, pinch him and mutter some teasing remark that would make Tommy want to laugh and kill him at the same time. Often the whole team guffawed while Heinsohn chased Ramsey around the practice gym in a fury.

Heinsohn's public image was that of a big rough guy with a fiery temper. It was true, but it was also true, as with most of the Celtics, that he possessed exactly the opposite qualities. He is a very literate man, even poetic when he wants to be, and has infinite patience. One day, in the early 1960's, Heinsohn left home in the morning after a long and trying argument with his wife. When a cop stopped him for speeding and took a long time writing up the ticket, Tommy knew he was going to be late for practice. He also knew that Red was going to be on his back about it for hours, and Red really knew how to make your teeth grind —especially Heinsohn's. There's a scene in *The African Queen* when leeches fasten themselves to Humphrey Bogart while he's in the river and almost drive him crazy. That's the way Red would get on you, and the only difference between him and the leeches was that he always let you know how much he enjoyed doing it. Heinsohn was anticipating this treatment while the cop dawdled, and at the same time he was still fuming over the argument with his wife. But he controlled himself. "I'm going to be late anyway," he told himself, "so I might as well take it easy." Taking a deep breath, he drove his car slowly out into the road, and lit a cigar to help him relax. *Bang!* It was one of Red's exploding cigars. It completely undid Heinsohn, and he still had to face the whole day, including Red and practice.

For at least two years after this, Heinsohn kept feeding Red perfectly good cigars, and Red made Tommy test-smoke every one for months. He was no dummy, and he knew revenge was on Heinsohn's mind. But after awhile he made Tommy test-smoke only occasionally, and with time his suspicions wore thin. Finally, after nearly three years and a thousand cigars, Red was trying to give an earnest talk to the team when Heinsohn slipped him the loaded cigar he'd been saving all that time. *Bang!* That's how patient Heinsohn is.

I'd have never gotten as much grief as Heinsohn did about the day that cigar exploded on him. For one thing, I wouldn't have told the story the way he did, and I'd never have come dragging into practice with that victimized look. On the Celtics, that was like throwing red meat to a school of sharks. Long before, I had developed techniques to minimize the abuse I got, even from Red. In December of 1956 I was more than an hour late for my very first game with the Celtics, after being completely lost in the Boston traffic. By the time I finally approached the Garden, I was really sweating; I had the hives about that first game anyway, and on top of that I didn't like what I'd seen of Red's temper. In the parking lot I decided I'd better fight fire with fire, so I started working myself up, and by the time I got to the locker room I was madder than Red could ever hope to be. I was so angry that it alarmed him, and he started trying to calm me down. I was careful not to calm down too fast, because I was afraid he'd remember that he was angry himself.

With my size and temperament I could avoid a lot of harassment by scowling or looking glum at the right time. I never had to carry basketballs or go out for Cokes the way the other Celtic rookies did, for example. I'd have done it if I'd been asked, but nobody ever did.

Later on, though, I got my share of ridicule. K.C. and Satch and Don Nelson were *always* on my case. They made fun of the way I rubbed my beard, the way I walked, the way I shot free throws, and almost everything else. They said my shots were so heavy that they bent the rim of the bucket. I'd come back from the shower and find one of them parading around in my long black cape or my Nehru jacket, making fun of my trendy wardrobe. K.C. always ridiculed me for the way I was portrayed in the newspapers, and Satch used to drive me crazy by mimicking the way I brood. I'd find him hunched over in the locker room with his fist on his chin, like Rodin's "Thinker," scowling ridiculously. They were imaginative, and I'd never know how they were going to come at me. Heinsohn and Wayne Embry also got some mileage out of me, and Ramsey teased everybody.

All these juvenile pranks and ridicule were integral parts of the Celtic tradition. They helped us get along with each other and revealed everybody's character in a peculiar but accurate light. I have always believed, though, that there are limitations to the kind of friendship teammates can have. We were special friends, but limited ones. I used to joke with Bob Cousy, and I admired what he stood for and the way he conducted himself. I thought he was the smartest man I'd ever played with, and I had too much respect for him ever to get sucked into the jealousy others tried to promote between us. Still, I can't say that I was ever close to Cousy; we never sat down and had a talk the way real friends would. The same was true with most of the other Celtics while we were playing. There is simply too much competitive pressure in professional sports to share your hopes and fears with somebody in the same business. You cultivate your strengths, keep merry and stay on your guard. Our kidding helped us to have fun and to win, but it didn't make us the closest of friends. That changes after retirement; then you had a better chance of becoming an ex-teammate's friend.

Laughs, kidding and ridicule are often great for a player's motivation, and motivation is the greatest mystery in any champion athlete. Heinsohn, for example, needed to be motivated by others, and though Red yelled at him for about an hour every day, it wasn't enough. Tommy should have been a much better rebounder than he was, and he never got into peak condition. I believe Red should have run him up and down the floor like a Marine drill instructor till he dropped. Tommy was so gifted and so smart that if he'd gotten into top shape and made up his mind that he was going to play every night, the only forward who'd have been any competition for him was Elgin Baylor. Not even Bob Petit could have come close to him. Petit was shrewd and worked as hard as anybody who ever played, so he could stay with Heinsohn and often beat him, but he had much less natural talent. He couldn't dribble the ball more than three times in a row, and his left hand was so bad that if he'd tried to wipe his nose with it, he'd have put his eye out. Still, I think Petit and Baylor are the best forwards I've ever seen.

Though I thought Red wasn't mean enough to Heinsohn, it seemed to me he was *too* mean to Satch and Nelson. He'd yell at them for no reason at all, as a pair, and he was cruel. He used to embarrass the whole team as he jumped up and down and yelled at them as if they were referees. This offended my sense of justice, and so one of my first reforms when I succeeded Red as coach was to begin giving Satch and Nelson the respect they deserved. That season, unfortunately, Satch and Nelson played like ghosts at first. I'd put one of them in the game, and a few minutes later would find myself thinking, "Wait a minute. We've only got four players out there." I'd look around, and for an instant I actually wouldn't *see* Satch or Nelson. It wasn't that they were goofing up, but neither one of them seemed to *be* there. I couldn't put my finger on exactly what they were doing wrong, but finally I'd boil over and yell at them. Then, of course, they'd play better. For weeks I tried yelling at them only when they were guilty of something, but it didn't work. Then I tried yelling at them when they were clearly innocent; some players, like Heinsohn, could become productively enraged when wrongly accused. But that didn't help either. Then it dawned on me that it didn't matter so much *why* I yelled at Satch and Nelson; I just had to do it regularly, at certain intervals, the way you take vitamin pills. After only a few months as player-coach, I found myself thinking, "Okay, it's seven-twenty. Time to yell at Satch and Nelson." Needless to say, Red became less of an ogre to me and I became more of one to the players.

Red's genius as a coach was mostly in his skills as a motivator. He was a master psychologist who knew that there are as many different ways to psyche people as there are personalities. He knew that he had to yell at Heinsohn shrewdly and personally, whereas he bullied Satch and Nelson in a cruel, off-handed, matter-of-fact way. With K.C. Jones, you had to be honest and leave him alone; he'd do the rest. I watched Red spend time with the Celtics who played the least, the guys at the end of the bench. He expected them not to smolder all season over their lack of playing time, but he always talked to them enough to remind them how important substitutes are to a team. He tended to be more supportive of them than of his regulars. Following his example, I tried to do the same when I coached. I told my friend Ron Watts, who almost never played, "Ron, I'm saving you. I'm saving you for the big one." I'd laugh, but he knew I cared about him. Sometimes even starting Celtics needed to be built up. With Bailey Howell, my approach was to say, "Listen, the reason we traded for you is that we have respect for your game. We know you can play, and we need you." These were just basic patterns. You couldn't say the same thing over and over to each one; you had to dream up new ways of getting the message across. Red used to brag that he could dream up a thousand different reasons for winning, but his real trick was that he could apply each one of those reasons to the right player at the right time.

So Red came up with the right players and enough motivation to win one championship. Now that might have satisfied the Celtics if we'd been in New York, where excellence gets noticed. When the Knicks won a championship just after Sam Jones and I retired, within a year or two there were nearly a dozen books out on them. Most of these proclaimed that the Knicks had invented "unselfish" basketball and a whole new style of defense. A few years later the Knicks won another championship and became a "dynasty." All this happened because New York is the center of the earth. In Boston, you have to win at least five championships in a row before it means anything.

Red wanted to win it all every single year, of course, but that goal produces a new set of problems. There are so many factors that militate against building a dynasty. A lot of them are external to the team. We had a very small "break-up dinner" after our first championship in 1957, just the players and the coaches. Not even our wives were invited. We cussed and told jokes. Red told each of us how much he wanted us to weigh at the beginning of the next training camp. We reviewed the season and laughed at each other and enjoyed our championship for an evening as we could only do alone. Unfortunately, it was the last such break-up dinner. As our championships piled up, our family dinner gradually turned into a huge Boston banquet. Formal, with no cussing. One year I'd just taken a seat in a banquet hall when an "official" of the evening informed me that I couldn't sit there because all the seats at that table had been reserved by "the committee." That's how things had changed.

Petty but erosive forces usually attack whatever it is that makes a championship team special. There's the entourage problem, for example. It's vital for the members of any team to deal with each other one-on-one, player to player, but successful professional athletes tend to develop sidekicks and hangers-on. Then they approach each other like dukes or counts, as the head men in their own cliques of supporters. If everybody has at least one friend who's a jerk (which I think is a law of human nature), then the sidekicks of one player are going to be offending that player's teammates, and if the players aren't careful, they'll find themselves fighting over what their friends do.

All championship teams create a feeling that other people want to associate with or feed off of. A car dealer wants to give a car to one Celtic, but he asks that *all* the Celtics attend the promotional ceremony. A sportswriter does an article on the team, but interviews the Celtics he likes and slights the ones he doesn't. Politicians, friends and advertisers are always around, but their intrusions are important only because such people don't know or care about what it takes to maintain a championship team.

Even apart from the outsiders, it's much harder to keep a championship than to win one. After you've won once, some of the key figures are likely to grow dissatisfied with the role they play, so it's harder to keep the team focused on doing what it takes to win. Also, you've already done it, so you can't rely on the same drive that makes people climb mountains for the first time; winning isn't new anymore. Also, there's a temptation to believe that the last championship will somehow win the next one automatically. You have to keep going out there game after game. Besides, you're getting older, and less willing to put up with aggravation and pain. I can't count all the times I used to heave up a mighty wish that we could slow a game down just for a minute and break the killing pace. But I knew that pace helped us win, so you have to reach down inside yourself and call up the reserves. Nobody knows just what those reserves consist of, but when you find someone who at thirty or thirty-five has the motivation to override that increasing pain and aggravation, you have a champion. Rarely will you see an athlete who hasn't put on ten or fifteen pounds over a full career, but even rarer are the ones who don't put on the same amount of mental fat. That's the biggest killer of aging champions, because it works on your concentration and mental toughness, which are the margin of victory; it prevents you from using your mind to compensate for your diminishing physical skills.

For all these reasons, our motivation had to *increase* a little every year, which made Red's job even tougher. We were always carrying the same amount of water up the hill, but with every championship and every year the hill got a little higher and steeper. Red was running around behind us like a madman, cussing, screaming and cooing us to the top. He had to be a little crazy.

Red and I had our own motivational dances and routines we'd go through, mostly in private. He yelled at me publicly only once —in a hotel in Yugoslavia, as I recall—and I yelled back twice as loud. It didn't work to yell at me, and he didn't have to anyway. The first half of my second season I played like a wild beast, helping the team to such a huge lead that nobody could hope to catch us in the regular season. Then Red called me into his office one day. This was to be my first pep talk, though I didn't know it at the time. "We've got the division sewed up already," he confided. "You know that as well as I do. I can understand that you're letting up a little bit because there's nothing to drive you. Well, you should be the MVP in this league, and in this game you can't turn it on and off. You have to play *all the time,* as well as you think you ever could. You know that. And I'd like to end the regular season winning big so that we won't have to do anything different in the play-offs." He went on and on, never raising his voice, alternating little morsels of flattery with appeals to my belief in excellence. That night I went out and broke the league record in rebounds.

By Red's standards, everything he did to help motivate me was subtle. Over the years we worked out all kinds of gimmicks. He'd call me into his office and ask my permission to yell at me the next day in practice, just so the other Celtics wouldn't feel persecuted. I'd agree, and the next day he'd cuss me all up and down the floor so ferociously that his regular victims like Satch and Heinsohn would feel sorry for me. Or we'd trade favors. I'd call him up and say, "Hey, man, I don't feel like practicing today. My arthritis needs some treatment." I hated practice.

"You want to go to the library, darling?" Red would growl.

"I didn't say that." I'd laugh.

"Okay," he'd say, "but you *owe* me one."

A month or so later we'd be out on a road trip facing a game that Red wanted to win extra bad, and he'd call me over in the locker room. "You owe me one, right?"

"Yeah."

"Well, I want it tonight." And he'd get it. It was only fair.

Over the years Red worked me over regularly. He'd make a casual remark to me about how well someone on an opposing team was playing. I wouldn't say anything, but the remark would fester in my mind because I didn't think the guy was playing *that* well, so I'd work extra hard the next time we faced that player's team. Only later would it hit me that Red's remark hadn't been casual after all. Everything he did was calculated. As I got to know him better I'd laugh whenever he started telling me that Bill Bradley was the greatest college basketball player who'd ever played. This meant we had a big game coming up with the Knicks and Red wanted me to help Satch guard Bradley. We'd both know what was going on, but it didn't matter.

Red didn't have to work hard to appeal to my pride because I was basically self-motivated. I showed up ready for (almost) every game, and all I needed were occasional boosts. An unusually high percentage of the Celtics were the same, driven by something inside them that didn't need much outside fuel. Cousy was that way, and so were Sharman, K.C., Ramsey and Havlicek. Sam Jones was a special case, but his motivation also depended largely on himself. There is no question in my mind that we won championships because so many of us had so much confidence that the air was thick with it.

But contrary to what people think, a self-motivated athlete is rarely one who "eats, sleeps and drinks" his sport to the point that all his self-worth, and even his self-respect, depend on his performance. The all-consuming players value themselves as people only because they play ball. Now if that's the case, you'd expect them to play their hearts out, right? Wrong. They don't, because such players usually don't like themselves. They choke or complain or have strange things going on inside their heads that injure their performance. In a kind of self-fulfilling prophecy, such athletes prepare an excuse for themselves against the time when they don't play well—or don't play at all.

Some top athletes *are* one-dimensional, I believe—that is, they have no belief in themselves outside of sports—and I don't think any champion completely escapes the feeling that his drive depends on a fear of being diminished elsewhere as a person. The long-distance runner is likely to worry that only perversity is making him run the tenth mile of his daily workout, and there are equivalent worries in all other sports. Every now and then, either you or your sport is going to seem worthless, and you have to deal with those feelings.

"You're a bum," is a phrase you hear constantly in sports from fans and writers, and players even say it to themselves. They take it personally and get all shook up about it. They'll grit their teeth, make a stupendous play at a crucial moment, and then say to everyone, including themselves, "See? I'm not a bum." Every aspect of Reggie Jackson's character and talent came under attack in New York in 1977 until he hit three home runs in the seventh game of the World Series and silenced all his critics. There was a lot of pressure in his head, but Reggie could still see the ball. You don't just go into a trance and wake up when the ball goes over the fence. Despite the pressure, Reggie's mind worked well enough to guess what the pitcher would throw, his eyes worked well enough to see it, and his body worked well enough to smack it out of the park. Those are the marks of a champion, but neither Reggie nor the fans nor the writers should fool themselves that his bat speaks for his character.

Any athlete will identify with his score, statistics or reputation, and it's a struggle to keep a sense of your self-worth that's independent of those elements. Many of the Celtics succeeded; we had an extra feeling of confidence beyond the game itself, because we knew we'd be all right no matter how the game came out. Ironically, this feeling of independence makes you play better, and also helps you assume what I call the star's responsibility.

I never ran out of the huddle to the jump circle when I played. Other players would be slapping each other and pumping themselves up, but I'd always take my time and walk out slowly, my arms folded in front of me. I'd look at everybody disdainfully, like a sleepy dragon who can't be bothered to scare off another would-be hero. I wanted my look to say, "Hey, the King's here tonight!" It was an act I developed over my first two or three seasons, and almost always somebody fell for it. When I sensed anybody on the other team thinking, "I'm gonna show that son of a bitch!" I knew I had him. My little show was aimed at the guards and forwards on the other team; I wanted them to drive on me and try to beat me all night, even if it meant they made me look bad, because then they wouldn't be playing their game. They couldn't guard one of my teammates as well if they were thinking about humiliating me. Part of my responsibility to the team, as I saw it, was to divert an extra portion of the opponent's attack on myself. My teammates would know that they could take risks on defense because I was ready to pick up their men if they slipped by and came to the bucket. Some nights I'd point to a guy on the other team and call, "Send him in here! Let him come!" I wanted the Celtics to let the players drive on through if he wanted to, because I thought I could block his shot. Even if I didn't, I might mess up his head a little.

Sometimes I'd make a speech out in the jump circle. "All right, guys," I'd say to the other team, "Ain't no lay-ups out here tonight. I ain't gonna bother you with them fifteen footers 'cause I don't feel like it tonight, but I ain't gonna have no lay-ups!" Or

I'd lean over to one of the forwards and say, "If you come in to shoot a lay-up off me you'd better bring your salt and pepper because you'll be eating basketballs." Of course I wouldn't say anything like that to Oscar Robertson or Jerry West; there are some guys you don't do that to. But many players would psyche themselves out if you gave them half a chance.

Star players have an enormous responsibility beyond their statistics—the responsibility to pick their team up and carry it. You have to do this to win championships—and to be ready to do it when you'd rather be a thousand other places. You have to say and do the things that will make your opponents play worse and your teammates play better. I always thought that the most important measure of how good a game I'd played was how much better I'd made my teammates play. In order to do this I would have to play well myself, to get the rebounds to start the breaks, to set the picks to get the shots and to score the points off their passes. But I could do these things and still neglect that extra load, which was what helped us win.

Some of my contemporaries in the NBA carried their teams in different ways. Oscar Robertson was like an assistant coach on the court. At a certain point in the third or fourth quarter he'd take over the game; you could see fire coming out of his nose, and he'd start yelling at his teammates. Getting them ready to make a run, Oscar would sit outside dribbling for a few seconds, and every time the ball hit the floor you'd hear his fierce chant: "Hey! Shit! Come on! Play! Goddam! Play!" Then he'd take off with his teammates all fired up, and you knew you'd have to hang on. Oscar literally *made* Wayne Embry into a good player. Wayne was a mild-mannered man before Oscar got hold of him and showed him what a monster he could be with all his size and strength.

After a few seasons with the Celtics, I noticed that Sam Jones could take over a game too. He wouldn't do it the way Oscar did, or nearly as often, but sometimes he gave off a feeling that he simply would not let us lose this game. He'd shoot, steal and score lay-ups, and when the other team tried to gang up on him, he'd feed the rest of us for easy baskets. Sam took on a glow that said, "This game's over."

But it only happened about one game in twenty, and I puzzled over it for a long time. I couldn't figure it out, so one day I asked, "Sam, why don't you play like that all the time?"

"No, I don't want to do that," he said without the slightest hesitation. He knew exactly what I meant, and he'd already thought about it. "I don't want the responsibility of having to play like that every night."

I was floored. "It would mean a lot of money," I said.

"I know," Sam replied, "but I don't want to do it."

Sam knew how good he was, but he made a choice and lived with it. Many players since him have refused to make that choice; they want the star's money without the responsibility. While I believe that players should be paid as much as the market thinks them worth, I also think the star's money carries the extra load.

I respected Sam's choice, but I didn't understand it. There were a lot of things about Sam I didn't understand. One night when we were playing in St. Louis he got the ball wide open at the foul line; nobody was near him, which is like giving the Celtics two points. But he just stood there two or three seconds and let the defense recover. None of us could believe what he'd seen.

"Sam, *why* didn't you shoot?" I asked, as if I was about to cry.

" 'Cause I couldn't see the bucket."

"You *what?*"

"I couldn't see the bucket," he repeated seriously, as though the statement made sense.

"What do you mean you couldn't see the bucket!" I screamed.

"I couldn't see it," he said. "The light was shining in my eyes, and I didn't like the way it looked."

I kept waiting for him to laugh, but he was serious, so there was nothing to do but shrug my shoulders.

When I first started coaching I called Sam over one day and said, "I want you to call the plays when you come up the court." It was a routine assignment.

"I can't call the plays," he said.

Something was wrong. "What do you mean?"

"I don't have the authority to call the plays," said Sam.

I tried to control myself. "Sam," I said. "I'm the coach, and I just *gave* you the authority!"

"Oh, no," he said, as if he'd caught me trying to pull a fast one. "You're the coach, but I still don't have the authority, so I can't call the plays."

He looked at me as if he knew he was in the right. I don't know exactly how I looked back at him, but I couldn't think of any response that seemed right, so I sighed. "You're right, Sam," I said quietly. "You can't call the plays."

I never could guess what Sam was going to do or say, with one major exception: I knew exactly how he would react in our huddle during the final seconds of a crucial game. I'm talking about a situation when we'd be one point behind, with five seconds to go in a game that meant not just first place or pride but a whole season, when *everything* was on the line. You're standing there feeling weak. The pressure weighs down on you so brutally that it crushes your heart as flat as a pizza, and you feel it thudding down around your stomach. During that time-out the question will be who'll take the shot that means the season, and Red would be looking around at faces, trying to decide what play to call. It's a moment when even the better players in the NBA will start coughing, tying their shoelaces and looking the other way. At such moments I knew what Sam would do as well as I know my own name. "Gimme the ball," he'd say. "I'll make it." And all of us would look at him, and we'd know by looking that he meant what he said. Not only that, you knew that he'd make it. Sam would be all business, but there'd be a trace of a smile on his face, like a guy who was meeting a supreme test and was certain he'd pass it. "You guys get out of the way," he'd say.

For many years I tried to figure out where this quality came from inside him. I never could, but I did know I could rely on his word whenever he got that look. Occasionally he'd even have it in advance. In 1966, Red's last year of coaching, we fell behind the Cincinnati Royals two games to one in the semi-finals of the play-offs. We'd promised the championship to Red as a farewell present, and to do so we had to beat Cincinnati two games straight. With Robertson playing like a demon and the first of these games on their court, things were looking grim. Sam drew me aside before that first game. "You get this one, Russ," he said, "and you won't have to worry about the one back in Boston. I'll take care of that myself."

I looked at Sam and saw he had that look, and I knew he meant what he said. He wasn't telling me that he was going to lay down on me in Cincinnati; he was just saying that he felt the moment coming back in Boston, and that game was salted away. I trusted him, and what he said uplifted me in both games. I had felt I was supposed to carry the team all the time, but here was Sam telling me he'd carry us half way. He was speaking in his championship voice.

Whenever the pressure was the greatest, Sam was eager for the ball. To me, that's one sign of a champion. Even with all the talent, the mental sharpness, the fun, the confidence and your focus honed down to winning, there'll be a level of competition where all that evens out. Then the pressure builds, and for the champion it is a test of heart. Heart in champions is a funny thing. People mistake it for courage, though there's no moral element to it. To me, you display courage when you take a stand for something you believe to be morally right, and do so in the face of adversity or danger. That's not what sports is about. Heart in champions has to do with the depth of your motivation, and how well your mind and body react to pressure. It's concentration—that is, being able to do what you do best under maximum pain and stress.

Sam Jones has a champion's heart. On the court he always had something in reserve. You could think he'd been squeezed of his last drop of strength and cunning, but if you looked closely, you'd see him coming up with something else he'd tucked away out of sight. Though sometimes he'd do things that made me want to break him in two, his presence gave me great comfort in key games. Under pressure, we had hidden on our team a class superstar of the highest caliber. In Los Angeles, Jerry West was called "Mr. Clutch," and he was, but in the seventh game of a championship series I'll take Sam over any player who's ever walked on a court.

Consistency under pressure is a certain kind of psychological steadiness that I first noticed at the 1956 Olympic Games in Melbourne. The U.S. track team had a sprinter named Bobby Morrow. Most people didn't think he was the best in the world because others had beaten his best time. But there was one thing everybody knew: Morrow would always run his best race in the championship heat. If the best he could do was 10.2 seconds in the 100-meter dash, you had to run a 10.1 in order to beat him; you'd never win running a 10.25. You couldn't go out there hoping he'd be upset or nervous or hung over or unprepared in any way. You might be faster than Bobby Morrow and completely convinced that you were, but you still had to go out there and prove it. Morrow matched his best time in heat after heat at the games, and wound up with two gold medals.

An athlete gains a special confidence when he thinks and performs like Bobby Morrow did, because he knows that win or lose, he'll give a champion's performance. The Celtics were that way, and so I never thought we'd lose a single play-off series—except in 1967, when I knew Wilt's Philadelphia 76ers were a superior team. Actually, I even believed we might win that one if we hung in there; there was no assurance that the 76ers would play their best under pressure, but they did.

Once you're ready to play like a champion in every game, you're entitled to hope for a performance that surpasses your own expectations. Every champion athlete has a moment when everything goes so perfectly for him that he slips into a gear that he didn't even know was there. It's easy to spot that perfect moment in a sport like track. I remember watching the 1968 Olympics in Mexico City, when the world record in the long jump was just under 27 feet. Then Bob Beamon flew down the chute and leaped out over the pit in a majestic jump that I have seen replayed many times. There was an awed silence when the announcer said that Beamon's jump measured 29 feet 2 1/4 inches. Generally world records are broken by fractions of inches, but Beamon had exceeded the existing record by more than two feet. On learning what he had done, Beamon slumped down on the ground and cried. To all those who saw it, this was an unforgettable moment in sport. Most viewers' image of Beamon ends with the picture of him weeping on the ground, but in fact he got up and took some more jumps that day. I like to think that he did so because he had jumped for so long at his best that *even then* he didn't know what might come out of him. At the end of that day he wanted to be absolutely sure that he'd had his perfect day. That's a champion.

All the years I played basketball I looked for that perfect game. I knew that it wouldn't come unless I was ready to play for every second the same way Bobby Morrow ran those sprints. I never had that perfect day, and I graded myself after every game to see how far in my own mind I fell short. The best score I ever gave myself was 65 on a scale of 100. It was a game in Boston in 1964, which I consider my best year. I got between thirty and thirty-five rebounds, made a high percentage of my shots, blocked a dozen shots, started a lot of fast breaks, intimidated my opponents and made them lose their concentration, and said the right things to my teammates to keep us playing confidently as a team. Above all, I felt inspired because my intuitions were right on target, running ahead of the game, and I felt in harmony with the sport. Despite all this, the game was not perfect. Errors stuck in my mind. I'd embarrassed myself missing free throws, looking like a shot putter; I'd missed five or six passes I'd seen but failed to make; and I didn't set five or six screens. Also, I'd failed to control certain impulses that can plague your game. On several occasions, for instance, I'd crashed the boards for a rebound that I *knew*, from both the angle and the shooter's habits, would bounce long to the side. I should have gotten those rebounds. All in all, I couldn't give myself a grade higher than 65.

This grading process never took me long. I could do it in less than a minute in front of my locker, in the shower or in the car driving home. Although I usually forgot the score of a game before I'd even left the locker room, the plays themselves would stay in my mind until I made a conscious effort to forget them. I could grade myself by watching the game again in my head, using that mental camera I'd discovered back in high school on my trip to the Northwest. This never changed, and neither did my conviction, once the Celtics became champions, that no one —whether Red, a teammate, an opponent, a fan or a reporter— could grade my performance as well as I could.

Basketball is not like Beamon's long jumping. A basketball player thinks and makes thousands of moves in every game that he falls short on by his own standards, however vague they are. Also, there are, by anyone's standards, clear-cut signs of failure; how can you play the "perfect game" if you miss a free throw or a field goal? But in addition, basketball is a team game, and this more than anything else changes the way performances should be measured. I never quite expected to have a day like Beamon's. Those scores gave me a way to push myself, to remind me of how much the game demands of any player. But it was not my motivation for playing the game, nor did it give me the greatest pleasure from it.

Every so often a Celtic game would heat up so that it became more than a physical or even mental game, and would be magical. That feeling is difficult to describe, and I certainly never talked about it when I was playing. When it happened I could feel my play rise to a new level. It came rarely, and would last anywhere from five minutes to a whole quarter or more. Three or four plays were not enough to get it going. It would surround not only me and the other Celtics but also the players on the other team, and even the referees. To me, the key was that *both* teams had to be playing at their peaks, and they had to be competitive. The Celtics could not do it alone. I remember the fifth and final game of the 1965 championship series, when we opened the fourth quarter ahead of the Lakers by sixteen points, playing beautifully together, and then we simply took off into unknown peaks and ran off twenty straight points to go up by thirty-six points, an astounding margin for a championship series. We were on fire, intimidating, making shots, running the break, and the Lakers just couldn't score. As much as I wanted to win that championship, I remember being disappointed that the Lakers were not playing better. We were playing well enough to attain that special level, but we couldn't do it without them.

That mystical feeling usually came with the better teams in the league that were challenging us for the championship. Over the years that the Celtics were consistently good, our rivals would change, as teams would come up to challenge and then fall off again. First it was the Hawks, then the Lakers, Royals, Warriors, 76ers and then the Lakers again, with the Knicks beginning to move. They were the teams good enough to reach that level with us some nights. It never started with a hot streak by a single player, or with a breakdown of one team's defense. It usually began when three or four of the ten guys on the floor would heat up; they would be the catalysts, and they were almost always the stars in the league. If we were playing the Lakers, for example, West and Baylor and Cousy or Sam and I would be enough. The feeling would spread to the other guys, and we'd all levitate. Then the game would just take off, and there'd be a natural ebb and flow that reminded you of how rhythmic and musical basketball is supposed to be. I'd find myself thinking, "This is it. I want this to keep going," and I'd actually be rooting for the other team. When their players made spectacular moves, I wanted their shots to go into the bucket; that's how pumped up I'd be. I'd be out there talking to the other Celtics, encouraging them and pushing myself harder, but at the same time part of me would be pulling for the other players too.

At that special level all sorts of odd things happened. The game would be in a white heat of competition, and yet somehow I wouldn't feel competitive—which is a miracle in itself. I'd be putting out the maximum effort, straining, coughing up parts of my lungs as we ran, and yet I never felt the pain. The game would move so quickly that every fake, cut and pass would be surprising, and yet nothing could surprise me. It was almost as if we were playing in slow motion. During those spells I could almost sense how the next play would develop and where the next shot would be taken. Even before the other team brought the ball in bounds, I could feel it so keenly that I'd want to shout to my teammates, "It's coming there!"—except that I knew everything would change if I did. My premonitions would be consistently correct, and I always felt then that I not only knew all the Celtics by heart but also all the opposing players, and that they all knew me. There have been many times in my career when I felt moved or joyful, but these were the moments when I had chills pulsing up and down my spine.

But these spells were fragile. An injury would break them, and so would a couple of bad plays or a bad call by a referee. Once a referee broke a run by making a bad call in my favor, which so irritated me that I protested it as I stood at the foul line to take my free throws. "You know that was a bad call, ref," I said wearily. He looked at me as if I was crazy, and then got so angry that I never again protested a call unless it went against me. Still, I always suffered a letdown when one of those spells died, because I never knew how to bring them back; all I could do was to keep playing my best and hope. They were sweet when they came, and the hope that one would come was one of my strongest motivations for walking out there.

Sometimes the feeling would last all the way to the end of the game, and when that happened I never cared who won. I can honestly say that those few times were the only ones when I did *not* care. I don't mean that I was a good sport about it—that I'd played my best and had nothing to be ashamed of. On the five or ten occasions when the game ended at that special level, I *literally* did not care who had won. If we lost, I'd still be as free and high as a sky hawk. But I had to be quiet about it. At times I'd hint around to other players about this feeling, but I never talked about it much, least of all to the other Celtics. I felt a little weird about it, and quite private. Besides, I couldn't let on to my teammates that it was ever all right to lose; I had too much influence on the team. We were the Celtics, and our reason for being was to win championships, so I had to keep those private feelings to myself. It's good I did; if I'd tried to explain, I'd never have gotten past the first two sentences. Anything I confided would sound too awkward and sincere for Celtic tastes, and I could just hear Satch and Nelson. The next time we lost an ordinary game they'd have been cackling, "That's all right, Russ.

It don't matter that we lost, because we had that special feeling out there tonight. Yeah, it felt real special."

The Celtics were a family, but it was a family bent on winning. Oddly enough, I think I shared more of my appreciation for championship basketball with my opponents, especially with those who were good enough themselves to elevate games. Throughout my career I spent a lot of time off the court with Wilt Chamberlain, Elgin Baylor and Oscar Robertson. We never talked much about basketball, which in itself was a relief, and we had nothing to prove to each other, which helped us relax. We never became intimate friends, but I always enjoyed being with them because they made the game so much fun for me. I felt we shared a special kind of camaraderie, like professional soldiers. We were in the same business, had the same kinds of problems, and didn't have to be on guard around each other.

Wilt Chamberlain and I carried on a friendship the entire time we played basketball together, even though the newspapers portrayed us as mortal enemies. There's a certain amount of show business in professional basketball, and the two of us were a promoter's dream. The sportswriters flogged their feverish imaginations and came up with headlines like BIG GOLIATH VS. LITTLE GOLIATH or THE GOOD GUY VS. THE BAD GUY, and devoted hundreds of columns to the question of whether Russell was better than Chamberlain or vice versa. You'd have thought we were heavyweight boxers going at each other, because our respective teams were largely ignored. Offhand, I can't think of any two players in a team sport who have been cast as antagonists and as personifications of various theories more than Wilt and I were. Almost any argument people wanted to have could be carried on in the Russell vs. Chamberlain debate, and almost any virtue and sin was imagined to be at stake. If we weren't a metaphor for something, we were at least a symbol of it.

As long as we were playing, I thought Wilt and I were amazingly successful in ignoring this. We used to dismiss the controversy by laughing that it was only making both of us a lot of money. We each tried to dismiss the talk in our personal relationship, and a few people supported us in doing so. Eddie Gottlieb, the owner of the Philadelphia Warriors, used to remind Wilt that it was all hype; at least that's what Wilt would tell me. I believed this about Gottlieb, for whenever the Celtics played in Philadelphia he would scream to the newspapers in advance that I was a criminal goal tender, getting away with murder and that I had to be stopped. When we arrived in Philadelphia I'd see these headlines, and in the game itself he'd scream at the referees so violently that he had to be restrained. I always thought he was even more of a firecracker than Red until one night when he came into our locker room before a game, took me aside and said, "I assume you're not paying any attention to all that stuff about goal-tending. It just helps to keep our seats filled and our flock growing." He was warm and humorous, and then he went out to the arena and in a few minutes was screaming about goal-tending again like a madman.

Wilt and I took Gottlieb's advice to heart, but even before that we had an instinctive respect for each other. We spent far more time socializing together than the newspapers ever told the public, and it was more pleasant than anyone wanted to believe. If a reporter found out that we'd eaten together, it was inevitably reported as some sort of psychological-warfare session, with each of us like fighting gamecocks, itching to get at the other, struggling for some subtle psychological advantage. If it had been like that, we wouldn't have met so often. We ate together almost every time our teams played; when he came to Boston, I'd invite him home, and when the Celtics were in Philly, I'd go to Wilt's. The NBA scheduled a Thanksgiving game for the Celtics in Philadelphia, and for four or five years running Wilt invited me for Thanksgiving dinner with his mother and whole family. I'd have missed those meals if Wilt hadn't invited me, and I was happy to reciprocate when I could. And we both knew that this respect and good feeling had nothing to do with the game. We would lean back from the table after a good meal, tell a few jokes, and then go right out and try to kill each other on the court.

Wilt was by far the toughest center I ever played against. He was awesome, and no matter what anyone says about his lack of team play, his teams always wound up in the play-offs staring at us. He always outscored me by huge margins—by twenty or thirty points a game—so I could never hope to compete with him in scoring duels any more than I could make twenty-footers from outside. I couldn't allow myself to get suckered into a game within the game; I had to do whatever it took to help us win. One year Wilt averaged an incredible fifty points a game, when I was averaging sixteen or seventeen. In that same year his team averaged one hundred and twelve points a game and the Celtics one hundred and ten, so I figured if I could knock a few points off his average, we should win most of those games. That's what happened.

Wilt always seemed to know what he was doing on the court. He realized what we were trying to do to his teams, and he knew how his were trying to stop us. I never questioned his perceptions of the game, but it did seem to me that he was often ambivalent about what he wanted to get out of basketball. Anyone who changes the character and style of his play several times over a career is bound to be uncertain about which of the many potential accomplishments he most wants to pursue. It's perfectly possible for a player not to make victory his first priority against all the others—money, records, personal fame and an undivided claim to his achievements—and I often felt that Wilt made some deliberate choices in his ambitions.

Wilt was always good enough to generate that special high. On rebounding alone, the game would begin to heat up whenever we were going for the ball. We had some high-octane rebounding, and sometimes the rest of the game would rise to those same standards. As a team, the Celtics always had a distinct personality of play on the floor, which the poorer teams would imitate and the better ones would try to challenge. Wilt's teams always challenged, usually with a style so different from ours that the variety alone made the games more interesting, and if we really made a simultaneous run at each other, the game would vibrate. It didn't happen as much as it might have, because Wilt was so domineering when he was having a good night that he rarely inspired his teammates. He alone and a few of the Celtics could put on a show, but it wouldn't be basketball at its best.

It was many years before our supposedly fierce rivalry entered our conversations. Of all the things said and written about us, Wilt told me that the theme he most resented was the casting of him as the "bad guy" and me as the "good guy." I agreed with him. Me, the good guy of basketball? I was almost offended myself. In any case, I didn't feel that our court behavior symbolized our character or morals.

As the Celtic championships began piling up, Wilt took offense at those who enjoyed labeling him a "loser." They said he "couldn't win the big one," as though there were some flaw or stumbling block in his character that prevented him from winning key games. This seemed to me nonsense; I think you keep winning games until you play a better team. It's that simple. I prefer to think that the Celtics were winners—champions, in fact —and that Wilt's teams were consistently the best ones we had to defeat.

In 1967, Wilt and the Philadelphia 76ers beat us, because they were better. They almost ran us off the court, and I got an instant taste of the "loser" syndrome. Though the Celtics had run off an unprecedented string of eight consecutive championships before 1967, the fans in Boston hooted me that summer in the streets. "What happened to you guys last year?" "All washed up, eh?" "I knew it couldn't last. You guys don't have it any more." I had to blink my eyes. Never had I felt happier that long ago I'd trained myself to discount the cheers and boos. During that winning streak I could easily have gotten an appetite for cheers. At last I understood why Wilt had been hinting that the "loser" label had begun to bother him. To be bombarded with such abuse for years is enough to nettle anybody. To Wilt's credit, it never seriously damaged our respect for each other while we were playing.

During my career with the Celtics they beat the Los Angeles Lakers six times in the NBA finals, without a single loss, and so had just as much reason to brood, but they never did. I always got along with Jerry West, and have always had a carefree friendship with Elgin Baylor. The Celtics and Lakers could be beating each other's brains out in competition, but Elgin and I still played golf together and shared movies and meals. We even tried out new recipes on each other. (His were better.) As with Wilt, my friendship with Elgin was partly a result of those highs that occurred in our games. Elgin and West could inspire the whole Laker team, and if circumstances and luck were with us, we'd have a run out there that would make our teeth chatter. It was contagious, and whenever we got it going Elgin would almost break into laughter. He loved to play.

If I sensed that our teams were in a high, I'd always keep a sharp eye out for Elgin, hoping he'd come at me. Of all the numbers going on between ten hot players, I most enjoyed the one between Elgin and me. He was a smart player who loved to take advantage of what we called "peekers." He'd stand facing the man guarding him, and whenever the player even thought about peeking behind him to check on the position of the other players, Elgin would sense it and be gone. He'd fly past, coming toward me and the bucket. We'd both take off and go up in the air together, with him wiggling around the way he always did so as to get me to go for some move and foul him. But I'd be waiting for him to let go of the ball; sooner or later he was going to have to carry or throw it across the arc to the basket, and so I wouldn't fall for his body fakes. But sometimes he'd fool me. I'd be waiting for him to let go, and waiting some more, and then he never would let it go. Elgin would simply dunk the ball. Whenever he did something like that, we'd both laugh. A play like that never broke a high; it was part of it. Elgin took advantage of my preference for finesse over muscle in blocking shots, knowing that I liked to deflect the ball in the air rather than try to check it in someone's grip. He had an instinctive awareness of the eccentricities of my game.

So did Oscar Robertson. Of all the players in the NBA, I had the most fun playing against him and his teams. He was so brilliant that he could orchestrate the Royals' offense and pump so much energy into it that all by himself he could push a game into a high if we could respond. He had a joy and ferociousness that nobody else could match. When he was cooking and dealing, the Celtic-Royal games had a way of revving up to a high for a few minutes at the beginning of the fourth quarter. Those few minutes were enough to make me feel good for a month.

In the middle of all that frenzy out on the court, Oscar and I would usually butt heads in ways I'd remember. On many an afternoon we'd eat a meal together, and then go out that night to kill each other. He knew that if he ran into me I was going to hit him, and he'd probably have been upset if I hadn't. And I knew that whenever I guarded him on a switch, Oscar would be dribbling with one hand and trying to club me to death with the other. This was what we called Oscar's "free foul," because the referees would never call it on him. Most of the established stars in the NBA had quirks that the refs let them get away with. For example, they tended to wink at my goal tending and the "Russell elbow." (I didn't like getting hit while going after rebounds. You wouldn't either. So deliberately, from my first year in the pros, I began to throw my elbows and knees around on the court. My strategy, which worked fairly well, was to get the referees to accept the flailing elbows as my "style" so that they wouldn't call fouls on me. When opposing players realized that I might hit them "for free," they became less inclined to bother me on rebounds.) And the referees let Bob Petit take a whole bunch of little steps just before he shot the ball. (I always protested Petit's steps, and one night a referee just laughed and said, "Well, maybe he was walking, but he didn't go very far.") Oscar's free foul was in keeping with his attitude toward the game. He'd gobble his way up your arm if he could. He always wanted something extra. If you gave him a twenty-footer, he'd *take* a fifteen-footer; if you gave him a five-footer, he'd *take* a lay-up and try to make it a three-point play. He always had the moves to take these advantages. Of all the photographs taken of Oscar shooting when he was in his prime, very few will show a defensive man hanging all over him. Somehow he could always get himself free.

Oscar came into the league with a big reputation, and I remember one night when we played the Royals in a Philadelphia double-header in his rookie season. At one moment when the game was flying, he stole the ball and took off on a break with only me between him and the basket. In a split-second he was coming at me, one-on-one. He was scheming and so was I. "This guy's a pretty good jump-shooter," I thought. "But he doesn't know what I can do. I'm gonna make him go for a lay-up." When he hesitated near the foul line for the jump shot, I would take a step toward him, faking a move to block his shot or to steal the ball. But what I really wanted him to do was to take the opening to drive by me for a lay-up, and I'd be able to recover in time to block it. So I timed my move for the beginning of his jump shot, but Oscar reacted instantly to the *start* of my move. While my foot was still going forward in my sucker play, he was already driving around me. His pulling up for a jump shot had been a fake in itself, and I couldn't quite recover in time the way I did with other players. I was trying to be one step ahead of him, but he was two steps ahead of me. As he ran back up the court, I thought, "Okay, you got that one, buddy," and I filed his move away in my little book.

Three years later when we were playing a game in Washington, D.C., the same situation arose. Again Oscar was in a breakaway, one-on-one with me. Because of that time three years earlier, I had worked on a move in which I could take a bold step forward, as if I was moving to block a shot, but my body weight would actually be shifting backward toward the bucket. This made my reaction time even shorter when I was trying to sucker guys into going for the lay-up. So I put this move on Oscar, and was two feet over the rim when the ball got there. Only something was wrong. Oscar had remembered, too, and he'd let the ball go from the foul line, even though it had looked as if I were coming straight at him to block the shot. He got me again.

I got him just as many times; I like to think more. One night in Cincinnati he stole the ball, and we were running side by side down the court. I knew he had a way of going up in the air and simultaneously swishing his ass into you in a way that would get the ref to call a foul on you instead of on him. He could move his ass sideways like a burlesque dancer and still make his body look straight. What he did seemed anatomically impossible, but he could get himself into contorted positions and still make the shot. He was an expert at drawing the three-point play. On this particular occasion I sensed that he was going to run into me at the foul line while shooting. So just when his body committed itself to the ass swish, I cut straight off at a right angle toward the stands for two giant steps, so that when he jumped toward me I was gone. Usually the defender obscured the view of this contortion, but this time I could clearly see his ass making a sideways detour between his chest and legs, so that he looked like a side view of a brace and bit. Oscar had a stunned look on his face in the air, and he was so embarrassed to be caught out that he shot the ball like a high-school rookie and didn't come close.

Oscar knew that he'd rarely get a lay-up off me, especially when the Celtic defense was set up for his attack, so he'd come right to the edge of the no man's land where my territory started, and take most of his shots from there. I'd made all kinds of efforts to get him to come into my turf, and he'd try to sucker me out, a little like the way Sam Jones played Wilt. We each knew instinctively where the territorial line was; it was about a yard wide just outside the three-second lane, and in a hot game we always had something going there. One night I was guarding him on a switch and he came just to the edge of my territory and stopped, holding the ball over his head. *He* knew that if he tried to take a jump shot I'd block it, because I had slipped a foot or so out into no man's land, and *I* knew that I couldn't come out any further because Royals were breaking for the basket behind me and Oscar would hit one of them. So he just crouched down low with the ball over his head, and I got down there with him; the instant he went up for a jump shot I'd go up too, and he'd have no chance. He faked a few times, but he knew I wasn't going to fall for them. I leaned away a little bit, but he knew better than to be suckered into a jump shot when I was that close. We just stared at each other, like two roosters, both of us twitching. All of this went on between us in the course of two or three seconds, and the net result was that because of all the hundreds of moves we'd tried on each other in scores of games, we were at a stalemate. Oscar just stared right at me, his eyes never moving toward the basket or another player. His arms didn't move either, only his fingers. With the only part of his body I wasn't watching, he flipped the ball up there blind. Plink! The ball swished through the basket while he was still staring at me. We both laughed all the way up the court. I got such a kick out of it that I sprinted out ahead of Wayne Embry, took a lob pass, and dunked it at the other end, still laughing. The game was sweet at moments like that.

One advantage I had over most other centers in the NBA was that I could run. Sam Jones was the fastest Celtic, but he could only beat me by an inch or two when Red had us running races up and down the court. In the last few years, however, I found it harder and harder to get up the speed to make the game fly, and I also discovered that I couldn't afford to be easygoing with the younger stars the way I'd been with Wilt, Elgin and Oscar. Players like Willis Reed came along and had me pinching and scraping for any little edge I could get. I used to talk basketball with Willis, which I'd never done with opponents before. One night we sat down to eat and talk, and I asked him how he played every center in the league. As we swapped yarns, Willis confirmed my hunch that he knew what he was talking about. He didn't play his opponents the same way I did, because he was a great big ox who loved to remind people how strong he was, but he was shrewd in his analysis. I've met very few players who consciously try to study and take advantage of the ways their opponents play.

I had enormous respect for Willis's game, but I tried not to let him know it. He was about eight years younger than I was, and to a lot of black guys his age, people like Elgin and me were heroes. They had grown up watching us, much the same way I had grown up watching Jackie Robinson, and in my older and more desperate years I wanted to keep such players thinking I was a legendary hero. Anything you can keep stirring in an opponent's head can give you an edge. So to a lot of the rookies and younger players I'd put on airs that would have gotten me laughed out of the Celtic dressing room. I wanted Willis to believe that I thought of him as just another young player coming along, when in fact I was treating him differently than any other center. In my last two years I knew that I simply could not play him in a full forty-eight-minute game without modifying my approach. As far as I could tell, Willis had only one weakness that might help me, which was that he played at a single speed—full throttle. My plan was to try to make him play even harder than usual in the first half, while I hung back, and then hope he'd sputter in the fourth quarter. When we were standing in the jump circle before the game, I'd try to make remarks that would drive him to play harder. "Willis, I'm an old man," I'd say. "I've got a wife and three kids and a big mortgage. Now I'm not asking for nothing, but I'd appreciate anything you could do to help me out tonight." And I'd look kind of pitiful, hoping this would make him think that with some extra effort the old man could finally be knocked off. In my thirteenth season this didn't work very well against Willis, and I barely kept up with him in the play-offs.

A thousand adjustments in my game helped the Celtics to our eleventh championship that year, but there were some factors that no amount of tinkering could fix. The grades I gave myself consistently went down, and the spells of inspired basketball became less frequent. I knew that sometimes this happened because I was coaching as well as playing, so I couldn't allow myself to let go as much. But a lot of it was that I just couldn't keep up. Some of my most frustrating moments in basketball came in those last few years, when it dawned on me that *I* was the reason a game wouldn't quite ignite. To want something that bad, something that's been precious and mysterious to you for so long, and then to have to acknowledge to yourself that you can no longer do your part to make it happen—well, it hurt so much that it undermined my motivation to play. I already knew that there are no final victories in sports. The games just keep going, and the only final victory you can have is to walk away from the last game intact. I knew that. I also knew I could survive without winning a championship every year, but I had no way of realizing how hard it would be. About midway through the 1968–69 season I decided that parting would be even more difficult if I kept going until I played like a mercenary, with no joy in the game. I told myself, and no one else, that I was playing my last season.

Not long after that we played the Bullets in Baltimore. With only a few seconds left in the game, the Celtics tied the score, stole the ball and called time-out—all within a few seconds of inspired plays. The arena was shaking with the crowd's roar as the team came running to the bench to plot strategy for the last shot. I was full of adrenaline, pounding my fist in my hand and yelling, "Now we've got 'em! Now we've got 'em by the gym shoes! Let's go out there and kill 'em!" The players jumped into the huddle, waiting for me to give orders. Suddenly I burst out laughing, unexpectedly to everyone, even myself, and I couldn't stop. It started off slowly, then built up speed and finally went out of control off into space, like a barrel going over Niagara Falls.

The players thought I had gone crazy. "Hey, Coach, what's the matter?" asked Bailey Howell urgently. "What are you laughing about? What play are we going to run?" The other Celtics chimed in.

I was wiping my eyes, recovering from hysterics, and shaking my head because a thought had just lit on my shoulder out of nowhere. I said, "Hey, this is really something. Here I am a grown man, thirty-five-years old, running around semi-nude in front of thousands of people in Baltimore, playing a game and yelling about killing people. How's that?" I looked at my teammates as if I'd really said something profound, and they looked back blankly as if I hadn't said anything.

We didn't make the last shot in that game; in fact, we threw the ball away and the Bullets won. That game confirmed my decision to retire; if there had been any doubt, it was erased. In all my years of laughs in pro basketball, I had never mocked the game itself. You can't give out what a game requires if you start focusing on its ridiculous aspects.

I preferred to go out on a winning team. Throughout my career the Celtics had used different slogans and goals each year to give us extra motivation. We had dedicated a championship to Cousy, one to Walter Brown, one to Red and so on. (For a few years in there we couldn't think of anything special, so we won those on general principle.) In 1969 we hoped to win a last championship for Sam Jones, who had announced his retirement. Privately, I dedicated myself to leaving just as happy as Sam.

In the finals that year we played the Lakers, who had added

Wilt to Elgin, West, and the other members of a strong team. There were some long runs of good basketball in that series, especially in the first game, which we lost. I can't quite say that I didn't mind losing that game, but it was close. But whatever glow I felt afterwards wore off in hours instead of months; I wanted to win this series too much to pamper that high.

As it so often did, that year the championship came down to the seventh game. Thousands of balloons were inflated, to be dropped to the floor of the Los Angeles Forum as a Laker celebration. It never came off. As the fourth quarter opened, we had a fifteen-point lead, but then the Lakers started making a long, slow run at us that threw the game up for grabs. They were hot, inspired, cooking and clicking. It wasn't that the Celtics were playing badly; we were just shy of matching them, and they kept nibbling away at our lead. There was a lot going on inside me. As both coach and player I was struggling to push myself above top form so that we could win; also, I was acutely aware that my career was ending, and I wanted to leave on a high. On both counts, the Celtics lacked the tiniest spark, and I wanted to give it to us.

With five minutes left in the game, we were ahead by thirteen. Wilt banged his shin and took himself out of the game. A few minutes later, when the Lakers had whittled our lead down almost to nothing, he tried to put himself back in. But his coach left him on the bench, the two of them ended the game arguing, and we won.

For my own selfish reasons, I was offended the instant Wilt left the game. I didn't think he'd been hurt that badly, and even if he was, I wanted him in there. We were close—oh, so close—to finishing with a great game. I was almost moaning. "Oh, man, don't do that. Don't leave," I thought to myself. "This is my last game. Make me earn it. Come on out here." Wilt's leaving was like finding a misspelled word at the end of a cherished book. My anger at him that night caused great friction between us later. I couldn't control it, even though I realized Wilt had no way of knowing how special that game was to me, and that in any case he had no obligation to care.

The only person I'd told that I was retiring was Oscar. That year the last time we played the Royals was in Cleveland, and as always Oscar clubbed me all night with his off hand. After the game I felt flooded with sadness about leaving the kind of games we'd had together. I sought him out when it was over and said, "Oscar, I'm not going to play any more, and here on the court I want to tell you how much fun it's been playing against you all these years." I felt all emotional and flustered. Oscar said, "Good luck."

Oscar was a champion athlete by my standards. So were Elgin, Wilt, Willis, Jerry West and many others. Only one thing kept them from earning more championship titles to show for it: the Celtics were there.

5

Starting Points

A basketball game starts and ends with a clock, and so does a basketball career. Outside of games, however, you don't often find handy reference points to tell you where events begin and end. Usually it depends on where you started from and your point of view. In 1964, during my second trip to Egypt, for example, I had to bend almost double to fit through the dark passageways inside one of the pyramids. As our group stood in one of the inner chambers, the guide stunned me by declaring that we were exactly at the center of the earth, at the spot where the time of day and time of year had once been fixed. This was in the days of the pharaohs, he said, before the Romans and then the British had won the right to claim that *they* were the center of the earth. He still resented the fact that international time is fixed from Greenwich, England, instead of from his pyramid, and he was angry that the world used the modified Roman calendar instead of the five-thousand-year-old Egyptian sun calendar, which he claimed was superior.

When I returned home I did some research on time and calendars. The guide had a point, I discovered, and I realized that my own idea of time was a hodgepodge of many cultures. There are no weeks in nature, much less weekends. All divisions of time are man-made, and many of them have been settled by war.

In that pyramid it dawned on me how much we take for granted our viewpoints on many fundamentals. The subject of time reminded me of the way I think of cultural bias, which to me is any slanted vision and is much broader than racism or discrimination. It's about the way people see—or don't see— things. During the early part of the civil-rights movement, almost anybody could detect racism in the television pictures of police- men clubbing black students in Selma, but few people detected the cultural bias against blacks that ran through all television programming itself. They didn't see it because their habits kept them from being aware of details that are to them part of the background. Such things are virtually invisible. In August, for example, no one stops to think about how its name comes from a Caesar named Augustus who controlled an empire. "August" survived through the centuries, passed along by other empires powerful enough to make their ideas of time prevail, so that today it is accepted as a unit of time everywhere, even though it comes from one of the most irrational calendars ever devised.

Bad calendars may not be a burning social issue, but how we think of time *is* important—or so it seemed that day to me in that pyramid. All those Caesars, pharaohs and popes didn't hesitate to declare that they were the arbiters of time and that their lands were the center of the earth. This is a common way for cultural bias to begin. There is a theory that when babies are born they cannot distinguish between themselves and the outside world. A baby *is* his whole world, until gradually he perceives that objects like his mother's breast are outside himself. Growing up is a process of learning that you are smaller and smaller in relation to the universe. One aspect of religious humility is learning that in one sense you are negligible, and yet part of the grand scheme. Those Roman emperors didn't get very far down that road.

When I was growing up, cultural bias for me was only a matter of black and white. That's the only way it could have been. I never met a Jew until I'd grown up, and never heard of mistreatment within the same race—white against white, black against black— until I'd left West Oakland. I would have thought such things were impossible; my whole experience was that bias was based on race. In Louisiana all blacks endured an accelerated maturity. It didn't take us long to learn that we were emphatically *not* the center of the universe; in fact, we learned that we lived in a land where we were just about nothing. We saw a completely different world from white people. In high school, in Oakland, one kid was so poor that he had to beg or steal his lunch money. He was well known among his fellow students because he smoked a lot of "weed." (Marijuana was called "weed" back then, before it spread to the suburbs and got upgraded to "grass.") This kid was popular, but when he was arrested for possession of marijuana we never saw him again. Another guy was convicted on three charges of selling marijuana, and the judge sentenced him to three consecutive terms of twenty-two years each, a total of sixty-six years. The kid went into shock; he didn't really know where he was or what was happening. Finally he managed to say, "Your Honor, I can't serve no sixty-six years."

The judge looked down at him, smiled benignly like a grandfather, and said, "Well, do as many as you can."

By the end of that day, the judge's words had been repeated to every black kid in West Oakland. The words stung, and I passed them on. The fact that a white judge had put someone away for sixty-six years just for smoking weed was big news on the black grapevine, but whites weren't even aware of the case; to them, we were invisible. The judge hadn't batted an eye, the newspapers didn't notice, and nobody saw it but the black folks.

Everything changed in the 1960's, when weed ventured out of the ghetto to be smoked by white, middle-class kids. Then, all of a sudden, cries went up against those horrible laws that had been on the books for fifty years. People said it was unthinkable to "ruin a kid's life" just because of a youthful experiment. Newspapers wrote editorials calling for reform, bar associations got upset, scientists took a "new look" at marijuana, and within a few years smoking weed was worth a ten-dollar fine instead of sixty-six years. This change didn't come about because of enlightenment, but out of the vanity of the dominant white culture. Never mind all the cases from the past; those black kids were still in jail.

In 1971 *Sports Illustrated* devoted a long cover story to the issue of why blacks had come to dominate certain sports—basketball, the sprints in track, the speed positions in football, and so on. The story was produced in-house by reporters on the staff. After reviewing the various "scientific studies" on racial characteristics, *Sports Illustrated* concluded that blacks were doing well in sports because they were "natural athletes." To support this old chestnut scientifically, they came up with the following: ". . . Blacks have a marked superiority in hyperextensibility, or capacity for double-jointedness and general looseness of joints. This may be because they tend to have more tendon and less muscle." (Translated, this means that genetically blacks have the ol' loosey-goosey shuffle.) Further: ". . . many observers who have worked closely with both black and white athletes contend that the former have a superior capacity to relax under pressure." (Translated, this means that whites get nervous because they have a lot on their minds, and that blacks have nothing on their minds to get nervous about.) The piece went on and on in this vein. It was simply an updated version, with a few pseudoscientific trimmings, of the old Confederate belief that blacks were more like farm animals than human beings.

Word of this article spread quickly among black people across the country, just the way the sixty-six-year sentence had electrified West Oakland twenty years earlier. Black readers denounced it, laughed at it and shook their heads in dismay—but they all noticed it. Among whites, the article seemed to go down quietly; in effect, they thought that though it might not be definitive, at least it tried to address a real question. Besides, the article confirmed their cultural bias. They would have become more upset if the article had contended that blacks do well because they have a superior ability to make innovations and adjustments in sports strategy, or because their culture is on the ascendency and has the edge over white decadence.

People react to ideas that prick their vanity by cutting across their cultural bias. If *Ms.* magazine published an article stating that women were becoming more successful in business because they were wearing the proper clothes, I don't think many of its readers would like it. Or if *The Wall Street Journal* published a front-page story on "Why White Men Make Successful Bankers," in which the only reasons given had to do with the way white men look, it would be considered ridiculous. To *Sports Illustrated,* however, it made perfect sense to say that blacks' prominence in sports must be caused either by physical or mental factors. It's doubtful that the mental one ever occurred to them, so they were stuck with the idea that we blacks win because we have long limbs and loose joints. ". . . Perhaps because of physical inheritance, no black has ever been a swimming champion, or even a near-champion." Supposedly that "physical inheritance" keeps black kids from swimming faster. But couldn't it have something to do with the fact that black families don't have many swimming pools, or that they were arrested down at the "white" pool up until a few years ago? Black kids do most of their swimming around fire hydrants, which is not an Olympic event.

I worked at basketball up to eight hours a day for twenty years —straining, learning, sweating, studying—but *Sports Illustrated* didn't mention such factors as a reason for blacks' success in sports. Or all the forces that turned my ambition to basketball instead of, say, banking. No, I was good at basketball because of my bone structure. All of which shows how far out in the twilight zone your thinking can drift from a weird starting point. All the racial upheaval of the 1960's had taught *Sports Illustrated* that it's okay to be racist as long as you try to sound like a doctor.

Of course nothing like the "white banker" article could ever appear in *The Wall Street Journal*—which is part of the point. It is a newspaper designed to reflect and inform the cultural bias of its readers, not to challenge it. One of the limitations that white people in this country face is that their biases are so seldom challenged. All the major news media, left, right and center, regularly shock me—and, I suspect, most other blacks as well. I regularly read articles that make me think, "Wow! Where is *this* guy coming from?"

When I lectured on college campuses, I used to call a volunteer out of the audience for a skit. I'd tell the volunteer to relax and not worry, and then I'd put my hand around his throat to choke him. "I'm a little bigger than you are," I'd say. "Now suppose I grab you around the neck like this and start squeezing hard." By this time the volunteer student would be turning red and hamming it up. "Now suppose my hand gets tired, so I decide to squeeze you with the other one. But while I'm changing hands you manage to yell to your friends out there, 'Help! This giant's choking me!' I'm cool and collected, though, so I just turn to your friends and say, 'Hey, what I'm doing is all right because this guy's a Nazi.' So the next time I change hands, you yell, 'I am not a Nazi!,' and pretty soon you may find your self in a debate over your political beliefs. After all, a lot of your friends would like to know it if you are a Nazi."

By this time, if the skit worked well, some of the students in the audience would be yelling questions and accusations at the volunteer. I'd keep talking, "Of course the debate continues only when I loosen my grip a little, and you can only debate the merits of your position on an issue that I've defined in the first place. Meanwhile, I've got my hand around your throat, and if I keep squeezing long enough, you're dead." At which point the volunteer would usually collapse dramatically on the floor.

That's a maneuver called "label and dismiss." I had labeled my volunteer a Nazi and dismissed the fact that I was choking him. It's a familiar technique to minority groups all over the world. The American television networks also have the power of labeling; they decide which of the day's million events will be labeled "important" and which will be ignored. For the important items they determine where the camera will take our eyes, as well as decide how people appearing on the news program will be identified, and how every issue will be defined. In other words, television labels everything.

In 1968, CBS telecast a special program on black athletes, at a time when many of them were debating whether to boycott the Olympic Games in Mexico City as a protest against racism in America. The concept touched raw nerves on three of the most emotional subjects around—sports, race and patriotism—so controversy ran high. When CBS asked me for an interview as part of the program, I inquired what the format would be, and learned

that a while string of prominent black athletes would be asked a
series of questions about the boycott, the Olympics and so forth.
Then our answers would be edited and paired off against each
other; for example, they might show my face and have a couple
of sentences from me, and then switch to Willie Mays and get
a couple of sentences from him. In short, it was apparent that the
issues and labels would be shaped by the producers. I refused to
go on the show, which made the executives angry. I wasn't going
to lend them my face and name for a few seconds on a subject
so close to my own struggle and identity, especially when I could
sense that their framework was completely different from mine.
It was obvious from their entire approach and from many of the
questions they posed. One of them, for example, was, "Should
politics be involved in the Olympic Games?" We were expected
to give a yes or no answer, which I thought absurd. My starting
point was that politics have *always* been involved in the Olympics. Flags are raised, anthems are played, judges are chosen,
countries and individual athletes are included and excluded from
the Olympics all the time—all on the basis of politics. The big
rhubarb always comes over *who* gets to engage in the politics, at
what level.

(That boycott eventually fizzled, but sprinters Tommie Smith
and John Carlos made their own show of protest by raising black-
gloved fists in the black-power salute while they were receiving
their medals. Millions of viewers were shocked, and the two blacks
were thrown off the Olympic Team instantly; as a result, they
became so infamous that they have had trouble finding employ-
ment ever since. Harry Edwards, who inspired the boycott, received almost as much hate mail as Smith and Carlos. Somebody
killed his pet dogs and left their mutilated carcasses on his lawn.
When this made news, even more people decided to drop man-
gled dogs in his yard. It caught on as a way to communicate with
Harry Edwards. As I've said, it was a very emotional issue.)

So much depends on your starting point. When I first went to
Africa, in 1959, the whole continent was preoccupied with an-
ticolonialism, and the most interesting country seemed to me

French Guinea, where Sékou Touré was—and has remained—
the leader. President de Gaulle offered the French colonies an
unprecedented chance to vote on whether they wanted to remain
colonies, join the French commonwealth, or become independent. As the only country to vote for immediate independence,
French Guinea found out how much the French resented being
asked to leave; they ripped telephone poles up out of the ground
and tore the railroad tracks out of the roadbeds. After more than
a century of French rule there were only a handful of educated
blacks in the whole country, and the situation was desperate.
When Sékou Touré asked the United States for economic assist-
ance, we said, in effect, that we'd like to help him, but that De
Gaulle was our ally and we didn't want to offend him. Touré then
went to Moscow, where the Russians happily granted aid, and
soon he found himself denounced in the American press as a
Marxist.

Throughout its colonial history, Guinean natives like Touré
had seen a world divided only into black and white, master and
slave. They had never debated the merits of Jeffersonian democracy as opposed to Marxism. The United States says, "You're
either with us or you're Marxist." The Russians say, "You're
either with us or you're an imperialist," and these two views then
define the world. Every form of government becomes either a
copy, variation or synthesis of these extremes, which is all that the
two empires will allow. For all we know, Sékou Touré may be
interested in nothing but permanent rule and big Cadillacs for
himself, or in nothing but enough food for his people. But all that
counts to the U.S. or Russia is his "political alignment" as defined
by them.

All empires claim for themselves the right to determine the
starting points for international debate. They like to determine
the answers too, and to get the ones that please them, but simply
establishing the ground rules is usually enough. Anyone who can
determine the launching point of an argument will usually win it.
If Daniel P. Moynihan can have the whole country debating the
habits of black fathers and mothers, as he did in the mid-1960's,
then blacks have already lost the fight to redefine their history and

status in this country. If Sékou Touré has to defend himself over whether or not he's a Marxist, he has already lost his chance to define himself as something outside the narrow vision of the two great political systems.

Americans are peculiarly blind to the importance of starting points because most of us have grown so accustomed to having ours accepted. When the Paris peace talks on the Vietnam war finally began in 1968, our press heaped abuse on the dispute about the shape of the negotiating table. In effect, our newspapers said that it was an idiotic argument; here we were trying to end a war, and all that the nitpicking Vietnamese wanted to do was fight about the shape of the table. What did this have to do with anything important; why couldn't we sit down at any old table and get on with it? Few people seemed to realize that this quarrel (about a starting point) was a fundamental one. In a sense, the whole war was being fought over the shape of the table because the war was about the shape of Vietnam—whether there was to be one Vietnam or two, and who had a right to speak for each of them.

I developed strong convictions about Vietnam very early in the war—about 1963. It wasn't because I was farsighted or interested in foreign affairs but because of Francis Cardinal Spellman's convictions about it. From what he said, I first suspected that the war had religious as well as racist overtones. Spellman was the spiritual father of the Vietnam war. He knew and supported the heavyweight officials in South Vietnam, which had a Catholic government, even though the country was overwhelming Buddhist. That alone was enough to make me suspicious, because I knew Catholicism had been introduced into Vietnam by French colonialists, and that the Vietnamese Catholics had tended to side with the French in the colonial wars. When the French left, many of those same Catholics sided with the Americans. It seemed to me a continuation of the colonial wars, about which, as a black man who opposed the colonies in Africa, I felt sensitive. It seemed to me that in effect the Vietnamese were saying simply that they didn't want Occidentals running their country. We Americans didn't see it that way, of course. As an empire, we insisted on defining the war as a matter of communism versus democracy, and we were powerful enough to *make* this the question. As it turned out, we weren't powerful enough to get the right answer.

In 1966 I had a chance conversation about the war that has stayed in my mind ever since because it made me feel less smug and threw my own starting points out of whack. Flying from Philadelphia to Los Angeles, I sat next to a black Marine officer on his way to Vietnam. We talked, and when the officer asked me what I thought of the situation there, I gave him my basic frame of reference: that I didn't like our role because in effect we were simply replacing the French colonialists.

The black officer disagreed with me strongly. "We have to help Vietnam to stop communism," he said.

I asked, "Which communism, Chinese or Russian?"

"Chinese, of course."

"What's the difference?" I asked.

"Well," he said, "Orientals have a low regard for human life, and that's what we're seeing in Vietnam. It's Chinese communism, all right."

"Wait a minute," I said. "How can you say that those people have a low regard for human life? Do you mean less regard than Westerners?"

"Yes."

I was getting a little steamed up, though instinctively I liked the man. "You're saying that they have less regard for human life than Occidentals, when America dropped atomic bombs on Hiroshima and Nagasaki, and when an Occidental like Hitler could kill six million Jews systematically? Or Stalin—he killed twenty or thirty million Russians. Do you mean to tell me that we're in Vietnam because these people have less regard for human life than Americans do?"

"Not for the individual," he said. "The individual has no meaning for them." We went on like that, with the officer trying to convince me that the Vietnamese were corrupt, fanatical and without moral principle.

I was beginning to have a seasick feeling that had nothing to do with the Vietnam war, and that I'd never quite seen clearly before. "This same situation is beginning in Africa, isn't it?" I asked. "Some of the black governments there are corrupt, and they're killing people too, aren't they?"

He sighed and said, "Yes."

"Well, what are we going to do about that?" I asked.

"If it gets bad enough and the Russians come in," he said, "we'll have to take over and run those governments for them until they straighten up."

After that remark I just made polite conversation on other subjects. But I was thinking to myself, "Here's a guy as black as I am, and if we were in Africa he might kill me for the same reason a Klansman would, because he saw me as a corrupt and lower form of human life—and he'd think he was right, too." This thought depressed me down to the soles of my feet. I'm not quite sure why, but I know that part of it was because I wished that blacks could have some sort of secure racial framework through which to view the world.

Yet I know that I couldn't look through such a framework. Here was a black officer who was looking at the world through the eyes of a white empire builder. He reminded me of the American blacks in Liberia, who had subdued and ruled the Africans there, behaving pretty much the way the Pilgrims did when they landed in America, according to the old jingle: "First they fell on their knees, then they fell on the aborigines." In Liberia, native blacks have unquestionably been persecuted, though there have been enormous changes there in recent years. (Imagine an American President appointing a couple of American Indians to his cabinet. That would be like what has happened in Liberia.)

But what happened in Liberia is no different from any other place I've heard about: the underdog culture is subdued and invisible, whether it's the Catholics in Northern Ireland, the native Taiwanese on Taiwan or the Indians in Paraguay.

At the time of that plane ride I had been reacting to white cultural bias virtually all my life. It was everywhere—in libraries, on television shows and on peoples' faces. There were few things white people could do without revealing a prejudice that was offensive to me, and I spent a lot of my time trying to combat bias in all its forms. I'd yell or laugh at it; it didn't matter which as long as the point was made. I'd shake my head gravely and say, "Well, I'll give you credit. What you just said may be prejudiced, but it sure is stupid," or I'd tell newspaper reporters that I found Boston to be the most segregated city I'd seen. I was always on defense, just like in basketball.

I ached for some offense. I wanted to captivate that black officer with an "I Have a Dream" speech, or offer him a passionate new philosophy that placed blacks at the center of the world. But I couldn't do it. There was no way I could spread the gospel and go on the offensive, any more than I could make twenty-foot jump shots. I just wasn't built that way.

Minority cultures have a hard time assuming center stage. After hundreds of years of the white colonialist being "The Man," it was tough for any native African to step into a role of authority. When he tried, his friends were likely to laugh at him and say, "Who do you think you are, brother? You're just plain folks like us, so don't be putting on airs like the white man."

After all those years that the white culture was blind to me because it thought itself the center of the world, it was impossible for me to insert blacks in that position. It would have been just as wrong and ridiculous. At the same time I could see why people want to see themselves at the center; it gives you a place to put your foot down, a point of reference for everything you do, say or believe. As for myself, I barely had a point of reference; I had no grand design, and I needed one.

That airplane flight took place just after a period—1963 through 1965—when I had been very lonely. I was away from home almost continuously, looking for something that my wife and kids could not satisfy. The glow had worn off basketball; I thought it was a child's game, and said so publicly. How could I "play" basketball as a grown man in the same way I had played it as a kid, when there were so many more important things going on? I wanted to help change the world, and was looking for a way to do it. The black revolution was beginning, and many other tides were turning. I got my feet wet in all of them, but I didn't become immersed in any.

Martin Luther King and Malcolm X had the most passion among black national leaders then, and I was drawn to both of them. When Dr. King's voice rose to that preacher's pitch, and he rocked back and forth in his shoes, all my old church days came back strong. Initially, however, I had the same reservation about Dr. King that I had about the Vietnam war: the white people in Boston liked him, and so I knew something must be wrong. To me, Boston itself was a flea market of racism. It had all varieties, old and new, and in their most virulent form. The city had corrupt, city-hall-crony racists, brick-throwing, send-'em-back-to-Africa racists, and in the university areas phony radical-chic racists (long before they appeared in New York).

I had no doubt about those people in Boston because I saw them every day. They constantly surprised me, since I'd thought of Boston as the city where Paul Revere rode for freedom. If Paul Revere were riding today, it would be for racism: "The niggers are coming! The niggers are coming!" he'd yell as he galloped through town to warn neighborhoods of busing and black home-owners. Most of the Irish Catholics in Boston were ready to pick your fillings out if you weren't the right religion or from the right clique—much less from the right race—and almost everybody else wouldn't acknowledge you unless you'd gone to the proper school and came from the proper family. I had never been in a city more involved with finding new ways to dismiss, ignore or look down on other people. Other than that, I liked the city.

Nevertheless, everybody in Boston rushed to speak out in favor of Dr. King, and the newspapers went on a crusade on his behalf. Virtually nobody opposed him overtly, though many were patronizing in their support. I was mystified. The only explanation I could come up with was that perhaps Dr. King's dream of a color-blind society based on love was being misinterpreted by Bostonians. To them, "color-blind" meant that blacks would be invisible, which would be fine with them and not much different from the reality. To them, the whole civil-rights movement would end when the South was just like Boston. As it turned out, when the movement headed North there was an instant, massive reevaluation, and the glowing editorials on race disappeared. Within ten years of Dr. King's "I Have a Dream" speech, the news in Boston was that white gangs were catching black folks on the street and burning them alive with kerosene.

In a sense, Dr. King's movement was built on the blind charity of white people outside the South. They were attracted to it because it was based on the philosophy of love, which was easy. Also, blacks were being nonviolent, which made the whites feel even better. That's where Dr. King and I parted ways. In the immortal words of the Old Man, "Nonviolent is what I am before somebody hits me." I doubt that I could have taken a beating even on national television, where the sight of my passive resistance might inspire somebody else, and I *knew* I couldn't take one in private.

Once I was nonviolent. I saw Charles Evers shortly after his brother Medgar was murdered, and made the mistake of telling him that I'd do whatever I could to help him down in Mississippi; all he had to do was call. It was a rash statement on my part— just how rash I realized when Evers called me right after the murders of Chaney, Goodman and Schwerner during the summer of 1964. His people were losing hope, he said; could I come down to Mississippi for a few days?

It was about the last thing I wanted to do. The whole state was an armed camp, full of tension, as close to open racial warfare as any place on earth, and the prospect of going there did not excite me. To make matters worse, I realized that I would have to be nonviolent on the trip. It was their movement, in their state, and if I agreed to go, it would have to be on their terms. I decided that there was no way I could live with myself if I backed out of my word to Charles Evers, so I went.

Fortunately, my teammates on the Celtics had cheered me up with the tender sympathy that was our trademark. "You'll be just fine down there, Russ," they'd drawl. "Just make sure you stay *inconspicuous.* Incognito is the key." That was a big help. In Mississippi, I felt about as big as a target range, and I had the feeling there were bull's-eyes lighting up across my shirt as I walked around Jackson giving basketball clinics. Basketball clinics! Half the state of Mississippi had taken cover behind pick-up trucks and magnolia trees, and there I was dribbling a basketball out in broad daylight—a perfect target. This experience alone was enough to convince me that I am not Dr. King's ideal nonviolent person. Nobody can incite such fear and hatred, and then hope to brutalize me without a fight. I was glad that my commitment to nonviolent principles was not tested on the trip. My philosophy may be one of love, but I have a don't-tread-on-me personality.

For me, all the more militant black groups of the late 1960's were mere imitations of Malcolm X. He spoke more truth, with less pretense, than any other black leader. Dr. King may have inspired more people, but Malcolm opened eyes. His sense of injustice was so keen that he pointed out areas of cultural bias that even its victims had been unaware of.

As a free-lance black man with no speeches to give misguided Marine officers, my opinions have usually been out of step with the doctrines that have sprung up along the way. After defending "militants" like Malcolm X in the early 1960's, I later wound up putting in a word for people who were called Uncle Toms, like Roy Wilkins of the NAACP. To me, historical perspective was forgotten for a time in the rush to stake out the newest and blackest positions. I disagreed with Wilkins most of the time, but I never doubted where his heart was. It was easy for me to imagine the atmosphere of the 1920's and 1930's, when he spent years trying to register voters in the South, at a time when he could easily have disappeared off the face of the earth without a whisper of notice. He did that work full time, when there was only a dim prospect of success, and no television coverage, star status, big grants or new styles to set.

I try to look at everybody by the light of the times they lived in, but for me that doesn't rescue most of the white heroes of yesteryear. As much as I attempt to conjure up the atmosphere of the American Revolution, I still can't respect Patrick Henry. He owned slaves when he made his famous declaration, "Give me liberty or give me death!" To honor this statement is to honor a frame of mind in which blacks are not people. The most significant word in that piece of rhetoric is "me"—"Give *me* liberty"

—and that kind of ego is usually a starting point for cultural bias.

People from almost every culture in history have decided that they were God's chosen people. Cultural bias gets strong when a group claims to be on intimate terms with God. They've got a pipeline to Him. Whatever they don't like, God doesn't like either. Whatever they want to do is right, because God wants them to do it. People wind up making God in their own image, and they rarely notice how strange it is that their God looks at things from their point of view. To me, that is the ego, a symbol of our pretensions. Everywhere I go somebody seems to look out over things, scratch his head and say, "Well, I must be God."

In Rhodesia there are beautiful, impressive ruins of temples and rock formations whose origins are unknown. Nobody knows how the ancient people living there possessed the technology to carve and move such huge stones. But almost any white Rhodesian you meet will tell you that some outside race of people came to Rhodesia a thousand years ago, built the temples and then left. No other theory occurs to them, because they assume that no people native to Africa could have constructed them.

It's often easier for us to deal with grand-scale abuses of the ego than with small personal ones. We find it simple, for instance, when we look at the big picture to see that often the United States has a blind ego when it surveys the world. In true empire fashion, it is important to us to be Number One: the best political system, the best education, the richest economy, the first in everything. We are so smug that we don't even acknowledge that we are an empire; we don't like the word because somehow it's beneath us. We prefer to think that our influence comes from virtue instead of power. It seems to me obvious that we have to close down the empire and scale down the grand view we have of ourselves. Of all the world statesmen I have studied, I admire de Gaulle the most (and in spite of what he did to French Guinea). He himself had a colossal empire ego, and yet he skillfully closed down the French Empire because he knew that his dearest pretensions were hurting his country.

I often wish I had that kind of control over my own ego. After all these years of suffering the ordinary tribulations of being a modern black man, I have come to think of control, for me, as either a laugh or a scowl. But sometimes I can't manage either of these. In Boston, there was a period when I was plagued by the "I didn't notice" liberals, a bunch of whom used to hang around the Celtics. For example, in conversation one of them might bring up the name of someone I couldn't place. "I don't remember her," I'd say. "Was she black or white?"

"I didn't notice," the answer would come, sweet and innocent, sometimes a little proud.

"You didn't *notice?*" I'd ask, amazed at the power of guilt. On good days I'd laugh, on medium days I'd scowl and on bad days I'd lecture.

Once I lectured a vice president of a brewery that had a big plant outside Boston. It was well known in Massachusetts that the company had gone out of its way not to hire a black at any level for over twenty years—not a token, not even a janitor. One night at a party this executive announced loudly that his company would not even notice the color of job applicants any more, and then he took me aside and confided that he'd like to begin their new policy by finding a black master brewer. Could I recommend a qualified black biochemist?

It happened to be a bad day. "Get out of my face," I said. "I won't even talk to you, you blind son of a bitch! If any black man has pulled himself up to be a biochemist in spite of all the people like you in the world, he sure as hell doesn't need me to speak for him." Five minutes later I was laughing at the memory of the look on that man's face. My reactions to prejudice have always been a mixture of laughter and rage.

I laugh now when I look back on one incident that offended me in 1958, my second year in the NBA. I was chosen the Most Valuable Player in professional basketball, and yet when the sportswriters voted, I was not even on the first All-NBA team. They had to trip all over themselves to leave me out, putting three white forwards on the team and no center at all. What ingenuity, and what a trivial place for prejudice!

Ego is fueled by fear and anger—fear of being small, anger at being unnoticed. The fear in many whites has driven them to all kinds of extremes to find ways of making people like me seem small. I made some independent and relatively intelligent comments shortly after moving to Boston, and the sportswriters there immediately assumed I was spouting Muslim doctrine. Where else could I have gotten any ideas? I certainly couldn't have come up with such thoughts on my own. They were trying to make me smaller, taking slices off my ego.

To me, the ego has always been a paradox—it is the point from which you see, but it also makes you blind. New perspectives on it bring the biggest revelations. I've looked back at things that I did as much as twenty years earlier and suddenly, as if I were coming out of a dream, be outside myself, looking down, confused, disoriented. Something had twisted the lens. Usually I'd be playing the victim, feeling innocent, but generally there'd be this sleepy little piece of guilt somewhere that made me unsure. Did I want to laugh or to feel sorry for myself? I'm sure people feel that way in Death Row and in divorce court. Golfers feel that way behind trees and in sand traps. I've seen hundreds of basketball players suddenly go befuddled and helpless when life kicked them from the blind side. Stars and rich people tend to have life run out from under them, poor people tend to have it run over them, and some of us can arrange to have it do both.

My own life has been one of future shock. My grandfather, who talked to me about slavery and drove a buckboard team most of his life, took a jet flight just before he died, in the year of the first landing on the moon. As a rookie, in 1957, I was the only black player on the Boston Celtics, and I was excluded from almost everything except practice and the games. Exactly twenty years later I was coach and general manager of the Seattle Supersonics, which had only two *white* players on the team—and they were excluded from almost everything but practice and the games. The black players left them out of meals, conversations, parties and anything else that makes a lonely road trip bearable. I told the blacks how unfair this was, and they made a token effort to change, but they said the white players were just too different. In basketball, it took only twenty years to go from the outhouse to the in-crowd.

I've picked fruit and worked in shipyards and thought of a dollar as something you got by adding up your savings. I've also thought of a dollar as the last decimal place, and have turned down job offers for $200,000 a year. I have been insulted countless times by strangers, but I have also turned down an appointment with the President. I have gone through a time of rage when I hated all white people; now I am married to one. There have been times when I felt as small and insignificant as the echo of a sigh, and there have been other moments when I was so high and mighty that I couldn't think because I refused to grant myself a mental interview.

At least fifty times I've had all of life figured out. I've stood in Boston Garden after making a big play in a play-off game and literally felt fifteen thousand people cheering for me—the whole Garden shaking with waves of emotion washing over me so strongly that it felt as if my spinal column were immersed in sparkling champagne. And I have felt the personal abuse of those same fans—sometimes right after the game. How can a young kid who gives his life to basketball prepare himself for the idea that the cheers and boos are not permanent? Or that you can't take one without the other? Or that the cheers and boos are really like mass love and hate—just a lot of energy being released? It's nothing personal.

As a kid, I went to see *King Kong*. When I came out of the movie my friends were all excited; they beat their chests and talked about how high the Empire State Building was. But I kept asking myself why King Kong, who had for many years killed and perhaps eaten young black women as peace offerings, didn't kill the first white woman put on his plate. Not only did he not kill her, he fell in love with her! I knew this was necessary for the plot of the movie, but it still struck me as strange that a great ape would fall in love with his food just because it was a different color. My friends thought I was peculiar for having such thoughts instead of indulging in the fantasy.

As I saw it, Kong's problem was not how he interpreted the white world but how the white world saw *him*. Everyone's relationship to him was based on fear and greed; they were trying to drag him out of the jungle and chain him. From Kong's point of view, these people running around, screaming and attacking him, were not normal. I think his was the problem common to all misfits—unusual physical specimens, eccentrics, anyone outside the norm. They have a skewed view of reality. Beauty queens tend to see dumb lust on the faces of men, and winos expect people to be repulsed or to avoid them.

The challenge to any misfit comes from trying to figure out the odd world around him. It's impossible to have a sense of yourself without reference to other people, and if you're different there's no convenient place to start. It's hard for me to understand other people because I see a distorted world. People show me a different side of themselves than they show others. Like Kong, I am a misfit —and a triple threat at that. Not only am I tall enough to make a lot of people uncomfortable, but I am also black and infamous as an athlete. No wonder I have my quirks.

I've tried to handle my ego the way I would any other part of my character: to acknowledge it but not to let it control me or make me into something I don't like. All of us have prejudices that grow out of our egos, but that's natural. Show me a person with no prejudice and I'll show you a person with no taste. The struggle is to keep the prejudice from turning into bigotry and hatred. Bigotry takes possession of people, and is mankind's biggest enemy.

Some people try to guard against egotism and bigotry by surrendering their point of view to others or to an institution. It doesn't work. I insist on having my own view and on taking responsibility for what I do. I believe any other approach is foolhardy, dishonest or worse. So I will always defend my ego, and at the same time try to keep it from running away with me. That is the tension in my life, my personal starting point.

6

Freedom

One day in 1966, during my first season as player-coach of the Celtics, I got a phone call from an executive with a large Madison Avenue advertising firm. After telling me who he was, and that his firm produced a large percentage of the ads on network television, he went into his pitch. "Mr. Russell," he said, "we want you to make an ad." He paused to let this sink in. "You know, the advertising industry has been backward in bringing blacks into the field. It's been wrong, and we've been talking it over here and have decided to correct the situation. It has been a long time coming, I know, but we want to get some blacks into advertising."

Whenever I hear a white guy start talking like this, I get nervous, so I said, "Uh huh," and let him continue.

"One of our accounts is Johnson & Johnson," the man said. "We're planning a new campaign for Johnson's Baby Powder that I think will be a winner, and we believe it's important that you be one of the celebrities to go on the air."

"How much does it pay?" I asked.

"Scale," said the executive. "It's standard across the industry."

By now I was a little less nervous, because I sensed where the executive was coming from. "Let me ask you a question," I said. "If there were several young kids in the ad with me, fresh out of modeling school, what would they be paid?"

"Scale."

"That sounds wrong," I said. "A kid just starting out gets paid the same, even though I've been working for ten years to build up a reputation that you want to use to make the ad work?"

"Well, it's not likely that there'll be anybody like that with you in the ad," the man said.

"I understand that," I said, "but in theory that's the way it would be. It doesn't make sense to me, so I won't do the ad."

"Mr. Russell," the executive said, sounding a little huffy, "there's a considerable amount of money involved here, but most of the people we've talked to aren't much concerned about the money. It's more a matter of prestige."

"Wait a minute," I said. "If I needed prestige, you wouldn't have called me in the first place. The only reason you called me is that I already have prestige, and you want to rent it."

"Not at all. Look, we're going out on a limb, and we need some black stars to help us. Don't you want to be the first black American featured in a national ad?"

"What do I want with a first?" I asked. "I don't need it. You don't want to pay me, right? That's what it's about in your business. And I refuse to pay again for what you said was your backwardness."

Our conversation deteriorated from there. The executive couldn't believe that I would refuse to do the ad, so he kept challenging my reasons. I kept trying to tell him that it didn't matter what he thought of my reasons; it was what *I* thought of them that counted. He kept insisting that I satisfy him with my reasons, as though I had an obligation to work for him unless I could convince him otherwise. We never quite saw eye-to-eye.

This was not my first dispute with advertisers and media people. Red Auerbach is a moneymaker if there ever was one, and he used to tell me about all the projects he had, like the $10,000 he was getting from a soft-drink firm to make a film, so I was upset when the same firm offered me only $2,500 for the same kind of film. The Boston stations got indignant if black players like myself refused to go to their station for free to promote their interview shows and newscasts, but I could never get any of them even to discuss the possibility of giving me my own show. When a television station in Boston wanted to hire a professional player from one of the city's teams as a sportscaster, its executives interviewed all interested players from the Bruins (there are virtually no professional black hockey players) and the white players from the Red Sox (baseball), New England Patriots (football) and Celtics. They didn't interview a single black and wound up hiring the place kicker from the Patriots. For these and other reasons, the Boston media seemed to me to represent the city fairly well.

Blacks will play games on themselves, too. One of them is "the brother act." When I lived in Los Angeles at the start of the seventies, semi-African clothes were in fashion, and everybody was wearing beads and a dashiki. A peddler on the street who was selling beads and necklaces grabbed me. "Hey, man," he said, "I've got some down beads for you. They're really together."

I didn't like what I saw. "I don't want them," I said.

And he answered, "What's the matter? Ain't you a brother?"

In all these cases, from Madison Avenue to the bead seller, I've found myself searching for ways to resist such petty little intimidations. Most of us today are like cows; we will quietly stand in any line or fill out any form if there's a sign telling us that's what we should do. As a result, the country is filled with people who either paint signs or stand in line. I don't like doing either one. My grandfather and father always said they preferred doing things themselves, and I agree with them. My problem is that I'm constantly running into people who expect me to do things that offend me and my sense of freedom, so I've spent a lot of time trying to establish a set of principles that will both protect my freedom and respect theirs. I've developed defensive tactics: I use the glower; I can play the silent sphinx; I use the wisecrack; sometimes I've even been downright rude. But often I've had to improvise.

Most people, especially the ones who despise the government in Washington, simply don't believe that policemen sometimes harass and beat up black people for kicks. Cops have sometimes given me a hard time too, so I've worked out some tactics. Once in

Boston, in about 1960, I was sitting in my car in a parking lot while a friend was inside getting a few sandwiches to go. When a cop pulled into the parking lot next to me, I knew he didn't like the look of that big car—or at least the look of me in it. He walked up to me and said, "Let me see your driver's license and registration."

I said, "Why?"

"Because I want to see them."

We stared at each other. I figured I had three options. I could show him my papers, sit there and let him hassle me a little before letting me go. That was standard practice. Or I could take the chicken's way out by saying, "Hey, I'm Bill Russell of the Celtics. I'm not one of those black pimps who drive cars like this. You don't need to bother me."

Or I could do what I did. I said, "Officer, you have no grounds for suspecting me of anything. If you want to see my driver's license, you'll have to take me to jail. If you tell me I'm under arrest, I'll go with you, but I'm not showing you my papers."

We stared at each other some more, and then he told me I'd better let him see my papers if I knew what was good for me, and asked me where I'd got the money to buy the car. I ignored the question. The officer called in my license plate on his radio for a check, and then strutted around while he told me about all the things he could do to me. Finally he got a report back telling him who I was, and he left.

You have to be more theatrical in Los Angeles, I discovered. Once, in the early 1970's, I was driving home after a radio show. It had been a good day, and I was cruising along down Sunset Boulevard in my Lamborghini, doing about twenty-five miles an hour, when two cops pulled me over not far from the Beverly Hills Hotel. The day was so nice and I was in such a good humor that I'd let my guard down. "Why did you pull me over?" I asked the policeman.

He looked grave. "We have a report of a car like this being stolen and we have to check on it," he answered.

"What kind of car is it?" I asked.

I knew instantly that I had him; he had no idea what kind of car I was driving. I saw him searching desperately back and forth along the side of my car for an identifying mark, but there wasn't anything to see; the Lamborghini has only a tiny emblem on the front of the hood.

The cop was sweating; he could guess and probably look stupid, or he could admit he'd lied.

"Well," I prodded, "what kind of car is on that stolen-car report?"

He stalled and sweated a few seconds more, and then had an idea. "Well, you might have been one of the Brinks' robbers," he said. He had a malicious smile on his face, as if he was proud of himself for coming up with the line. It was his way of telling me that it didn't matter why he'd stopped me. "Get out of the car," he snapped.

"I understand now," I said as I unfolded myself from the car. "I'm often confused with the Brinks' robbers." I looked down at the cop and his partner, then raised my hands high in the air.

"Put your hands down," said the cop, glancing around to see if anybody was watching. "Come on, put your hands down."

"No, no," I said. "I ain't going to have you shoot me here on the street and then claim I was going for a gun." I reached even higher.

By this time we were drawing a crowd. It's not often that folks on Sunset Boulevard see a black giant standing out in the street reaching for the sky like a villain in a Western. I turned toward the gathering crowd and shouted loudly, "Don't shoot! I want these people to see that I'm going slowly for my wallet so that you can see my driver's license!" With my right hand still high in the air, I dropped my left one very slowly, fished out my wallet gingerly and dropped it on the top of my car.

"Okay," said the cop. "You can put your hands down now." By now he was almost pleading.

"Oh, no," I repeated. "I'm not going to put my hands down so you can shoot me and say I was going for a gun." I looked around at the crowd. "Yeah," I said loudly, "this is stop-the-nigger-in-the-expensive-car time."

After searching my wallet the policemen asked me if I was the Bill Russell who played for the Celtics. The crowd was already buzzing behind us, and some people had recognized me, so suddenly the cops laughed and apologized. It was a "routine mistake," they said, and as they left, one of them told me I didn't look like a Brinks robber after all. I didn't say anything. They had stopped me for nothing, and I had given them back some of their own hassle.

I can't really say to what degree I've relied on my name to protect me in incidents with the police, but I know that it has saved me in many cases. There's nothing I can do about this, and I know that my view of the relationship is permanently skewed. If another black man had acted the way I did in these two incidents, he might have wound up with an extra scar or two. That's why I shy away from giving advice; I don't think you can see a situation from another person's perspective when you have as many abnormal items on your bio sheet as I do. All I can say is that I regard moments like these as personal attacks, and that I'll do whatever I have to in order not to submit to them. I can't really know what I would do without my name, but I like to think that I wouldn't act differently.

Notoriety doesn't always work in your favor. I've gotten out of many scrapes by being recognized, but I've gotten into just as many for the same reason. I regard my twenty-year ordeal with autographs, for instance, as a struggle between notoriety and freedom. I always felt funny about autographs, even as a recognized basketball player in college. At first I didn't pay much attention to the feeling; I just signed my name because it was what everyone did. But in the early 1960's I noticed that after a session of signing fifty or sixty autographs, I felt strange about it for two or three days—as if I'd just come out from under an anesthetic and couldn't remember why I'd had an operation.

It's hard to step back and look detachedly at the custom when you're in the middle of a crowd. I'd be surrounded by all kinds of people. Some of the kids were so innocent, reaching up with their pencil and paper, that it shook me. Others were little monsters, out hunting scalps. They'd swarm from one player to another, never hesitating to complain if I didn't get to them fast enough. Women were usually shy and would manage to offer a compliment while I was signing. The men always made excuses; they didn't usually ask for autographs, they'd say, or that it was for their kids. They always seemed to need to say this, as though it was humiliating to ask another man for an autograph.

Typical autograph seekers are a mixture of shyness and rudeness. I've had them interrupt my meals in a restaurant by putting their pen and paper in my food, always by accident. It happens because they scuttle up to their target with their arms extended and their eyes turned aside. Nobody looks each other in the eye at an autograph session; it would be out of character. The process is like an assembly line, and I never had a single conversation while signing my name.

I finally stopped the practice at about the time I quit smoking —and in the same way. I do things abruptly. I try to think them out in advance, but when I've made up my mind I don't hesitate. When that first Surgeon General's report came out in 1964, I had been smoking for at least fifteen years. As I recall, the report was to be formally issued on a Monday, and on the preceding Friday the newspapers carried stories that the Surgeon General would declare that smoking causes cancer and that each cigarette takes an average of seven minutes off your life expectancy. After reading this I realized that nobody had ever explained it to me in that way before. When the report came out on Monday, I was already a nonsmoker; I had quit over the weekend and haven't gone back since.

Not long afterward I also kicked autographs cold turkey, and it didn't take long for the wrath of the sports world to descend on my head. My decision seemed to offend more people in Boston than anything I'd ever said about racism—which must be a sad commentary on something. One Boston writer launched a campaign in his column to have me fired from the Celtics because I was insulting the sovereign sports fans of Boston. People would come up to me on the street and snarl. "You have to sign autographs," they'd say. "That's the price you pay for being in the public eye!"

I wouldn't reply, because I don't like hostile conversation, but

I'd be thinking, "Wait a minute. Who decided that's the price I must pay? Somebody's trying to lay a decision on me arbitrarily, without consulting me, in an area that involves me personally. I don't have to put up with it unless I like being intimidated."

Or strangers would say, "Not signing autographs, eh? Well, *who do you think you are?*" As though signing autographs were an exercise in humility for celebrities, administered by the fans as therapy. In the autograph business, either the fans are prostrate and the stars are high and mighty, or vice versa. There's no such thing as an even keel, which is why the whole exchange is phony. Sometimes I'd answer the people who called me uppity by saying, "I don't think it matters to you who I think I am. But evidently it does matter who *you* think I am, and if I deviate from what *you* think I should be, you get pissed."

One year when I was squirming for an alternative to autographs, I had some small posters printed up with a photograph and a quotation from something I once wrote: "We learn to make a shell for ourselves when we are young and then spend the rest of our lives hoping for someone to reach inside that shell and touch us. Just touch us—anything more than that would be too much for us to bear." Whenever I felt especially bad about not signing, I'd get the person's name and address and mail him or her a poster. It was a compromise, but I thought it was better than an autograph. I never signed for some people and not for others because I wanted to deal with the issue as a matter of principle. It is the same one I struggled to live by when I played basketball: to keep my life separate from the praise or rejection of the crowd. I didn't play for the cheers or the boos. I considered myself an artist who did something he loved, got satisfaction out of it, and took responsibility for it.

With the Celtics I tried to play so that at the end of each season basketball and I would be even. Nobody would owe anybody anything. Each year I gave my best because that's what anyone does who cares about a game and wants to win, and the fans always got their money's worth. In all my thirteen years I asked for only one no-cut contract to guarantee my place on the team; I didn't want to work anywhere I wasn't wanted. I leaned

over backwards to make sure that there were no misunderstand-
ings about what was due, and at the end of the season I wanted
everything to be square. The people who came to the games
wouldn't owe me any money or testimonial dinners, and I
wouldn't owe them any exhibitions or autographs. The same
would be true of the owners and the other Celtics. That way,
whatever happened between people apart from the game could
develop freely.

There are many fundamentally nice people who ask for autographs and want little more than a chance to express kindness
toward me, but in order to accept their kindness I would have to
increase the risk of growing dependent on it. I'd also have to
expose myself to people who dislike me, and to violate my belief
that there should be no glories or obligations imposed on people
other than by their own choice. As I saw it, I had to make a choice
between these people and me, and I chose myself. It seemed to
me the best way for me to be at peace with myself.

Of course there are still a lot of people who will insist that I'm
supposed to sign autographs, no matter how I rationalize it. But
since they deny me free choice, they make it easy by reminding
me that apart from all my abstract principles, autographs are
usually a pain in the ass. Sometimes they create funny situations
though. I was standing by myself in the Cleveland airport, waiting
for a flight, reading a newspaper and keeping to myself. Suddenly
I became aware of a little round man staring up at me.

"Hi, Wilt," he said.

I knew I was in trouble because the guy had an aggressive,
know-it-all look to him. I didn't answer.

"Hi, Wilt," he repeated. His grin told me that he was going
to needle me until I responded. He was like one of those kids who
blows in the cat's ears. When I still didn't reply he looked irritated. "What's the matter, Wilt? Aren't you going to speak?"

"My name's not Wilt."

"Yes, it is," he insisted, as if he was correcting me in school.

I gave him my Grade A glower, which has a big batch of
smoldering Black Panther, a touch of Lord High Executioner and
angry Cyclops mixed together, with just a dash of the old Sonny

Liston. It usually works instantly, but not that day. For a minute or two we fought each other to a draw, with me glowering and him shaking his head up and down. "Yes, it is," he said again as he finally drifted off.

I knew I hadn't seen the last of him, and about five minutes later he was back. "Why didn't you tell me you were Bill Russell?" he demanded angrily.

"You didn't ask."

"You could have saved me a lot of trouble," he complained, acting put upon. Then he took a long breath, shook his head from side to side at all his troubles, and reached into his pocket for a pen and paper. "Sign this," he said.

"I don't sign autographs," I said.

"You *what?*" he asked. For the first time he was off balance.

"I don't sign autographs."

"You *have* to sign autographs," he sputtered. "I'm part of the public. We *made* you, you know."

This made me smile. The man was the closest I'd met to central casting's version of the tough, abrasive fan. "Pardon me, sir," I said with a smile, "but it seems that the next logical step here is for you to kick my ass."

He stepped back. "What do you mean?"

"Well, I was just standing here, not saying anything, not bothering a single soul. Then you come along and start a conversation I don't enjoy. So it seems to me that the next step is for you to kick my ass, because if you're not going to, you may as well leave me alone."

There have been hundreds like that man, but incidents don't always have sour endings. Once on a golf course a middle-aged lady asked me for an autograph, and when I declined she was upset until she had another thought. "Well, would you mind if I introduced you to my dog?" she asked. I said of course not, that I didn't mind meeting anybody. Whereupon she formally introduced me by name to her dog and went off happy as a lark.

I've noticed how often people are irritated when somebody else practices freedom. It upsets them, and they fall all over themselves to stop someone from doing whatever it is that *they* don't like. They try intimidation, and if this doesn't work they'll use rules, laws and even guns. I have seen this happen in sports all my life. It seems funny now, but in 1959 the NBA owners met to vote on a rule banning facial hair on the court. The reason was me; I'd grown a beard—not much of a one, but noticeable. Then Wilt grew one, and the league was faced with the first two hairy athletes in modern professional sports. The reaction couldn't have been any worse if we had taken up arson as a hobby. When Bill Walton broke into the NBA with the Portland TrailBlazers fifteen years later, his comments about J. Edgar Hoover caused a stir in the whole country. Walton criticized the FBI for illegal surveillance and harassment of him, and for other things that have since been proven largely true. But the FBI had a better image then, and Walton's comments made a lot of people angry. They said he should shut up and play basketball.

My impression of most of Walton's critics was that if you probed deep enough you'd find that their motivation was based on his half-a-million-dollar salary, and that he ought to shut up about the FBI and be grateful. That's saying that Walton's free-dom to speak his mind has been bought, which is nothing more than high-priced slavery. Intimidations come from every direc-tion. When you're young and poor, you're counseled to lay low because you can't afford to offend anybody; when you're success-ful, you should ignore what offends you because otherwise you'll seem ungrateful. For a country built on individual freedom, we sure are full of loopholes.

Of course you'll find oddballs and bizarre doings wherever freedom is practiced; that's part of the idea. But to me most free acts are not really weird in themselves; what makes them appear strange is that free acts are always warped by the forces of con-formity. Freedom is always under attack. It never travels alone, but is always dodging rocks and barbs.

Like most people, I've always had the urge to wander off the beaten path, but this went relatively unnoticed until sports put me in the public eye. Once that happened, it wasn't long before acts that seemed simple to me became so distorted by the public reaction that they seemed peculiar even to me. That's the way it was with my beard and with autographs, and later that's the way it was when the Celtics retired my number. Red wanted to hang my shirt from the rafters of Boston Garden, along with other Celtic "immortals." I didn't like the idea at all; I figured I'd retired myself, and my number could do whatever it wanted. To return to Boston and stand in the Garden while the crowd cheered in nostalgia and a number was raised to the ceiling to make me a basketball "immortal" wasn't my notion of a good time, and I didn't like it for the same reason I didn't like signing autographs for even the nicest people. Basketball was behind me. I knew what I had done better than anyone, but it was private. To the extent that memories were shared, it was with other players, not with fans. From my very first year I thought of myself as playing for the Celtics, not for Boston. The fans could do and think whatever they wanted. If they liked what they saw, fine; if not, the hell with it.

Bob Cousy's last year helped me to see things more clearly. He had announced his retirement in advance, and toward the end of the 1963 season we had an emotional "Farewell, Bob Cousy" night in every city around the league. Cousy went through hell, and the ceremonies didn't seem to have anything to do with the various ways he and the rest of us were trying to handle his retirement. We were his friends, and we didn't believe in funerals, but to the crowds he might as well have been dying. Fans seem capable only of expressing and receiving the rawest emotions. As I sat there watching Cousy go through all this, I thought to myself, "I'll never go out that way," so when the time came I kept my retirement plans a secret.

I knew I wouldn't be comfortable at a ceremony to retire my number, either—quite apart from the fact that such ceremonies seem a little tacky to me. But Red didn't see it that way, and he kept calling me every few months to arrange a time for the ceremony. Usually, he'd run a fast break on the phone—joking, talking, hatching schemes and thumbing through his date book for a convenient date. He has a persuasive way of looking ahead; he likes to ask little questions that presume you agree with him on the big one. So he kept trying to focus on the "when" question while I was still stuck on the "whether." It's an old salesman's trick. He'd known for years that I don't want any part of the ceremony, but he's nothing if not persistent.

Finally Red got smart. He learned that I had to be in Boston for an ABC telecast of a Celtic game in March 1972, the first time I'd been back to the Garden. He knew I couldn't get out of it, so he planned a surprise ceremony. Hearing about his scheme, I went straight to Red's office when I reached Boston. From the way he was grinning he must have figured he had me trapped. He looked like an unrepentant con man. "What's going on, Red?" I asked. "You know I don't want my number retired. Why are you pulling this?"

"Relax," he said. "The whole ceremony won't take more than a couple of minutes. You deserve it, and I promise it won't hurt. You should enjoy this, Russ. It's in your honor."

"We've been over this," I sighed. Red was still smiling. "I really don't want it, and I've told you so for years. I can't imagine how you can feel you're honoring me by doing something that offends me and makes me uncomfortable. If you go ahead in spite of my wishes, it's got nothing to do with me."

"I have to go ahead," Red said. "I've already retired those other guys' numbers, so it's only fair to retire yours."

We had a problem. Red and I are both stubborn, and we might have embarrassed each other in public if we hadn't worked out a compromise. Finally I agreed to the ceremony, and Red agreed to do it without a single fan present. We had our own little moment before the game—just Red, some of the Celtics I'd played with, and me. With that crew all the schmaltz was ruled out in favor of so much horseplay that we never could control ourselves long enough to pose for a serious picture. The next day newspaper readers saw a bunch of cackling Celtics alone in a cavernous Garden. A lot of people wrote in that Russell was being weird and outrageous again. Maybe so.

I have tried to avoid intimidation in all kinds of situations, both trivial and important. I have a compulsion to be my own man, but I haven't always been a Rock of Gibraltar about it. For example, when I became player-coach of the Celtics, I discovered that I had acquired many new friends. One of the reasons they turned up was that I could get them tickets to the games. In the first round of the play-offs that year, when we were expected to win easily, I got loads of tickets. I asked a new golfing friend of mine if he wanted some, and he refused them, but in the next round, when we were playing Wilt and the 76ers and tickets were at a premium, my golf buddy said he wanted *nine* tickets. It was too much trouble for him to come by for the tickets; he wanted them left at the press gate, so I took some extra time and saw to this. In fact, for the first play-off game against the 76ers I had gotten thirty-six tickets for various new friends. Afterward, when I asked my golfing friend if the tickets were okay, he said they were all right but that he didn't like having to sit next to another friend, so for the next home game I switched seats around. Then the golf buddy said he wanted better seats, a little closer than the rest of my friends, so I worked on that. By the end of the series I was getting to the Garden early because I had a whole game before the game—making sure nobody was upset about where they were sitting.

We lost that series. I can't blame it on all the sweat at the ticket office, because the 76ers had a better team that year, but I did blame myself for being a chump. I didn't want those people to think I didn't like them or that it was any trouble for me to throw my weight around in the front office, so I invited myself to stand in line for them. It took the whole series before I woke up to see that intimidation is not always hostile; often it comes from friends, people around you and close to you. I had tried not to trade on my athletic status to ingratiate myself with people or to wrangle favors, but I was right there playing the big star in the ticket office, helping those people attack what I wanted to stand for.

Once Mahatma Gandhi said something like, "It is not my aim to be consistent with what I have said, but to be consistent with the truth as it reveals itself to me." I agree with that remark. I have never been absolutely consistent about anything, even though I've tried. But it was revealed to me that those people weren't going to get any more tickets to the play-offs, and they never did.

That time my vision was bad; I didn't see what was going on. But there have been other times when I saw my freedom being attacked and couldn't stop it. I opened a restaurant in Boston back in the early 1960's, when the Celtics were at their peak and had hired contractors to do a complete remodeling job before the place opened. On the day work was finished, there were a dozen Boston city inspectors milling around the place, and not a single part of my restaurant passed inspection. The fire inspectors wouldn't approve the counter tops because they were made of a Formica base. Everybody knows that Formica won't burn, but it turned out that in those days the only surface that would pass inspection was made by a Boston company in which the fire inspectors had an interest. Other inspectors gave me similar excuses about the plumbing, wiring and kitchen. Most of them were simply waiting for a payoff, and there were other guys milling around who offered to take care of the payoffs if I gave *them* a payoff.

I was a greenhorn about all this, so it offended me, and all the inspectors went home empty-handed. My friends tried to explain the facts of life to me, but I wouldn't listen. Over the next few days I looked for an honest way out, but I got nowhere, so I wound up calling up some of the political big shots who had been friendly. Apparently the politicians made the inspectors' phones ring, because they filed back in, one by one, and approved my restaurant without a word. In order to win round one against corruption, I had to stoop to a little influence-peddling of my own.

Round Two wasn't far off. Shortly after the restaurant opened, one of the policemen from the local station dropped by and insisted on seeing me. "The captain sent me over here to get some food," he said.

"Good," I said cheerfully. "Just give your order to one of the waitresses and she'll take care of you."

When I walked away the cop followed me, but I wasn't going to make it easy for him. He caught up with me and said, "Look, this is for the guys down at the station who work this area, and the captain doesn't pay for it."

"Well, then, he's not going to get it," I said.

The cop looked more surprised than upset. "You telling the captain no?" he asked in disbelief.

"You got it," I said.

Round Two wasn't so hard. It was simply a matter of calling the bluff of the police, who had built up a tradition that each local station got free meals at neighborhood restaurants. I didn't get any favors from the cops after that, and they went out of their way to give my customers parking tickets. But they didn't threaten the business.

Then came Round Three. My restaurant was packed almost all the time, and we sold a lot of food and liquor, but somehow the receipts always came up way short. It didn't take me long to notice this. Somebody was picking me clean, and it didn't take much detective work to discover that it was mostly the bartenders and cashiers. The problem was easy to solve, I thought naïvely, and I replaced a few people. Nothing changed. I watched like a hawk to find out how it was being done. Overflow crowds kept spending money every night, but every morning I hit bare metal in the till.

The first hint that I was over my head came to me when I started *losing* money. The next one came when a rich, street-tough black dude came to see me. He said he'd heard I was having trouble and wanted to give me some advice about how to handle sticky-fingered employees. Some people he knew had caught a bartender stealing money and had taken him out back and broken his leg with a baseball bat. Then, while the guy was lying there on the ground, they gave him money for cab fare, told him to go to the hospital and get himself fixed up, charge the medical bills to the restaurant, rest awhile, and come on back to work when he felt like it. After that, the folks running the restaurant didn't have any more trouble with bartenders.

As this story unfolded, I decided that I was in the wrong line of work. Quickly my restaurant was up for sale. Corruption had kayoed me in the third round.

I'm not a crusader who wants to stomp out evil everywhere. But I do take it as a duty to defend the freedoms that exist within our society, especially my own. All corruption is an attack on people's freedom but so are many other aspects of life today. For example, inflation seems to me a form of corruption. So many people go to work in the morning already gritting their teeth that I know they can't be taking pride or joy in their work. Something tells me those people are doing shoddy work, while conspiring half the time to impose a price increase on somebody else.

You may be able to duck the forces that attack freedom for a while and get away with it, the way I did with my restaurant. You may even be part of such forces and not know it, but sooner or later they are going to attack *you*. When I was growing up, Mr. Charlie used to talk to me about the killer tiger on the loose. If I saw that tiger attacking somebody else, he said, and I stood by because it wasn't me, I had no right to complain when the tiger got hungry for my hide. The tiger didn't care who it was biting; it would get around to everybody sooner or later. It's in your enlightened self-interest to help keep the tiger off others.

When I was young we had the pushers in the slums, selling heroin and marijuana. By the time I was a little older the pushers were in the suburbs and penthouses. It took about twenty years, but it happened. In the Watts riot of 1965 the National Guard shot down blacks in the ghetto, and in 1970 the Guard was shooting white college kids at Kent State; it only took five years. The forces against freedom always spread, but whites don't see that the same force that attacks blacks will one day turn on them.

Those same forces spread out over the globe and then boomerang. When all the testimony came out about what our country had done to the Allende government in Chile, I had a sinking feeling that we had let loose something that was too nasty to stay abroad. As I see it, Nixon and Kissinger said, "There's a danger of communism in Chile, and the Chileans are acting like kids. They don't know what's good for them, so to hell with their elections and Constitution! We'll straighten them out!" Nixon and Kissinger decided that the Chileans would be better off with a right-wing dictatorship than a left-wing democracy. I wonder how long it will take for this approach to return home. How long before somebody in power says, "The average television show appeals to the mentality of a twelve-year-old. What do the voters know about anything? We've got to take over and run things right." Maybe it's already started happening.

What they did in Chile "to promote democracy" is incompatible with everything I've learned since I was a little boy. Ideas are like the wind: they're free. You can't really impose an idea like democracy on people in the first place, because that's not the nature of ideas. You may think you're promoting a better idea, but what you are really imposing is yourself. You can lay guns, bulldozers and bribes on a country until you have it in your power, and then you can claim that its people like your ideas. But the intimidation came first, and it really doesn't have anything to do with ideas. The best way to promote an idea is to simply let it circulate. If word spreads that it's a good one, you won't have to bully anybody; they'll come to you. In fact, if the idea is good enough, they'll be trying to sneak in your house to steal it.

Nixon's and Kissinger's attitude about the Chilean people is a common one in this country. We tend to look upon everybody around the globe as children trying to play like grown-ups. We feel that we're sober and responsible, whereas everybody else is acting silly in front of the mirror. This attitude is a road map to grief. It's the way we thought of the Vietnamese, and the way many whites thought of blacks for hundreds of years. Even today what most whites write about blacks has the undercurrent of the child-rearing parent.

Whenever I sense someone speaking about somebody else with a parental attitude, I figure somebody's freedom is about to be attacked. It doesn't matter whether they're kind or stern parents; the parental mind-set paves the way for them to deny somebody else's rights. The attitude is convenient because it's a way for people to soothe their consciences about not treating others equally. It was true of all the colonialists, from the Romans to the British, it was true of Nixon and Kissinger in Chile, and it was even true of the man who wanted me to advertise his baby powder.

In a similar vein, I worry when I hear people crusading in the name of their kids. The most explosive social issues in recent years, such as abortion, pornography and busing, have been debated according to their impact on kids—or at least what people claim will be their impact on kids. "I can handle pornography myself," you'll hear the parent say, "but I don't want my kid exposed to it." That's the voice of someone who's about to attack somebody else's freedom.

People have persecuted homosexuals for eons in the name of God and kids. Homosexuals, it's claimed, are vampires who replenish their ranks by preying on youth. "We have to protect our children!" is the cry. But homosexuals *are* our children, and we should treat them so; as adults they deserve the full respect given heterosexuals. I have my own fears and insecurities about sex, but I don't think it's my right to impose them on the world, or to hide things from my children; I have too much respect for them to do so. My duty to them is to love them and to help them interpret the world so that they will be able to make free choices and act on them. I worry a great deal about my children, but the best medicine for those worries is in their strength and independence, not in their ignorance.

When people are angry or afraid they tend to rally around an institution for protection—the flag, the army or the Church, for example. Or if they feel a recession coming, they'll huddle inside their company. This is natural, but at these times such people are the least free. They don't think much, don't take much responsibility and become drones. I have said that I could never identify with Thomas Jefferson and the other founding fathers because most of them were slaveholders. Still, I can appreciate the fact that they revolted against the major institution they knew—the European state—and also fought a rear-guard action against the European Church. They were on their own. What institutions they had were largely built by them, and they respected themselves and each other at least as much as they respected any institution. I admire that. These days many people are so emotionally involved with their institutions that they don't even see them for what they are.

• • •

The Basketball Hall of Fame is an institution of sorts. Its first members were selected in 1959, when I was already playing professional basketball, so I am its contemporary and an observer of its creation. Fifteen years later the Hall's selection committee chose me as the first individual black player. When my selection was announced I issued a statement saying that for personal reasons I preferred not to be inducted. I said I had no quarrel with the Hall; I simply did not wish to be a part of it, would not consider myself a member under any circumstances. I did not explain the reasons for my decision.

To most people the Hall of Fame is the ultimate in sports. It's like athletes' heaven—something you dream of and strive for throughout your career. If you are good enough and lucky enough to rank with "the immortals," you are "enshrined" into the Hall of Fame. To many fans, the very mention of the Hall sets off tremors of awe, and players themselves are subdued about it. There's so much sentiment surrounding the institution, it's unheard of to refuse when the angels come to carry you off to glory.

So the sportswriters jumped all over me; to many of them it was blasphemy of the highest order. From all over the country they called and challenged me to explain. All I would say was that my reasons were personal. Which didn't stop the writers; a couple of them simply guessed at my motives, and then tried to discredit them. One writer was more straightforward; he wrote that he didn't know what my reasons could be, but whatever they were, they stank.

The fans took up where the writers left off. A lot of them sent me letters that looked as if they were written by a nasty six-year-old, with misspelled words calling me a Jew and a nigger in the same sentence. On a higher level, a bank president from Ohio wrote to tell me that I owed him and the whole country an explanation.

Most of these fans and writers assumed that I think the Hall of Fame is racist. I do, but there's more to it than that; if I refused to have anything to do with every American institution that I thought racist, I'd be leading a hermit's life. What it came down to was that I thought of the Hall of Fame in the same way that I thought about autographs and having my number retired. I took fairly consistent stands on all three; in each case, my intention was to separate myself from the star's idea about fans and fans' ideas about stars. I have very little faith in cheers, what they mean and how long they will last, compared with the faith I have in my own love for the game. The Basketball Hall of Fame is the biggest cheer of all, and it means testimonials, dinners, souvenirs and memories. As an ex-athlete, I don't think that diet is good for me, or for my relationship with others.

When I was deciding what to do about the Hall of Fame, I'd occasionally catch myself and think, "Hey, lighten up. You're making too big a deal out of this. Just put the best face on it, and let it go." But on top of everything else I have another gripe against the Hall of Fame. It's jaundiced, I'll admit, but I think it's accurate. When I played basketball I had the misfortune to associate with a number of the Hall's founders and earliest members, before they were turned into stained-glass windows, and the experience soured me.

All of this amounts to a series of personal beefs, I know, and perhaps I should have risen above them in making my decision. But I always said my reasons were personal.

One of those beefs grew out of a dispute I had with a man named Mokray, who was the statistician for the Celtics. He and I did not get along. I did a lot of unpleasant chores for Mokray on his word that they were Walter Brown's wishes. Then, in a chance conversation one day with Brown, I discovered that he didn't know anything about all these favors. On top of everything else, Mokray had lied to me.

Mokray wrote some of the NBA's promotional brochures. One of these listed annually the leading professional and college players—fifty or sixty of them, their statistics, a photograph, and a short biographical sketch. Always included were the NBA All-Star team, the All-Pro players, the statistical leaders and the team leaders. Except for me; he wouldn't put me in. In 1962 I was named the Most Valuable Player in the NBA and was a member of its championship team, yet I was not even mentioned in Mokray's *Basketball Stars of 1962*. This didn't ruin my life, of course. I sulked about it for an hour or two and then it was over. But since Mokray and I saw each other around the Celtics' offices fairly often, I would be reminded of him. I wondered how anyone could call himself a professional and censor anybody the way he did. The way I saw it, I would never let our quarrel interfere with the way I played basketball, and he shouldn't let it affect the way he promoted the game.

In 1965 Mokray was enshrined in the Basketball Hall of Fame. It was one of the major shocks in my sports education. I had known Mokray for almost nine years, and in all that time I thought he never did anything except keep statistics and be a jerk. His selection made me curious about the Hall of Fame, and I discovered that he was in good company there. Abe Saperstein, for instance, was a member because of what he had done with the Globetrotters. As I've mentioned earlier, I don't even think that the Globetrotters play basketball; they're part of a show. Moreover, for years when blacks were trying to break into major-league sports, Saperstein worked against the aspirations of an entire race just to keep his little franchises.

Then there was Adolph Rupp. I know many players who had been coached by him at the University of Kentucky, I'd met him myself, and nothing I ever saw or heard of him contradicted my impression that he was one of the more devout racists in sports. He was known for the delight he took in making nasty remarks about niggers and Jews, and for his determination never to have black players at the University of Kentucky. He held to this until his top-ranked all-white team lost the 1965 NCAA finals to an unknown team of blacks from Texas Western.

Apart from his racism, I acknowledge that Adolph Rupp did a lot for basketball, and perhaps he deserves to be in the Hall of Fame. But I did not want to be associated with him or anybody else of his racial views. I saw that as my free choice to make.

The Hall of Fame did not descend from heaven on a golden platform. Its rules were not written on clay tablets. Far from it. The Hall of Fame was created in 1959 by a group of white men, all born about the turn of the century, who decided to declare themselves the Hall of Fame Committee. Rupp was there, along with people I personally admire, like Walter Brown. They all knew each other. They wrote their own rules to perpetuate themselves and their chosen successors as the controlling powers. And by and large they elected themselves and their friends to the Hall of Fame, along with some players. The patterns were clear, although I had never noticed them. In 1964, the year before he was himself elected, Mokray served as the chairman of the Hall of Fame Selection Committee.

I know that an institution has got to start *somewhere*, but in the long run respect for it will depend on how it is built. If the people who wrote the American Constitution had decided that they would be the members of the first Congress, and that each congressman would always appoint his own successor, I doubt that the Constitution would have lasted very long or commanded much respect. A lot of people would have said, "Hey, they can have that Constitution. They wrote it for themselves, but it doesn't have anything to do with me."

That's the way I feel about the Hall of Fame. Aside from racism or my own feelings about the cheers and boos in sports, I don't respect it as an institution. Its standards are not high enough. It's too political, too self-serving. I'm not trying to take it away from the people who run it. They've done well, and I'm sure there are many people who have more instinctive respect for the Basketball Hall of Fame than they have for the U.S. Congress. I'm just saying that the Hall of Fame is separate from me. It's theirs. I think of it about the way I think of the Ten Best Dressed List. Some people in New York got together and came up with that gimmick, and it's become such an institution that I'm sure many people believe it's the final word on fashion. I don't; I think it's just what a few people in New York say.

What I said and did about the Hall of Fame was for me. The only possible lesson for anybody else is that some people may accept institutions too readily. They accept authority blindly, without a second look, and when they do, they forfeit their rights and even their opinions to the sign painters in our society. When Walter Cronkite says, "That's the way it is," he really should say,

"That's the way it looks to me and the folks at CBS." Anyway, that's the way it looks to me.

Ironically, in spite of my convictions, the Hall of Fame "enshrined" me. They have one of my old Celtic uniforms in their museum up in Massachusetts, worn by a white mannequin.

Certainly my idea of freedom is not saying no to everything. If that were true, I could never have subordinated myself to basketball the way I did. Nor is it to keep people away from me; more important than any game is to touch and to be touched. Nor is my idea of freedom to be able to do whatever I please whenever I want. All my life, and particularly in the last fifteen years, I've tried to develop a personal philosophy built on the belief that I cannot be free until I accept responsibility for what I do. Until I get to that place, I can do all sorts of terrible things to people and to society in general while claiming an excuse—that it's not my fault, that something else is making it happen.

Many people today who profess to live by freedom spend most of their time trying to impose themselves over the rights and opinions of other people. Others who profess to live by freedom constantly allow themselves to be imposed on. Still others say they are religious but spend their time doing mean things to people. None of this would go on that way if people could accept responsibility for what they do. I have an extreme view of it, I guess. I alone am responsible for being a good human being. My religion is not, and neither is my family nor my race nor the institutions around me.

Let's accept the premise that there is some sort of magic in the universe, an inspiration for whatever there is, and call it a god. And god is part of you and you are part of god. Then how can anybody be mean to the person next to him when they are both part of god? How can you say, "Well, god created everything, but I'm better than you"? Or how can you say, "Well, god created everything, but he put me here to run it"? I have never understood that. Instead, I think you look at it all and you say, "I'm glad I'm part of this, free to make myself a place."

7

Women and Blues

Professional basketball went out of my life in 1969, but it had a lot of company. Within a few months of my retirement I also left behind my life in Boston and everything that went with it—including my wife of thirteen years, my three children, my Boston friends and my material possessions. Everything in life seemed an encumbrance to me, so I made a clean break and took off like a nomad.

It was a time of excitement mixed with fear. Every breath I took felt a little frosty. I was excited because I was venturing into the outside world after thirteen years in a compression chamber. Fans were about to become people, and I was about to become a person instead of a star. I wanted to read everything I could get my hands on, and to poke around in every layer of life. I felt liberated and tingly, the way college seniors are supposed to on graduation day.

At the same time I was a little fearful. I sensed that in many ways I was far behind other people who had led more normal lives, and with debts to pay. I thought I owed something, but I wasn't sure what it was. After striving for all those years to keep my mind, emotions and identity independent of basketball, I realized that it had still been an anchor and source of strength. On the court itself I knew exactly what I was doing. Now that certainty was gone; it would no longer serve to shield me or settle any arguments. In my head I had known that basketball was not meant to protect me, but I'd never had to live without it. It's one thing to know that you're not really walking if you use crutches; it's quite another to throw them away. In the back of my mind I feared that anyone as gifted and obsessed as I had been about something like basketball was bound to be retarded elsewhere in his life—maybe everywhere else.

As a basketball player, I had thought of myself as an advanced student, a revolutionary and a champion, so perhaps it was inevitable that I believed myself to be a novice in other aspects of life. If I was ten years ahead of the game, I was at least that far behind with women. Every ounce of me knew that the lights had gone out on my marriage about 1959, but it took until 1969 for me to do something about it. I was always struggling to catch up, and making mistakes. My confidence was low, my instincts were bad and my judgment was even worse. Over the previous ten years there had been many sweet times and many heartsick ones; I had been consistent only in never quite being on top of my life off the court. After retiring, I was free to start over and concentrate on my personal life, to make up for all those years of being behind. This was part of the excitement of starting over fresh. On the other hand, I knew I had a habit of getting in over my head; it was a characteristic that ran all though my past.

When I married Rose in 1956 I was twenty-two, fresh from the Olympics, and didn't have the slightest idea what I was doing. I knew only that Rose accepted and cared about me apart from basketball, which was a great breakthrough for me. I loved her, and I have never since felt that it was a mistake to marry her, because it seemed so right at the time. I wasn't trying to force a relationship to work against my better judgment; at the wedding I had all the feelings you were supposed to have, and I wanted to put that emotion into our lives together. Our marriage gave me such a rush of good feeling and romance that I thought I could leave it home like a keepsake and go on about my business. The feeling was so special that I simply assumed it had nothing to do with the rest of my life. It never really occurred to me that marriage and the other parts of one's life went together, or that married people should share that life like friends. Friend and wife were mutually exclusive terms to me. I don't know what Rose's attitude was because I never talked to her about it—which is exactly the point.

Back in those days it was acceptable to play Ulysses. You could take off, wander around the world for a few years, and then come home and expect to find things exactly as you had left them. That's what I did. I went off on road trips with the Celtics, visited friends, gave speeches, explored politics and became involved in civil rights. Later, I went off to Africa for months at a time; still later, I took off for weeks without knowing where I was going until I got there. When I returned, Rose and I would take up our conversation exactly where we had left it, and neither of us would mention the trip.

Rose never pried or asked questions—I suspect because she was a little scared of me. If so, we were quite a match. For years I had two bizarre fears involving her. I was frightened that the time would come when I wouldn't be able to open a jar for her. I didn't know what I'd do if she bought one that I couldn't open. I knew it was a strange fear, and sometimes I would laugh at myself about it, but the feeling persisted.

My other fear was that Rose would ask me a question I couldn't answer. I could never figure out what would lie on the other side of that moment, and I didn't like to think about it because it made me feel fragile.

Neither of these fears was ever more than a shadow, and they never materialized; staying away from home so much helped minimize my risk. Not surprisingly, I avoided discussing all subjects that interested me, figuring that these were precisely the ones for which I didn't have all the answers. Therefore, Rose and I didn't talk much about what concerned us, which did not strike me as unnatural for a number of years.

The hurts and antagonisms that grew up between Rose and me over the years were minor compared with the limitations we had from the beginning. I myself was one of the main limitations, and

I drifted away. A large part of me often wanted to think and act like a little boy, but I never considered acknowledging this to Rose; around her, I felt a compulsion to be strong and confident. Most of the time I managed to convey these attitudes by force of personality, but it was a pose. In fact, my whole life seemed to me a pose, which I needed to both maintain and destroy at the same time. So, piece by piece, I disappeared. Although our formal separation did not occur until 1969, the real move had been made years before.

My faithfulness to Rose lasted through my first two seasons in Boston, when I was even more shy about temptation than I was with Rose. The other Celtics, who were curious about my personal life, thought I was square. They were right. When we were on the road I stayed in my hotel room most of the time, and at home I'd go down to the basement most nights and play with the electric trains I'd assembled. Electric trains had been an obsession of mine ever since my boyhood in Louisiana, and with my first bit of Celtic money I started building a set-up that fulfilled all my fantasies.

But trains couldn't hold me forever. I had too much energy, and I heard too much from my teammates about how they spent their spare time. One night I simply told Rose I was going out. Nothing more was said, and I went out on the town. On that very first occasion I ran into Iodine, who turned me every way but loose.

I called her Iodine because she was such strong medicine that she could clean all my wounds if I didn't mind the sting. Black, with light copper skin and red hair, her beauty was striking, but what really made people sit up was the way she carried herself. When she walked into a crowded club, she was noticed by everyone there within a minute. She came from such a different realm of life that I could not understand her power until I'd spent a lot of time watching her move in her element. She kept gangsters and politicians wrapped around her fingers without ever working at it, and on the night I met her, she added a young athlete to her string.

Having been in the Olympics, NBA championships and in the

press spotlight for several years, I thought I knew something
about the big time. My rule of thumb was never to show interest
in anything or anybody, because I know that hustlers work on the
greed and desire they see in your face. This tactic had worked
fairly well until I ran into Iodine. After five minutes at her table
I realized that I didn't know anything. Iodine was the queen of
streetwise, a virtuoso on her subject, as anyone could tell by
watching her hold court. She swapped information with relish,
completely at ease. People sought her advice on every subject
from fights to marriage to race horses to business deals. She was
always ahead of the game, and you could tell she enjoyed playing.

Iodine understood how a a big, corrupt city like Boston worked
—everything, that is, that wouldn't appear in the papers or on
television, which is most of it. She knew all the pimps, gangsters,
whores, union bosses, liquor dealers, fixers, loan sharks, big-time
ghetto blacks, fences, and guys in the car-theft racket. She also
knew how each of them made their accommodations with the
police, Irish pols, WASPs and Italians who mattered. She knew
who was up and who was down, who was in trouble and who was
on top, who had a future and who did not. She knew all this
because people wanted to tell her everything, and because she had
a genius for reading faces. After a glance at a person she could
tell you his strengths and vices.

That night Iodine introduced me to the people who passed by
her table, and after each of them left she would turn to me and
give me the lowdown on them. I sat there in amazement, trying
to nod my head sagely, and putting on a good front with everybody except Iodine. Since I was with the Celtics and with her,
nobody tried to mess with me when I was first getting my street
legs.

In introducing me to black society in Boston, Iodine helped me
to understand the first fact of life for a young black man earning
thirty or forty thousand dollars in Boston back in the 1950's: that
my economic peer group consisted mostly of pimps and gangsters.
That was a necessity. There was no choice in the matter. If I
wanted to do anything that required money, most of the people
who could pull their own weight with me were gangsters. My only

other choices were to pay for everybody and have an entourage, which didn't appeal to me, or to form horizontal relationships that were unrelated to money, which is hard to do anywhere.

As it turned out, Iodine became a buffer between me and the black high rollers in Boston. She told me which ones would try to get a hook into me and about those who wouldn't try to capitalize on their friendship. She tried to steer me to what she called the soft-core guys, the "class" gangsters, because she knew I was too straight to be chummy with the ones who had ice in their eyes. In time, I learned how to spot the guys who respected privacy, who could laugh and play in their off time and not push it further. I wasn't interested in hearing what they did for a living, and by the same token I didn't want them questioning me about basketball all the time. I found some characters I could get along with, and I like to think they'd have been successful in different lines of work.

I believe Iodine learned something from me, too; at least she said she did. Most of the street people Iodine knew didn't buck the white folks much. They knew that whites would leave them alone if they ran their games in their own neighborhoods and didn't mind taking harassment from the cops every so often; it was a kind of unwritten agreement. As a result, most of the black men didn't have a great deal of self-esteem. They could laugh at the white world or sneak around it, but few of them faced it straight on. In Boston, in the late 1950's, the idea that a black man could be successful without either hiding or kissing ass was an obscure one, at best. But I was trying to do it, and time after time I violated the basic rules of Iodine's world, and it both stunned and fascinated her. We studied each other. As awed as I was when she displayed her street knowledge, she'd be equally taken back when I gave no ground to anyone, black or white. She never flinched at the worst intimidations of black people, but always became upset when I told a white policeman to get out of my face. By Iodine's rules, I often made stupid mistakes, even among blacks. I *was* stupid, but I was also tough—which is the worst possible combination. It leads to a great deal of aggravation, and that's exactly what I found. We nursed each other along and became a couple in no time.

But though we learned a lot, the basis of our relationship was never education, or pre-civil-rights ghetto sociology. Our relationship was never equal. She could turn me inside out and upside down. She taught me about passion. She was so good to me that sometimes when I was making love with her the tears would roll down my cheeks.

That was the medicine. The sting might come any time. Sometimes in bed at night it felt as if all my nerves had unplugged from my brain, and I'd be way out there where no words or familiar thoughts exist, when suddenly a scream would shatter me. "Stop it!" she'd yell. "Stop it, goddam it!" As big as I am, she'd throw me across the bed.

I'd be somewhere between Jupiter and Mars, and it would be all I could do to ask weakly, "What's the matter?"

Iodine would shrug her shoulders and say, "Oh, you were just having too much fun," and the next thing I'd know she'd be swishing out the door, leaving me there on the bed with about as much vitality as a pile of chicken bones.

This was only one of her little ways to keep me in line, as she called it. She had hundreds of them which she'd spring on me when I least expected them. Normally Iodine was cool, full of subtle smiles and gestures, and I could almost see her mind working. But when I was least expecting it, Jekyll would vanish and Hyde would take over. She'd pitch a fit of some kind, then shake the dust off her feet and take off. As an animal, she'd have been a mustang; as a food, she'd have been one of those hot chili peppers.

One night Iodine got drunk and decided that I had been looking at another woman. (I probably had.) She sat in her car outside the restaurant I owned, staking me out, waiting to follow me. I left in my car about midnight, and soon caught sight of her in my rear-view mirror. Pretending I hadn't seen her, I took her on a full tour of Boston. We went down side streets and through alleys, with Iodine always a block behind. Finally we ended up at a red light three blocks from where we'd started a half hour earlier. I was sitting there chuckling to myself, when *Wham!* my body went forward and my head backward as I heard the crunch of metal. Not only had Iodine rammed me at full speed, but she was still going! She pushed my car right through the intersection, red light and all. "My God!" I remember thinking. "This is dangerous!" And it was, considering the way people drive in Boston. When she got tired of pushing me, she backed off to ram me again. I took off at full speed, trying to dodge her, and we had a hair-raising chase through the streets of Boston at eighty miles an hour, tires squealing and jumping curbs. I came around a corner onto Columbus Avenue and was doing at least sixty when I made my move: I slammed on the brakes and skidded into an intersection. Iodine did just what I expected; she speeded up even more and headed right toward my car. Was she going to get me! At the last second I hit the gas and turned right at the corner. Since she was going too fast to make the turn, she went flying through the intersection, slammed on her brakes at the next block and turned right; she was going to circle the block and catch me. But I backed up into Columbus Avenue and took off behind her, then cut off on a side street before she sighted me. I got away with only frayed nerves.

I hadn't been home long enough for my pulse to slow down when I got a phone call. Iodine had rammed the Mustang into a building at fifty miles an hour. There were no skid marks, and the police had arrested her for drunken driving. It cost me $300 to have the police let her go without being booked or connecting me to her or the car. She hadn't been injured, and had jumped out of the wreck, full of fire and alcohol.

Iodine never left skid marks, and nothing slowed her down for long. Long before this incident I knew that I had no business being around such a woman, but I couldn't help it. We were always fighting, but it never mattered to me; nothing did. Sometimes I'd want to see her so bad that I hurt all over, and that's when she'd go off on me. One day she announced that she was moving to New York, and the next day she was gone. She got a job in a bar, and soon captured some of the heavy rollers down there. For months I had no idea where she was; then, just as abruptly as she had left, she called and told me to come see her. I didn't ask questions; I just went. There was a long spell when I was commuting to New York almost every free day I had. Sometimes I'd make a deal with Red to get out of practice, leave in the morning as if I was going to work, catch an early flight to New York, spend all day and evening with her, and then take the last flight back to Boston. I had a key to her apartment, but I always called ahead. Only once was I stupid on that score. I kept running into people on one trip, and circumstances prevented me from calling, so naturally I walked in and found her in bed with another guy. "I should have *known* better," I moaned, as the other guy scrambled up and left. Then came the bad part: Iodine convinced me that the two of them had gone to a party, gotten drunk, and passed out on the bed, naked under the covers, without ever touching each other. They were innocent as babes, she said. She convinced me because I wanted to be convinced.

Iodine was the first person who could make me believe things I knew weren't true, make me do things I didn't want to do, say things I didn't want to say, and go places I didn't want to go. Sometimes I was on the edge of nervous exhaustion from too many consecutive days of pressure basketball, trips to New York, trouble at the restaurant, and the effort to keep up the appearance of a home life. Inevitably, whenever I wanted to spend a day sleeping and playing with my kids, Iodine would call. "Come on down here today," she'd say.

"No," I'd answer firmly. "There's no way. They'd have to ship me in a crate. I'll come tomorrow."

"I want you here today."

"All right."

Nobody else could do that to me. On the plane I'd start talking to myself. "You realize you're way over your head, Russell, don't you?" Then I'd nod in agreement with myself. There wasn't the remotest possibility that I could handle Iodine, and I knew I was going to get my ass kicked in New York in one way or another, but I'd go anyway. As usual with women, my reaction time was measured in years instead of in minutes.

•   •   •

My experiences with Iodine made me think more about the differences between the sexes. I speculated on why women so often did things that seemed strange to me. They must come at life from a fundamentally different perspective, I decided, but I wanted to know just what this meant. I started cataloguing the differences. The discrepancy in marriage, for example: how I could run off and have affairs while Rose stayed home? Why was an unmarried woman of thirty called an old maid while an unmarried man of the same age was congratulated on being a confirmed bachelor? I also thought about violence. Any woman must be aware that if push comes to shove the man she's involved with can beat her up because he's bigger and stronger. No matter how sophisticated she is, or how deeply she has suppressed the idea, it must be down there somewhere. Subconsciously the woman must know that even if she's right—or *especially* if she's right— there can come a point when the man gets that glaze in his eyes that tells her she's gone too far.

Iodine never paid the slightest attention to my theories about women, and I never detected the slightest sign that she was physically intimidated by me. One night when she was angry with me she didn't hesitate to stab me in the arm with a pair of scissors, and she meant business; she plunged them all the way into the bone. The Celtics were in the middle of the play-offs at the time, and I had to find a cooperative doctor who would keep his mouth shut. He stitched up the wound just below the shoulder. But there are very few bandages you can hide under a basketball uniform, so when reporters asked me about the injury I told them I'd gotten immunization shots for a trip abroad I'd planned after the season. Iodine thought it was all very funny; she said she wanted to see if the Celtics could win a championship while I played with a hole in my arm.

After a few years in New York, Iodine returned to Boston as suddenly as she had left, and I came up with the brilliant plan of keeping a mistress on the side, just like they do in Latin countries —and occasionally elsewhere in the NBA. So I set Iodine up with an apartment, car, clothes, the works. This created even more excitement and drama, because it gave us so many more things to fight about. Each of us was determined not to be possessed in any way, but since each of us *was* possessed, there was usually enough friction for a spark. And there was enough powder in our personalities for big explosions. We'd have passionate fights, followed by even more passionate moments of bliss. I always knew there'd be surprises, but I never knew where they'd be coming from. Once when we'd made up after a fight, I felt so peaceful that I took off with Iodine and drove all the way to California. Then we went down to Mexico, flying high; and for a month there wasn't the hint of a cross word between us. But as we headed back east, Iodine said she was having such a good time that she wanted to take another week. Bracing myself, I decided to take a stand. I'd already been gone a month, I pointed out, and I had to go home and see Rose and the kids. She protested, and I set myself for an explosion. I was proud of how prepared I was. But Iodine crossed me up by simply falling silent. She did not speak a word to me for three days, all across the country. No matter what play I tried, she behaved as though I were not there. Then, about the time I let my guard down, she exploded back in Boston.

Never once did Iodine ask me to leave Rose; it was not her style. She simply wanted me to ignore Rose, and to keep the passion level high, whether in fighting or loving. Between my passion for her and my loyalty to my family, she split me in two. I felt that often she quarreled with me just to keep her voltage up. She took a toll that's still painful to remember.

Iodine went out of my life in her usual tempestuous style. Over the years the ache I felt whenever we were apart never diminished, but the pain of being with her kept growing. I became sullen, and it became harder and harder for her to touch me. Finally, at the end of one angry phone call she yelled, "Fuck off, motherfucker!" and hung up. They were the last words I heard from her for twelve years. At first I refused to call her back because I thought she'd only repeat her last message. Then, as the days and months wore on, I made myself refrain. It took all the will power I had because it was the first considered judgment I'd ever made about a woman.

At the end of 1976 Iodine wrote me a letter so sweet that a

grandmother could have written it. She said she'd seen me on a public television show—"Russell Raps with Kids"—and simply wanted to say hello after all these years. I shook my head and called her. She was the same old Iodine; the words were sweet and soothing, but I could hear the hot sauce still bubbling at the bottom of her voice. But we said good-bye before there was any explosion, and I was happy to have the relationship end peacefully at last.

About 1960, during one of my cold spells with Iodine, I took up with a New York stripper named Kitty Malone. She was altogether different from any person I'd ever known. As deeply as Iodine got under my skin, Kitty touched me in a way I never could have imagined. Every day I spent with her was full of discovery.

This all happened at a time when I had no "road women" and was still not a part of the road life of the team. Iodine in Boston was more than enough, so on trips I kept to myself and rested. But one day one of my teammates told me that his New York lady Pepper, a stripper, had a girlfriend who worked with her and who wanted to go out with me. He invited me to double date with them after the next Knick game in New York. I was taken aback, and told him that I'd think about it. I'd had my doubts about this teammate—small doubts, but real—and now here he was making an odd gesture toward me: a married white man fixing up a married black man with a white woman. In those years, with Ike in the White House and Elvis Presley widely considered obscene, this kind of thing was just not done, even by Celtics. Still, after mulling it over I decided the gesture was sincere. I became even more impressed after Kitty told me that my teammate had said that I was the Celtic player she would find most interesting. We learn about each other in strange ways. I had played basketball with this man for years, without knowing that he even liked me.

The next time we were in New York, Kitty and Pepper finished their work at the club while we finished ours at Madison Square Garden, and then we all met in a bar. I managed not to spill anything or sit on anybody, and otherwise kept pretty quiet. Kitty was a tall, stately brunette, with green eyes and skin you could almost see through. She had seen a lot in years of hustling, and there were tiny crow's feet at the corners of her eyes. She could look careworn, but when she laughed it was like opening a bottle of champagne. Her face would grow younger then, as it did when she denounced some injustice, which she did frequently. Rarely do people seem generous and loving when they're in a fighting mood, but Kitty was one of them.

She was also a talker. On our first night together she told me that she identified with athletes because, as a stripper, she knew that her career would end early because of age. But she was already in her thirties, six or seven years older than I, and was discovering that her body was not as fragile as she had feared. I told her that I thought her body was holding up just fine.

The key to survival, Kitty claimed, was to develop interests that kept you going after your body gave out. Most strippers relied on men, but she had other interests in reserve.

"Like what?" I asked.

"Like books."

"What kind of books?"

She started telling me as we drifted all around New York, strolling down to Greenwich Village after midnight. She kept talking all the way up to her apartment, where I found books piled high in every room—on her kitchen table, around her bed, in her closet. I felt as if I'd been transported back to my favorite room in the Oakland Public Library, and told her so. She asked what kind of books I'd liked, and I told her about Christophe and books on slavery. Soon she was rummaging around for books *she* had on slavery.

"Why do you care so much about slavery?" I asked.

"There are lots of different kinds of slavery," she said, "and some of them haven't even been written about yet."

"That's because most of the people who write books don't know what it is," I said. "They don't feel it, either."

From there our conversation took off like a plane and ranged just as far. We couldn't talk fast enough. As the night wore on, we actually found ourselves sitting up straighter in bed rather than slouching down among the pillows. She asked me repeatedly if I wanted something to drink, and I said it could wait. I asked her if she wanted to sleep, and she said it could wait.

We were still talking when the sun came up. Kitty had given me the first of many revelations: that there was something to do after making love besides going to sleep. I was amazed and delighted that she wanted to talk. As long as I knew her, our conversations always lasted for hours; we talked the way kittens play with a ball of yarn.

I left Kitty's apartment that day with a few books under my arm and a lot of ideas in my head. The notion that I could become friends with a woman was startling; friendship had never been a factor with Rose or Iodine. Over the next few years Kitty changed my life, by making me aware of things I'd never paid any attention to. Almost everywhere I went I'd find a book in the mail with a note from her: "Read this. Don't make any judgments, just read it." I'd read them and then visit her for another one of our talk marathons, which we had far more often than the Celtics played the Knicks. I found excuses to make detours. Whenever my head started filling up with ideas, I'd think, "Well, I better go talk to Kitty." The thought always made me smile.

We discussed the McCarthy era, on which Kitty was an expert. She knew all the dates, characters and details; she was a freak on the subject, the way some people would later become about Watergate. It was just one of her many interests, and she got me absorbed with it in spite of myself. Frankly, I had slept right through the McCarthy era; the hearings on television hadn't meant much to me at the time. When Kitty first started talking about the Senator, I agreed about the injustice of what he'd done, but I didn't do so enthusiastically enough for her. I did it the way people do when they say casually that they're against injustice—which usually means they don't know what they're talking about. The fact was that despite Kitty, I didn't really much care about McCarthy. She and I had met at a time when blacks were catching hell in every way, and the only injustices that touched me were those committed against me and other blacks. This attitude finally surfaced when I huffily asked her why I should care about what had happened six years before to an ex-Senator and a bunch of white people.

Kitty said, "Bill, if whites aren't free, you know damn well that blacks aren't going to be either, no matter what else happens. That's why you should care." She reminded me of Mister Charlie saying that justice is a tiger.

Kitty was a freethinker, motivated by outrage and a boundless curiosity. She was aware of all kinds of little stories before they made the front pages, keeping up with them and predicting that they would become important. Long before the state jailed him for publishing erotic photographs that would seem as mild as Walt Disney by later standards, she mentioned Ralph Ginzburg and *Eros* magazine. She got all charged up about it. At the time I was so straight that I thought Ginzburg's magazine was nothing but pornography, and I didn't really care what happened to him. At first I didn't say this because I thought my prudish views might offend Kitty since she was a stripper. But slowly I found myself siding with Ginzburg in spite of this. Kitty said the state would undermine freedom to convict him, and that's just what it did. He went to jail for something that was not even a crime when he'd done it.

I cared about politics before meeting Kitty, but my thoughts were generally selfish and confined to matters that affected me personally. I had no sense of the nuances of politics, or how issues here might relate to others far away. After Kennedy was elected President, and long before Vietnam amounted to anything, Kitty pointed out to me that Cardinal Spellman had introduced Kennedy to Diem and Nhu. This would be important because of the weight of the Catholic Church swung in both Vietnam and the United States. That introduction was *real* politics, she said. By then I trusted her enough to believe her, and when we entered the war in a big way later, I decided she'd been right once again.

Kitty taught me that if you isolate your own problem from all others in society, your chances of solving it are slim; serious problems require wisdom, and wisdom requires perspective. I often found myself thinking that my Celtic teammate had set me up with a hell of a lot more than I'd counted on in a burlesque queen.

Sometimes we'd talk all night on religion, music or love. Kitty said that the opposite of love was not hate but indifference, and that the opposite of hate was also indifference. "I hate indifference," she once said, laughing.

"Myself, I really don't care about it one way or the other," I said, laughing just as hard.

We used to roam up and down Bleecker Street at a time when the Village was filled with protest songs and drop-outs. Bob Dylan and Joan Baez were performing there, and we stopped in often at The Bitter End. I thought we made a handsome couple sitting there among people who were dropping out from one thing or another. "What do you think of this scene?" Kitty asked me one night as we walked along Bleecker Street, which was crowded with young people.

"They remind me of the beatniks I knew out in California in the mid-fifties," I said, "except that these people seem to care about whether others agree with them. The beatniks didn't."

Soon I was telling Kitty of the times I'd spent in college at the coffee houses on North Beach in San Francisco. I'd hardly been a beatnik, but I'd been drawn to their culture, just the way we were drawn now to Bleecker Street. Night after night, I'd sat in places like the hungri i to hear Mort Sahl, Pete Seeger, Josh White, and Stan Wilson and the Limelighters. My nights in such places had stretched through the middle of the 1950's, at a time when the white society seemed dormant.

I didn't really understand it until I talked with Kitty, but those coffee houses showed me that whites were capable of protest and sadness too. It was a breakthrough for me, because since childhood I had seen them as distant, cold and oppressive. What I saw of them on television and at USF didn't help; they just didn't seem real. Those coffee houses opened up a new way of thinking for me, because I saw that at least some white people got the blues, were irreverent and weren't tight-assed. Most of the white folks at USF walked like moving fence posts, while the beatniks looked more like sloping question marks. Together Kitty and I analyzed the different ways people walk and carry themselves. She showed me how to relate the anger and dissatisfaction I felt as a black to similar feelings in whites, and to think about different forms of freedom.

For nearly two years I carried on a dialogue with Kitty whenever I could, and I continued to see her even after Iodine reentered the scene. Kitty was always amused by my talk of Iodine. Then one summer I didn't see either of them for four solid months because my farm in Liberia kept me away, but the books from Kitty continued to arrive in the mail. She sent me Frantz Fanon and colonial histories of Africa, and I read every one of them.

During the next basketball season I saw Kitty again; the following summer in Africa the books stopped coming. When I returned home I learned she had moved. No one seemed to know where she'd gone, and her friends would say only that strippers have to be on the move. Whenever this had happened before, another book would arrive a few weeks later with a new address on it. This time no package came.

It took me more than a year to believe that Kitty was gone. I had lost the one person in the world who would listen to me on any subject, and who would talk with me until dawn without ever dropping an eyelid. She vanished without a trace, and for five years I heard no word of her. Then a man I knew in New York said, "Remember Kitty Malone?"

"Where is she?" I asked, jumping half way down his throat.

"She died."

The man and his friends told two stories of how she died. One was that she had been killed in an automobile accident; the other was that she died of a heroin overdose.

Hearing that a lover has died is one of the hardest squeezes the heart can take. The news about Kitty sent me reeling, and the grief had an eerie feel to it. I felt guilty that I had let Kitty drift away so far. On top of that, her death made me realize how little I had really known about her. We had spoken millions of words, but I had never even suspected that she could be taking drugs. All I had really known about her personal life was that she'd had two great loves, both of whom had died. This had put an end to her desire for love, although she could talk cheerfully for hours about it as a concept. Kitty and I were lovers who were not in love, but our friendship had consumed me by opening so many doors that I never realized how large a part of her I never saw.

From Kitty's life and death I learned that it is possible to feel full and empty at the same time, to feel full of discovery and yet know very little. This touched and puzzled me so much that I talked about Kitty to friends and acquaintances long after she died. I was very protective of her memory. On several occasions, people made the mistake of asking, "Why did you go out with a girl like that in the first place?" It was all I could do to keep from breaking such people in two. Kitty had reinforced my hatred for snobbism. We always introduced each other as friends; to me she was a friend first, a woman second and a stripper only a distant third. I felt about her the same way I wanted others to feel about me: that I am first and foremost a person, and that no label can encompass all the mysteries about me. I didn't like friends to introduce me as a "basketball player," even when I was playing; I preferred to be known as a man who played basketball. Similarly, with women, I tried not to pay any attention to the labels of occupation, status or class.

No woman has taught me more than Kitty Malone, and she left me one legacy that changed my entire social life. In showing me that it was possible to be friends with a woman by getting past the opaque mirrors between the sexes, she taught me how to make friends. Since Kitty, the vast majority of my friends have been women. I found it much easier to get past the barrier of sex with them than to hurdle the barrier of competitiveness with men. After I had spent myself on a basketball court, I didn't want to compete any more until the next game. But with men I found it impossible to escape this. It didn't matter whether we were talking, eating, playing cards or just walking down the street; I always sensed competition underneath. Sometimes I thought that's all there was to relationships between males. Even after I retired from basketball, men always seemed to be trying to prove something—usually that they could kick my ass in one way or another, no matter how famous I was.

Constantly, but without much success, I have looked for men I could be with where competition wouldn't be an issue, where neither of us owed the other anything, had any score to settle or any point to prove. Oddly enough, I felt something like this at times around Oscar Robertson, Wilt Chamberlain and Elgin Baylor. We were so fiercely competitive that in a way we were above competition. We were in the eye of the hurricane, a calm place right in the middle of the maelstrom. But these were special friends, linked to basketball; in day-to-day life I was always misreading people. I'd think that maybe some guy and I understood each other, and then find that he wanted to use me in some way, perhaps just to prove something to himself. Often I felt like the old gunfighter. The better he was at his craft, the fewer friends he had, and somebody was always trying to knock him off.

In one sense I wound up feeling like the opposite of the male stereotype. The cliché is that men have little to say to women apart from the war between the sexes, and that they get their relaxation and friendships from men. Because I felt more at ease with women, I spent most of time hanging out with them. It was one of life's major revelations for someone who had spent his youth fighting an urge to tremble and run away at the mention of a woman's name. I discovered that if a woman was smart and had a tale to tell, she could be a strong comfort. We could reveal ourselves and take chances with each other in ways that were both peaceful and exciting.

But to be friends with a woman you first have to get past sex. It didn't take me long to decide that friendship is usually hampered by sex and everything that goes with it—possessiveness, hopes of children and of a future. I had to keep those elements under control in myself and in the women I wanted to keep as friends. It helped that I was married all those years, which was some protection (though often not enough), and sex always had to be gotten out of the way somehow. With Kitty it had been easy; she made love as if she were a friendly traveler, as a way to say, "You are here. I mean you no harm. Talk to me and I will answer in the same spirit." She was soft and kind, and made love the way a friend should. In fact, she made you feel that you couldn't really be much of a friend to someone without making love to him. One kind of gentle intimacy flowed easily into the other.

With other women, sex meant different things, and we had to deal with it in different ways. Sometimes it would be a barrier before but not after our first time together. We'd say, in effect, "Okay, we've done that. Now let's talk and not worry about it anymore." In search of female friendships I had more than I could count that began in pure lust. With other women it worked out that we never made love at all. That was all right too.

I never took the initiative in approaching a woman. Somewhere inside me I was still the boy who couldn't get a date all through high school and most of college. But though I never really overcame that feeling, I didn't have to. Women would approach *me,* which was contrary to everything I'd been taught. The first few times it happened I was bewildered. "What is this?" I'd think. "You're kidding!" And when the woman persisted, I'd think, "What's the catch?" I'd be worried that as soon as I responded in kind, she'd laugh at me. I never learned to read intentions. Subtlety never got through to me; women had to be obvious. Occasionally, but not often, I found a friend, which meant talking and sharing through the night. Sometimes I would be lucky enough to have such friends in many cities. Some of them have lasted, and we still talk; others, like Kitty, have gone.

As for "pure" love, I spent years walking into crowded rooms around the country, looking into each woman's eyes to see if she were The One. Knowing that I didn't have the slightest ability to tell what was on a woman's mind, I was still convinced that one day I would look into someone's eyes, that she'd look back and that somehow we would just *know.* I was a victim of Western romance.

Toward the end of my basketball career, women seemed to be going by me in a blur. I was still married to Rose, though I did not yet understand her. I had never had the slightest idea what

Iodine was going to do, and I also knew that I had been blind to many important parts of Kitty's life. It's a sad feeling to see how foolish you've been over the years. Looking back, I saw that Iodine and I were just lovers, that Kitty and I were just friends, and that Rose and I were just married. All this made me feel cold as I tried to take stock of myself in my last years of basketball. By then I knew of a million reasons against trying to spend a lifetime with one person. I tried never to let my prejudices control me, but even when looking at people from the angle most favorable to them, I couldn't help finding reasons why I couldn't stand being with them for a day, let alone a lifetime. Heading for divorce myself, I didn't think it remarkable that the divorce rate was high; in fact, what seemed remarkable to me was that couples lived together as long as they did. *The* match is hard to find. Unless a woman was an angel who'd fallen off a Christmas tree—in which case she wouldn't bother with me—there would be odd spots in her that I would have trouble matching with all the odd spots in me.

I was confused. I decided that there were really only a few ideas about love that I felt certain about, and I hoped to build on these and refine them. I believed, for example, that you cannot earn love, which is one of the reasons it's so strange. You can earn respect or money, and in some cases you can even make people like you, but you can't earn love. It lies outside justice and logic in a place where no rules apply.

I also believed that you have no choice of the people you love. You can't manufacture it if it's not there, no matter how strongly you believe it should be, and if it is there, you can repress it, but you can't make it vanish. And it's so risky to let loose those mysterious, uncontrolled feelings that most of us try to clamp down on them. I believe that most people have a harder time letting themselves love than in finding someone to love them.

All of us have a place inside ourselves that we believe is ugly and grotesque, and this hidden place is the part of our personality hardest to acknowledge to others. Your efforts to achieve self-knowledge may reveal it to you, but when you love another human being you are frightened to let her see that hidden place because you fear that she will draw away from you in disgust. But that hidden place is the most human part of you. Many of us live our whole lives married to people without ever revealing that ugly place. They love their partners because they believe that he or she *might* accept the ugly spot if it were ever revealed, but they don't quite trust them enough to expose themselves.

During my last year in Boston I was thinking and writing about the protective shells we erect around those inner places. The excitement and romance of love comes when you decide to let someone reach around that shell and touch you. When you let another see that ugly spot, and she accepts you anyway—and perhaps can even convince you that the secret inside your shell is not ugly at all—we experience the sweetest moments we can ever know.

But it's also one of the most dangerous moments, and life doesn't always work out as hoped. The two things that have always been most important to me have been personal freedom and the desire to be touched, and sometimes the two of them have been in direct conflict. If somebody hurts you, lets you down or oppresses you, you want to assert your freedom from that person. The desire for freedom is overpowering, like a drowning man's need for air. You have to reach inside yourself for all the strength and independence you have. It takes a lot of strength not to drown and not to be a slave, and the fight can be lonely. You have to be on guard, but being guarded makes it harder to be touched. I have lived a large part of my life walking that edge.

8

Second Wind

All my small worldly possessions fit into one suitcase, lying in the back of my only large worldly possession, the Lamborghini. I drove it from Boston to Los Angeles in five days at excessive speeds, picking up half a dozen tickets on the way, and moved into a furnished apartment near Hollywood, which rented at $160 a month. I was mildly concerned about certain money problems, such as the fact that I didn't have any, but I decided that if you're going to start over, you can't do it half way. Poverty was just one more novelty to me after years of glitter and money. Simple chores seemed exciting to me. I went out and bought a small stereo set for $108, and it sounded just as fine as the elaborate system I'd had wired into my house back in Boston. Every day I went to the supermarket in the next block to buy vegetables—only vegetables. I'd decided to become a vegetarian, in the hope that it would help me grow less aggressive and competitive. I wanted to go with the flow. The vegetables worked just fine, except that every once in awhile I'd fall off the wagon and gobble down eight pounds of red meat at a sitting. Still, on the whole it was a good start.

I didn't really know how to classify my style of dress in Los Angeles until I read a newspaper story about the epidemic of hijacked airplanes. I dressed exactly like the official composite description of your typical hijacker: jeans, sandals or sneakers, old work shirt, dark glasses. In the description the hijacker was supposed to look ill at ease in his clothes, and to be looking around furtively. That was me. I was surprised I wasn't arrested, until I realized that half the people in Los Angeles looked like hijackers. As much as I ever could with my size, I blended right in.

I called on every old friend I could think of and wound up spending a lot of time with Jim Brown, who was well into his movie career. As always, Jim's primary interest in me was to devise some sort of game at which he could kick my ass or die trying. For years he had been trying to get me to play one-on-one basketball against him, thinking that he could outrun or run over me, and I'd always refused. Now I not only refused but also told him I didn't play such games anymore because I'd become a vegetarian. Jim took a long puzzled look at me and then shook his head sadly. It was Los Angeles, he sighed; he'd seen it happen before.

But soon Jim's face brightened. Golf, he said. Golf is a gentleman's game. Even vegetarians could play golf without disturbing their harmony. So within a few days after arriving on the West Coast, I was out on the golf course with him. The game had always been difficult for me. Because of my height, the ball looks tiny down there on the ground, and my swing travels through such a giant arc that the slightest error spells disaster.

On our first round I shot well over a hundred, and Jim was miserable. I was so bad that he couldn't think of any handicap for me that would make a fair bet, and without a bet he couldn't work up any competitive fever. That fever makes him get up in the morning, and Jim wouldn't argue with anyone who said he was the most competitive man in America.

"I have an idea," he said in the clubhouse. I saw instantly that this idea, whatever it was, had his competitive instincts all revived. The fever doesn't get him excited—in fact, he calms down—but you can tell that the furnace is going between his ears.

"What's that?" I asked.

"Let's go out for another round, and I'll beat you with only one club."

This took me by surprise. "You gonna putt with it?"

"I'm gonna putt with it, chip with it, get out of sand traps with it, drive with it—everything. One club's all I need to whip you."

I was intrigued, and my feathers were slightly ruffled. "What club would you use?"

Jim's face broke into a half grin, which he controlled. "My four-wood."

"Your four-wood!" I said. I laughed, which was a mistake, because then I had to take the bet. "You're on," I said. The vegetables inside me groaned in revolt against all this competitiveness, but I consoled myself with the idea that it was only golf.

Jim shot ninety with his four-wood. He made chip shots and putts that I wouldn't have believed possible, except that I know his will is so strong that it can make his body do anything. That's when the fever in him gets so hot that he can hardly talk. His chin gets that Mount Rushmore look, and you can see that every ounce of fury, strength, concentration and will power he has is focused on his objective. That's how he can hit a shot stiff to the pin from a buried lie in the sand with a four-wood. I played way over my head, and still couldn't quite catch him.

Though I was now a vegetarian, the idea that Jim could beat me with only one club bothered me. It was the principle of the thing, I told myself, and so when I had to return to Boston not long afterward to clear up some details of the divorce and my retirement from the Celtics, I played golf every day. I took lessons, sweated and went to driving ranges. When I got back to Los Angeles, I had Jim Brown out on the golf course within twenty-four hours. He gave me six shots a side, and I shot eighty—which was about ten strokes better than I'd ever played before. At the end of the day I was deep into his pocket by the standards of our small gentleman's wager: he owed me $125. Jim was chafing, but it wasn't because of the money, which was nothing to him; it was the principle of the thing for him, too. As he was reaching into his wallet to pay off, I said, "I don't want your money now. Pay me the next time you see me."

Jim looked at me oddly, saw that I meant it, and then shrugged. "Whatever you say," he said.

I made a point of not mentioning that money to Jim for more than a year. Then one day I sprang it on him out on the golf course. "Hey, man, where's my hundred and twenty-five dollars?"

He looked more puzzled than ever. "Why'd you wait so long to ask for it?" he asked.

"Well," I said, "when I moved out here, everybody knew that I was a friend of yours, and so they kept asking me, 'Do you play golf with Jim Brown?' And I've always answered, 'Yeah, that sucker owes me a hundred and twenty-five dollars.' I got to say that all last year, and that alone's worth more than the money."

"You're crazy," said Jim, as I broke out laughing. "I'm gonna kick your ass for that." He probably did.

So golf became my new sport, and at times it has consumed me. I knew it was a compromise of my principles, just as the chicken and fish I ate were a compromise with vegetarianism. But I could live with it, I decided, because it was such mild competition. Compared with professional basketball, playing golf is like a Quaker prayer meeting, even when you're playing with Jim Brown.

At night in L.A., Jim and other friends introduced me to Hollywood life. I started learning how to pretend. On meeting people for the first time I'd say, "How you doing?" And they'd always answer, "Well, I've got two pictures going right now. On the first one, we're making the final cuts, and then it will be all wrapped up." Everybody is just been offered parts in two movies, one opposite Marlon Brando and the other with Faye Dunaway, and is on intimate terms with the Mr. Big who's going to finance something. They've always got something going, and if they don't, they have a hot prospect, and if they don't have a hot prospect, they're hanging out with certain well-known insiders who have something going *and* prospects, so everything is fine. "By the way," they'd say, "how are you doing?"

"Well, I'm doing fine," I'd answer. "I've got a couple of scripts I'm looking at right now." If I wasn't careful, I'd fall right into the pretending game within five minutes. It's infectious.

Of course everybody else had a script, too, usually two or three at a time. This crossed all racial, social and economic lines. Down at the car wash or the beauty parlor the people there would have scripts. They acted funny about them, too. A lot of them would *complain* about all the scripts they had to read, but I got the feeling that they did all their complaining in public.

I hired a Hollywood agent, took bit parts in a few television series, read scripts, played golf, went to the supermarket and sorted out my memories. One of my reflections at the time was that in many respects I had led a sheltered life. Even on the Celtic road trips I'd often stayed in my room by myself. When I did go out, it was always with the lady friend I had in that particular town, and we both knew that I'd be flying out the next day with the team. We could talk and love all night, but the limits were clear; I was on the move. In L.A. all this changed. First of all, I resolved to explore as much as possible. I pushed myself to be more open and outgoing, and to discover what I could learn from every kind of woman. Soon I had a variety of romances going at once, and I realized that there were no natural limits. Since I wasn't leaving town every night, I had to make choices, to decide whether to pursue a relationship or cut it off. Sometimes I'd want to see more of a woman and would be rebuffed. That was a complication. Or I'd be seeing one woman and another would show up unexpectedly, which was another kind of complication. Everywhere there were complications.

For the first time I realized how bad I'd always been at ending anything, from my marriage on. I'd never really had to; I could just drift down the road, and things would take care of themselves. Now I had to handle them myself, which meant I had to make judgments that I didn't really want to make. I also realized that once I was unmarried and unmoving, it wasn't easy to have the undemanding friendships with women that I'd found so liberating since the days of Kitty Malone. Now I discovered that they often had an ulterior motive of some kind, and that we'd wind up arguing about it. Women were no longer the escape from the competitive undertow I'd felt with men. I was often down in the psychological trenches with them, and it took almost as much energy to hold my own as it had to compete in the NBA. Often, I'd find myself laughing over some bizarre tumble I'd taken, and wondering how long I could go on. This is Hollywood, I'd tell myself, and plunge right back into the fray.

But after a while I decided that it wouldn't hurt to get out of L.A. for a spell, for both personal and financial reasons. I called a lecture bureau that had been dangling a college-speaking tour in front of me. Within a few weeks I took off on a forty-seven-day trip around the country, in which I made thirty-one speeches on college campuses. It was the first tour I was to make over the next few years to many campuses.

All of a sudden I was back on the road again, except that everything was new. There was none of pro basketball's routine —same teams, same cities, same game. In any competitive sport the key is repetition. There's no getting around it; whatever you do well, you do it over and over again. That repetition is the heart of your game, and new elements come and go only on the side. In contrast to my background in sports, what struck me about those campus appearances was how different they all were— Catholic colleges, military academies, agricultural and drama schools, huge cosmopolitan universities and tiny Mennonite ones. I had to be ready for any question. What did I think of the split in the Black Panther Party between Bobby Seale and Huey Newton? What about the Scopes trial, the draft, Vatican II, the Italian Communist Party or the firing of Walter Hickel? What did I think about Norman Mailer's ideas on women's liberation? I had to keep up with every subject. On the plane from West Virginia to Nebraska, I'd be reading *Time, Newsweek,* the *Atlantic Monthly, Rolling Stone* and the *National Review,* but I could never read enough. The students' questions were like a saucer of fleas; you never could predict which way the next one would jump. I loved it, though at first I got so caught up in the spontaneity of each session that I'd say the first thing that popped into my mind.

Once I was giving a speech at a school in Wisconsin, and as usual questions were flying: should the university accept research contracts from the Pentagon; should the French-Canadians become a separate nation? Then a kid stood up and asked me a hostile question. "Mr. Russell," he said, "why is it that you come off so well in comparison with Wilt Chamberlain, when you and I both know that he's better than you were by far? And that the only reason your teams won is that he never played with anybody? And that you guys were always lucky while Wilt always got hurt? And that last year you wouldn't have won if Wilt hadn't been hurt in the last game of the play-offs? Why don't people see that?"

Here was a live one. For more than a decade I'd brushed off much harsher questions than these, but that had been worlds ago, back in the NBA, and his question caught me off guard. "Well, I'm going to deal with the points you've made, other than your overall opinions," I began. "Now, you say he never played with anybody. If you're a basketball fan, the names I'm going to mention should mean something to you. The first year Wilt played, with the Philadelphia Warriors, he started with Paul Arizin and Woody Saulsberry at forward, two very good players. Saulsberry was one of the best defensive forwards ever. And the guards were Tom Gola and Guy Rodgers. That's not bad . . ." Then I listed some of Wilt's play-off teams. ". . . In 1968 the 76ers had three forwards, Lucius Jackson, Chet Walker and Billy Cunningham, and their starting guards were Hal Greer and Wally Jones. That doesn't seem bad company. Last year Wilt was with the Lakers. He started with Elgin Baylor, Keith Erikson, and Jerry West. That's not bad either. I don't see how anyone can say he never played with anybody good. Now, you say he got hurt . . ." I paused. Until then, I'd been letting my irritation show, but I hadn't said anything out of line. Now all my anger at Wilt from the last game of my career came back to me, and I lost my cool. "I want to tell you something," I said, hard and cold. "In the final game of the championship series last season, Wilt hurt his leg when the Lakers were making a run to catch us in the last few minutes, and he took himself out of the game. But the Lakers kept the comeback going, and they cut our lead down to two points with a couple of minutes left. So Wilt made a miraculous recovery and wanted to come back into the game. Now in my opinion, if he's hurt so bad that he can't play in the seventh game, he should go straight to the hospital. But if he's hurt and then five minutes later recovers, there's something wrong with that injury. You can't quit like that and win championships. Wilt's coach didn't put him back in, and I wouldn't have either."

In a few short seconds it was out. I hadn't realized that reporters were in the audience, but within hours a wire service spread a story that I'd called Wilt "a quitter." It was the first public evidence of the animosity between us that everyone else had believed in for years. Reporters called Wilt, who said he was shocked by my comments and took a few retaliatory potshots at me. Most newspapers trumpeted triumphantly that the respect that we'd professed for each other all these years was finally exposed as fraudulent.

As far as I'm concerned, that respect was always real. Those comments were the only serious public criticism I've ever made of any player among my contemporaries. I never believed in criticizing the performance of others because we were all in the same business. We all have egos and feelings, and I didn't want to add to anyone's discomfort. If I held someone else's game or character in low regard, I kept it to myself.

Never again did I lay into Wilt, but I will admit to having kidded him occasionally. I don't know what this means, except that I feel worse about some of the pranks I've played on him than I do about that outburst in Wisconsin. For example, a few years after I left the Celtics, the Lakers were paired with the Knicks in the play-offs, and I was covering the series for ABC with Keith Jackson. The two of us were sitting in a plane on a flight to L.A. when an elegant lady stopped in the aisle and said to me in a sugary voice, "I just *love* your house."

"Pardon me?" I said.

"I live in Bel Air too, and I think your house is just *beautiful.* I drive by it all the time."

She was referring to Wilt's "dream house," I realized, and so I lowered my voice in the standard Wilt imitation. "You like it?"

"It's *gorgeous.*"

"Well, I'll tell you what," I said. "I'm having a party tomorrow night, so why don't you and some of your friends come on by. I'd like to give you all the *de luxe* tour."

"Really?" she gushed. "I'd *love* to."

"Right on," I said. "I'll be looking for you." By this time Keith had turned his face away to keep from laughing.

"We'll *be* there," she said, "and I sure hope we can beat those Knicks."

"Don't you worry about that," I said. "If West and Goodrich will just quit shooting so much and get me the ball so I can do some dipper dunks, I'll whip them myself. I guarantee it."

"Oh, *good.* I'll see you tomorrow night. I can't *wait."*

As the lady drifted off, I turned to see Keith chewing on the corner of his airsick bag. I'll have to admit I laughed myself.

Still, I don't think such incidents had anything to do with the deterioration of my friendship with Wilt. While we played against each other, the respect was mutual and genuine. He was my toughest competition, and because of our status we shared something that made us friends. I knew that, and I think he did too. I also admired Wilt for the way he conducted himself on the court. In all those years, under all that pressure, I never knew him once to play dirty. The games were rough, but no rougher than they're supposed to be. There are very few men who played the game as cleanly as he did. Also, he never did anything to hurt me —and I don't mean just throwing elbows. He was careful not to add to my discomfort while we were playing, just as I tried not to add to his. I think we both knew that, and it was part of our bond. We irritated each other a few times, but in the great scheme of things over all those years, what is that? Nothing.

The trouble was that we're both extremely touchy, and had little to sustain our friendship other than basketball. Neither of us is good at apologies, so when the bad blood grew up between us after my Wisconsin speech, we just let it ride. We bounced off each other's irritation and got our pride up. I'll be the first to admit, in general, that I'm about the last person to admit, in particular, that some grudge or injury is too silly to carry on. If I'd been born in a different era, I'd have been forced to change my ways or to fight duels on a regular basis.

When I hit Los Angeles, I was in a state of pure chauvinism —and not just male chauvinism; it was bigger than that. I wasn't trying to lord it over anyone, but I was satisfied with who I was and what I had done. This air, concealing certain raging insecurities, gave me just the right presence in Hollywood. I seemed to embody many paradoxes simultaneously. I would have adventures day and night, with confidence that nothing could knock me off balance, and at the same time withdraw into myself and worry about the dark place inside me. Sometimes I was an old-fashioned loner, convinced that craftsmen and honest men like my father were nearly extinct; at other moments I was contemporary and stylish, setting a pace. I'd be liberal, even radical, in politics, and then ultraconservative. Often I was kind and generous, occasionally cold and unkind. I was struggling to anchor my life on moral principles, but was willing to try almost anything. I loved to read and talk about serious ideas, but was drawn to the approach of *Mad* magazine. (In fact, when *Mad* did a humor spread on the way I conducted television interviews, I considered it one of the greatest compliments I'd ever received.) They also ran a series called "Snappy Answers to Dumb Questions," and I borrowed many of these answers to keep strangers at arm's length. At the same time I wanted to be touched.

Even kids divided me. Many of my happiest moments had been around children—Africans, Latin Americans, blacks, whites, any kid except a junior autograph hound—and yet my own three children were virtual strangers to me when I left Boston. I had to become closer to my kids, of that I was certain, and it was the first strong, unconflicted feeling I had in L.A. At the ages of thirteen, eleven and eight they started spending summers with me out there. I remember those times as ones of heartache and perplexity. I wanted to squeeze and hug them until the tears ran dry, just to make up for all the time I'd missed, but caution made me hang back because I didn't really know how to handle them well. Even a full-time parent would have had trouble with them at such ages, I believe, and there I was getting to know them while I was trying to sample every life style and golf course in the vicinity. Looking back, a lot of our times together were funny. I was quite unconscious of the contradictions in my behavior, but the children weren't. They didn't hesitate to point out how strange it was that I'd make them fasten their seat belts in the car as we drove out to a motorcross course, where we all rode motorcycles and half killed ourselves. It was perfectly logical to me, but the kids got on my case. They hit me with larger questions, too. It wasn't long before one of my sons confided how much he'd always admired my fancy cars, clothes and friends; therefore, he announced, he wanted to let me know that it was his ambition to become a pimp. I didn't know whether to laugh or cry that this was his interpretation of the role model I provided. My daughter, on the other hand, blind-sided me from the opposite direction. She always responded to the side of me that didn't smoke, drink or compromise in the search for a life of principles, and she told me in no uncertain terms that I shouldn't have any overnight girl friends. It was immoral, she felt, and she didn't mind letting me know it. So I had a son who looked to me for a pimp's luxury and a daughter who looked to me for a saint's purity, and both of them were regularly disappointed. I think all three of them were a little afraid of me in those Los Angeles years, but that didn't stop them from posing questions that no one else would ask.

All the whipsawing I took was nothing compared with what the kids dished out to my women friends. If they liked her, they'd say, "Oh, don't do that. Daddy's last girl friend did that," and if they didn't like her, they'd say, "Oh, don't do that. Daddy has another girl friend who always does it." They had an uncanny ability to zero in on a woman's weakest point and pick at it, dropping the most ruthless comments with the most innocent faces. I had to do a lot of retreating, throat-clearing and hurried repair work. I noticed that at least one of them would take an intense dislike to any woman who came over more than twice. This was natural, I figured; they didn't want anyone to replace Rose, their mother. The situation reminded me of the way my brother and I had made life miserable for all Mister Charlie's women friends after our mother had died. We didn't want him to go out with anyone, and we alternated in driving them crazy. Looking at things from the parent's point of view for the first time, I realized how unfair we had been to Mister Charlie. We had done everything we could to keep him from remarrying, and then when we grew up we moved back East and left him behind in California. Fortunately, Mister Charlie had the good sense and strength to ignore us and remarry.

Those summers with the kids brought me the first inklings of what was going on inside me out in Los Angeles: there were so many "me's" running around all over the place, and frequently they'd collide with each other like cartoon characters. When this happened it was a shock, but it also made me laugh.

Those little people inside me had an enormous amount of energy, and always ran at full speed. If any one of them got tired, there was another one waiting to take off. That's the way it felt, at least. I took a hard run at vegetarianism and golf, and an even harder run in my personal relationships. When those weren't enough, I added lecture tours, and later network sports commentary for ABC. I was also trying to get to know the kids and to keep up with current events. All these still weren't enough, so I started *The Bill Russell Show* on radio, broadcasting during the afternoon rush hour. It's hard to convey how much fun I had on that show. I'd just let loose and explore the world on the air. "Hello out there, you sweating commuters," I might say. "The traffic picture is hopeless. You're going to be out there a long time, so you might as well get used to it and relax. Think about all the things you're glad you're *not* doing. While you're thinking, here are some sports scores: three–six, one–six, zero–four, four and two. And here are some cities to go with those scores: New York, Baltimore; Atlanta, Oakland; Chicago, Detroit; Kansas City and Dallas. That's the sports."

Strangely, I had enough energy to do all these activities. Sometimes I'd do a few college lectures on my way to cover a basketball game, and while on the road, I'd do the radio show by telephone every afternoon, then spend half the night talking to friends around the country. (That's when I learned the value of dialing direct.) When I flew back to L.A. I'd go straight to the golf course, then to the radio studio, and then over to a friend's for dinner and a talk through the night. I was living at full speed, with everything I'd ever had in the NBA—competition, road life, challenges—except championships, but also with everything I'd missed while playing basketball. Or so I thought. Occasionally I had glimpses that there were gaping contradictions within me, but I ignored them. There was no way that I was going to come to grips with them then. The hardest task I know of is to detect the paradoxes within yourself clearly, sparing yourself nothing, and to give up the hypocrisy of thinking that you can have everything by stretching yourself to embrace every ideal *and* its opposite. I had no desire to resolve any of those clashes at that time because I was having too much fun.

Of course there were human casualties as a result of this new life. Mary was the main one. We had loved each other for several years, and had more or less made the transition from Boston to Los Angeles together. She came for longer and longer visits, and finally stayed. Through many trials and changes she was the first woman of consequence in my life who was simply a woman instead of a phenomenon (like Rose, Iodine and Kitty were, each in her different way). Instead of becoming some larger-than-life force, such as Marriage, Passion or Friend, Mary was a little of each. She was a beautiful, intelligent woman who loved adventure. Around my friends she usually was reserved, but she had a sharp eye for character and was always open. After an evening with people who were strangers to her, I could hardly wait to ask her what she thought of them. Then she'd talk; when we were alone, would she talk! We were like an orchestra; I'd start off with a little bass fiddle, and then she'd sweep in with the violins. I could be alone with her; there'd be no other forces in the room. Most women, I'd found, demand certain emotions and attitudes from you, and if you don't show them the side of you they expect, something bad will happen. You can feel it as soon as you enter the room: parts of you are stifled before anyone says anything. Years later you may find yourself thinking, "I'm not really myself when I'm around her." This never happened to me with Mary. However I wanted to be, she made me aware that she loved me, and she was the first woman since my mother who had been able to communicate this to me. I could feel the human contact, not just hear the words. Her love for me was so unqualified that it touched me inside the shell I'd built up over the previous twenty years.

Mary seemed to be self-contained. She could come to the radio studio and sit silently for hours, watching and thinking. Some of the technicians at the station never even realized that we were together. On road trips she'd sit and read for hundreds of miles, with her mind way off somewhere. Many of the books she liked were in foreign languages, mostly German. She would retreat into herself the way I do, and then project feelings that would squeeze my heart. Once when we were driving east from California, I looked over at her not long after we had crossed the border into New Mexico. Tears were falling into her lap, and I got so scared that I almost drove off the road. It was the road signs, she said. We had passed a number of big gaudy signs advertising Chief So-and-So's Souvenir Shop, and Mary was crying at the idea of hundreds of years of Indian dignity reduced to hawking pots and beads. She started talking about Indian culture, and pretty soon our orchestra was going strong.

Mary insisted on making a lot of my clothes, standing on a chair to measure me. At first I resisted; I'm particular about my clothes. But I became more attached to what she made than I'd have thought possible. When I was alone on a speaking tour, in a motel somewhere between Idaho and Arkansas, and put on one of Mary's suits, it was like having her arms around me. I could feel her measuring me for that suit, and remember the jokes I'd cracked while she was doing so. Before long I found myself looking forward to wearing her clothes; they were like getting fresh flowers every morning. In comparison, even my tailor's work began to feel as cold as a suit of armor.

Mary spent a lot of time waiting for me. I was gone more than I was there. I'd come home and see her for a few days, then vanish again for a week. Sometimes I'd withdraw, occasionally I'd go away with another woman, and often would run off to play golf, work or ride a motorcycle. I'd fly by, always expecting her to be the same, always amazed at how good she was, and then take off again. During those years I was bouncing from one activity to another so fast that Mary could never get a fix on me for long.

She would be everything in the world to me when I was in her company, but soon I'd become obsessed with other people or places, and leave. It never occurred to me that she might not be as happy without me as she was with me. I was rushing along from moment to moment, and I assumed that everyone else was doing the same.

About every six months I'd wear Mary out. She'd hang on while I cartwheeled through all my moods, and then would fly back to her family in Boston for a few weeks to refuel, build up her confidence, and then return to try again. All she wanted was to love me and have me love her. It was a period in her life when everything else seemed insignificant, and she was caught, much the way I'd been enmeshed with Iodine. I simply wasn't capable of being what she wanted me to be because I was not in control of myself. I loved her, but I loved everything and nothing, all at once.

Finally, when Mary had taken all she could, she announced, as usual, that she was returning to Boston for a while. As always, I was jolted, and I asked her to be sure to come back. As usual, she promised she would, but I think both of us knew she wouldn't. Something was broken. Relationships between lovers have a certain resilience, but one day you take it too far, and it's not able to bounce back. Unfortunately, that's the point where a lot of people become so frightened that they try to save the situation by getting married. Mary was too strong for that; she simply left permanently, to protect herself.

I was hurt when Mary left, but later on it hurt even more. She could handle me as long as I was there, but she could not cope when I was gone. I was going too fast to see this, so I ran over her. If you're strong-willed or oblivious, you can do that to somebody just in trying to get from one place to another. It's almost like running over a deer on the highway. You don't mean any harm—though it would be hard to tell the deer this—but you've collided at the wrong place and wrong time, and before you know it the damage is done. It's best not to look back or cry, so you keep going.

My spirits sank when I realized what Mary had given me. She'd made me believe that I could love and be loved again, and was the first person since my mother that I felt I could trust completely. I knew she would never lie to me; in fact, she was so honest that if anybody else lied in her presence, she'd turn red. She was just as honest when she revealed herself to me, and in accepting what I revealed of myself to her, which made me feel better than I thought was possible. I knew that other women had loved me, but it never hit me the way Mary did. There are some things you know, and other things that have an impact.

I didn't realize it then, but it was from Mary that I learned to start friendships with women from a broader base, simply because she had shown me the feeling I wanted with a woman. Once you've experienced that feeling, you can't accept less. At least I thought that I now knew what I was looking for. She had given me a great deal, and in return I had given her a lot of pain. I had broken as strong a feeling as she could have, and had destroyed what I wanted more than anything else. For a long time after she'd gone, I felt so much guilt and loss that I actually wished I'd never met her.

I was well into my four Los Angeles years before I realized that sometimes I have a domineering personality around women. In my mind it had always been so much the reverse that I couldn't see how my silence, words or presence could threaten the atmosphere between us. I realized I would have to give women space to allow them to express themselves, and that I'd have to do it consciously, because it didn't come naturally. Even when I was afraid inside, I could intimidate people. It had happened for years with Rose, I realized. "Hey, you can be downright dangerous," I told myself.

Once I had this insight I went right on behaving the same way, except that I tried to warn women that I was a hazard. They should be free and easy in our relationship, with no expectations. But this resulted in a string of weak relationships that reminded me of the "do-your-own-thing" period of the 1960's, when everybody did his own thing in so much the same way that it was like a series of soap operas. We'd frolic together for a few months, and then, in spite of everything, sooner or later we'd have the same conversation.

"You want to get married?"

"No, I don't want to get married."

"Why? Don't you love me?"

"In a way, I love you. You know that."

"Well, then, why don't you want to get married?"

"I just don't want to get married."

"Well, I have to stop seeing you, then."

"Why?"

"There's no future in it."

"Well, what's wrong with just enjoying it now? You can worry so much about the future that one day you'll look up and you won't have a past."

"But if I hang around with you, I won't have a future," the woman would say, and that would be the end of it.

There was another conversation that wasn't much different. "What do you want from me?" I'd ask.

"Nothing," she'd say.

I'd shake my head. "Uh oh. That means *everything*. Nothing means 'nothing in particular.' You just want it all."

I felt so isolated during this period that I was happy to see the mailman every day. For all my running around, there was nothing and no one left for me to touch except the space that Mary had left. I was close to feeling sorry for myself, which set off alarm systems in my head. I could see Frank Ramsey flashing his toothless grin at me on the court, and hear Mister Charlie lecturing me when I was little. If there was one thing that Mister Charlie had never stood for, it was self-pity. He called it the most evil emotion in the world and said there wouldn't be any of it around his house. I think blacks have an advantage in dealing with self-pity because we've had so many opportunities to confront the impulse. Mister Charlie's method of handling it was to fight it by making a virtue of independence. He and the Old Man had a saying: "If you see me in a fight with a bear, don't help me. Help the bear."

I've tried to live up to this, but there are limits. In L.A. I gradually came to the conclusion that somehow I was going to have to learn to trust some people; otherwise I was going to slide toward self-pity, no matter what. I could tell people over and over again to help the bear, but I'd still be feeling half-way sorry for myself. Also, in order to trust somebody, I decided, I'd have to get over the notion that I'd ever be able to resolve the conflicts among all those little people running around inside me. For a long time I'd lived by the idea that if I kept struggling with my contradictions, somehow they'd all dissolve one day into a consistent personality. The teetotaler in me would reconcile with the hedonist, the liberal with the conservative, the competitor with the Zen Buddhist, and the independent with the lonely. When all of these conflicts were resolved, I'd kept telling myself, I'd be able to trust people more easily because I'd know myself better.

Finally I had to let this fantasy go, and to accept the fact that I was going to continue to be all those little people. None of them was going to vanish because they were all essentially me. The part of me that hated being stereotyped as a basketball player was going to go right on acting up, and so was the part that loved the game. The part that craved new challenges wouldn't go away, and neither would the part that yearned for a place to come home to. I knew I wanted a monogamous relationship with a woman, and at the same time I sensed I was incapable of it. I was like a bird of prey who'd been circling for years, soaring because he loved flying, but also because he could never quite find the perfect place to land. For the first time I began to see that I was close to reaching the limits inside me.

That's when Sam Schulman called me, early in 1973. As principal owner of the Seattle Supersonics, he had a problem. His team had one of the worst records in the NBA—and also one of the highest payrolls. Season ticket sales had dropped 50 percent from the year before, there was dissension about salaries, and some players wanted to jump to the ABA. On top of all this, Sonic stockholders had sued Schulman for running up large debts to the several coaches he'd fired in mid-contract. Now he was looking for a new coach once more, and asked me for some recommendations. I gave him three or four names, but he found something wrong with each of them. When I said I couldn't think of anyone else, he asked, "What about you?"

"No," I said. "I don't want to do it."

"Why not?"

"Well, everybody knows that you never let your coaches alone. You stay involved just enough to make a mess."

"I'm not like that," Schulman said. "I never interfere."

"Well, I'm just not interested."

"Can I call you next week?" he asked.

"If you like."

The next week he telephoned again. "Why don't you take the job?"

"I don't want to do it."

"What would it take to get you to do it?"

"I don't know," I said. "I haven't even thought about it."

"I'll tell you what," Schulman said. "I'll call back tomorrow, and you tell me then what it would take."

I figured that the best way to get out of this situation was to make up a list of ridiculous contingencies that nobody would accept. So when Schulman called the next day, I laid it all out, right down to the particular kind of car I wanted furnished on road trips. I wanted complete control of the franchise, including a noninterference clause that would make it a breach of the contract for any officer of the corporation to speak or act for the Sonics. I also mentioned a stack of money that would have made me blush, if I could blush. When I finished, I was surprised that Sam was still on the phone. But he didn't give me the slightest excuse to back out; he simply said, "Okay."

Which is how I let myself be maneuvered into a new job as coach and general manager of the Supersonics, a move that put me back into basketball. At first it felt more or less like an accident, almost as if I'd lost a bet. I'd gambled that Schulman would turn me down, but when he didn't, I had to go through with it. But then the challenge of the job began to grow on me. My job was much more than rebuilding a bad basketball team; it was also to rescue a franchise that was in shambles. I'd have to really stretch myself to run the whole business. As long as I'd been around basketball, I'd never done anything like this before.

I felt good about the city of Seattle from the day I moved there. It's is the only place I know where rich old Republicans aren't always making speeches about how hard-pressed they are. It's also a place where hippies feel normal; they don't threaten anybody and nobody threatens them. When I was with the Sonics I had a number of friends and supporters among the town's enormous hippie community. I suppose they valued my outspokenness more than they resented my crass materialism.

On the basketball court itself I was faced with an uphill fight. As I sat in the coach's chair for the first few exhibition games in the fall of 1973, I shook my head in amazement. It was more than just a bad team; it was completely devoid of personality. Whatever the opposing team wanted to do, we'd accommodate them, whether it was fast breaks or slowing the game down to a walk. We were like a young girl at her first dancing lesson trying to follow her partner's lead. We followed, all right; we were always fifteen or twenty points behind.

In an early exhibition game, one of the Sonic players pulled up for a twenty-foot jump shot while one of his teammates was standing alone under the bucket, screaming for the ball. This missed opportunity was an obvious mistake, but I didn't realize how bad a one until half time. In the tunnel on the way to the dressing room, the player who'd taken the jump shot yelled at his teammate who'd been standing under the bucket. "Hey, man," he shouted. "Don't start messing with me while I'm shooting!" That's how bad things were.

My blueprint for building the team was a lot like Red's for the Celtics, with one major exception. The Celtics had been able to build a team during the 1950's without being financially healthy, but by the 1970's the competition for players was so intense that a poor team couldn't keep the players it needed. I realized that the Sonics couldn't lose money and build toward a championship at the same time, so in the first year I concentrated on the business side of the franchise. We needed new television and radio contracts and every conceivable scheme to encourage support. There was a lot of hoopla, and I deliberately kept myself out front publicly during that first year, hoping to divert attention from how bad the team was. The team's record improved by ten wins the first season. The next season, 1974–75, the Sonics made the play-offs for the first time ever.

By the spring of 1976, after we'd made the play-offs again, we were a respectable team, and we were young. With our two first-round draft picks that year, we got Dennis Johnson and Bobby Wilkerson, who I thought were good enough to start on a championship team. By trimming our roster, we obtained extra first-round picks in 1977 and 1978. From those four choices I hoped to develop at least two top-notch players. My plan was to build a nucleus of self-motivated players. You can't win consistently without such players, and when you have them, you can encourage stability and togetherness on the team by letting them know that they'll have a job with you as long as they keep performing up to their own standards.

We were on the brink of contention except for one problem —and the problem was me. In the third year, after two good seasons of struggling, I became discouraged because I couldn't treat the players the way I'd wanted to and had promised to, if I wanted to keep winning. All along I'd told them that I'd treat them the way I'd wanted to be treated myself. I'd talk straight with them and wouldn't tell them just what they wanted to hear. I'd try to tell them the truth to their faces, to say nothing personally critical of them in public, to tell them everything I knew about how to win games and how to develop a winning attitude. But I had to assume they had the basic motivation inside them.

It didn't work. One reason, I think, was that I carried my commitment to honesty too far—to the point that the rigid standards I was trying to attain for myself began to interfere with the team. Once a Sonic player came up to me and delivered a speech I'd heard many times. "Coach," he said, "I know I can play, but it doesn't seem to me that you like my style, so why don't you just trade me and let me get on with my career?"

I looked him right in the eye and said, "I can't trade you. I've been trying to for a month, but nobody wants you."

Now that happened to be the truth. I believed that this player had a destructive personality, and I'd had been doing my best to get rid of him, but it wasn't the smartest thing to say because the player couldn't handle it. He saw me as someone trying to attack him, when I was trying to help him see reality. From high school on, most gifted athletes are so accustomed to being treated dishonestly that reality is a shock to their systems. I was trying to toughen up my players' egos, but I should have known better than to carry it so far.

As is true with most losing teams, the Sonic players had fragile egos, and they spent a lot of time looking for reasons not to play, pointing fingers at each other and blaming everyone but themselves. The older players in particular were always comparing pay checks with their teammates and everybody else around the league, looking for excuses not to make an effort. There's always going to be salary jealousy in the NBA, but we carried it overboard. It didn't just happen at contract time; it ran all through the season, gathering momentum from a thousand small and imagined insults. In the heat of a game, I actually had players tell me that they weren't getting paid enough to go after rebounds in the fourth quarter, and others who told me they'd make sure we'd lose games if they didn't get a raise. In order to win in such an atmosphere I had to start yelling, saying things to people that I'd never have stood for when I was playing myself. The situation was very different from my coaching days with the Celtics, when I had to yell at a few players to push them. On the Sonics, the players who showed signs of self-motivation became infected by the attitudes of the rest of the team.

Of course each generation is different, and I tried not to expect the Sonics to be like the old Celtics. If they had been, they wouldn't have needed an expensive new coach like me in the first place. They seemed young to me and I seemed old to them, but we kept trying to adjust to each other through the end of the 1976 season. Then something happened that made me snap. The players met alone, as NBA teams do, to divide up their play-off money, and the prevailing faction voted to keep every dime for themselves. They withheld even the complimentary amounts customarily given to such support people in the franchise as the trainer, people in the front office and assistant coach. One player hurt his knee before the season was over, so they reduced his share. Two teammates had been hurt all year, so were voted nothing. One healthy man had not had much playing time, so they wanted to reduce his share. I couldn't believe it. The money involved was a trifling sum compared to what they made.

I felt so badly about the situation that I called in a couple of the players and asked the team to vote again, even though it's not really any of the coach's affair. But the result wasn't much better the second time around. The majority of the team was determined to act in a way that flew in the face of simple decency, let alone creating a team that could play and win together. It hit me then that not only was my program for the team failing but that I didn't like most of the players or want to be around them.

That's when I should have resigned. In all honesty I should not have coached any more. But I thought maybe things would get better. Instead they got worse, and finally I realized that I'd run up against another limit in myself. Once the challenge of rescuing a franchise had worn off, winning basketball championships was not worth enough to me to tolerate being around people I didn't like or respect. Since it is my habit simply not to talk to people I don't like, I found it harder and harder to have discussions with many of the players. It was obvious to them that I didn't like them, and naturally they didn't like me either.

Early in my fourth season with the Sonics, I knew it would be my last. I was withdrawn, not giving the players what I knew, not being as good a coach as I could have been and should have been. Under the circumstances it was a credit to them that they won as often as they did. I just wanted to get out. My daughter Karen and I would ride to the games together, and I'd be so glum that I wouldn't speak a word the whole way there or back. Staying on with the Sonics that last year was the biggest mistake I've ever made, and it was the most difficult year in my adult life. On the last day of that season I was as relieved as a GI coming home from war.

●   ●   ●

When I'd left the Celtics, I'd felt as if I was running off to seek my fortune; this time I thought I was beginning to find it. Limits were on my mind, as they had been for a long time. A few years earlier I'd decided that I couldn't hope to resolve all the contradictions within me, and that the best I could hope for was to keep any one of them from dominating me. Physical limits are the easiest ones to accept. If I jump into the Pacific Ocean and start swimming due west, everyone would expect me to have problems before I reached Japan. It's not so easy to accept mental or emotional limitations.

It's difficult, for instance, to accept the idea that it's dangerous to stretch feelings. Anything people have and enjoy, they tend to want more of it. The impulse applies almost everywhere. If someone has an exhilarating day in which everything goes just right—reaching new heights with a lover or understanding something for the first time after great struggle—he wants another day just like it, and then one even better. Usually the result is that the original feeling is distorted and finally ruined, so that something that should have been a source of happiness becomes one of discontent. It is extremely difficult to grasp that special feeling when it comes, and to treasure it as a separate and discrete moment that happened, a gift for that day.

That's a limit. Another one that I accepted years after leaving sports is the concept that happiness is limited by whatever is inside you. The basic joy I received from basketball came from within, and I think that this applies everywhere in life. Like friends and lovers, my teammates filled places inside me, but I would never have put any of them in the predicament of thinking that what they did or said would determine whether I was happy or not. I can't say to someone, "If you love me, I'll be happy," because it's not true. How you and I get along may be one of the biggest parts of my life, but it's not my *whole* life, and I don't want it to be yours either, because that feeling exerts tremendous pressure on a single point. Recognizing the limits of what you can demand of people produces a feeling of release. You're pulling your own weight, touching them and offering yourself without loading all your fears and troubles on them.

The starting point for love is that first you must love yourself. Unless you do, there is no frame of reference for loving anyone else. If you believe that you're unlovable, how can you accept it from others? It's worth a whole lifetime of work to reach the point of saying, "I take responsibility for my own outlook, and I accept and love myself." The reward comes in those moments when you are able to give love and accept it at the same time. They are only moments, but they are the most precious ones there are. And no matter how much money or fame you acquire, how tough you are, or how many idols you break, nothing but self-acceptance can bless those moments.

At times I have been happy with expressions of love that were indirect. Once, just after my forty-fourth birthday, I overheard a neighbor of mine ask my teen-aged daughter Karen if I were a good parent.

"Yeah," she answered offhandedly, "he's good."

"Why?" the neighbor asked.

Karen looked at him as though he were stupid for having to ask. "Because he loves me so much," she said simply. After so many years of distance from my own children, her answer overwhelmed me.

Feelings like that have a way of building up for a long time before I see them. Emotions have to percolate in me. It took me years to acknowledge that I have to make choices, and to plant myself somewhere for love to grow. And it took me seven years to marry Didi. It began as a kind of Cyrano relationship in which I acted as a surrogate for a friend of mine by long-distance telephone. (Never has anyone been more sincere on television than I was in those ads for direct dialing.) For the first few years it was a grueling assignment to try to woo her for my friend. I wasn't very good at it because she thought I was a boring jumble of words. I wasn't sure about her either. Then, after about three more years on the telephone, we actually met.

Didi is far too private for me to write much about her. I'll say only that she is beautiful to me, and that we want from each other the same things we want to give each other. That's rare, and so is the fact that we're friends.

After all these years learning things about myself, one thing I've learned is that I still don't know much about women. Often I don't have the slightest idea what Didi is going to do or say from one moment to the next. Like me, she's both very bright and very stupid at the same time. She has a bunch of conflicts inside her and is one of the few people I know who shares my unorthodox view of marriage. We don't expect marriage to work wonders or to change all our glooms into joy. It just makes life better. To me, marriage is very much like the new putter I bought one year. I already enjoyed golf more than I can say, but for some reason that putter took my game into unknown heights, and I couldn't wait to get out on the course. Similarly, I already loved living, but marrying Didi enhanced all the things I enjoyed doing, and made them better than they'd ever been before.

Didi and I share the notion that limits and adventure can go together, and that's how we got in trouble on Mount Rainier. One day about a year before we were married, I drove over to the base of the mountain and suddenly had the impulse to climb that monster even though I'm terrified of heights. I wasn't going to conquer *any* mountain, just this particular one, and then I'd never need to climb another. It was one of those feelings you don't argue with.

So one day the two of us went trudging up Mount Rainier, accompanied by friends and guides, weighed down with gear of every description. I was especially nervous because, in the previous day's training for emergency procedures, I'd failed every time in the "ice arrest," and gone flying into the make-believe cravasse while the trainer shook his head sadly. This shook my confidence, and I didn't have much to start with.

Good sense was also in short supply. We'd managed to wait until the last possible week of the season, in October, when the snow line was already down to Camp Paradise at 6,000 feet. This meant we had to climb to the summit at 14,400 feet through fresh snow of ever-increasing depth. I didn't understand what a hardship this would be when they told us, but I soon found out for myself. It was like walking through deep sand on a beach with a sixty-pound pack on your back—except that you're going uphill.

By the time we reached 8,000 feet, a couple of Empire State buildings above the base camp, I had already passed the kind of terminal fatigue I used to get on the third day of Red's training camps. At 9,000 feet we broke through the clouds, shutting out the world below, and saw the peak of Mount Hood in Oregon. Above us was a brilliant blue, and below were white clouds. The whole universe was simplified into two colors so bright that even with sunglasses you had to squint to take them in.

By now I had burned through to new layers of fatigue, and I could feel the capillaries in my lungs pounce on each breath of cold air. At 10,000 feet, Didi and I straggled into the half-way camp, called Muir, half an hour behind the other climbers.

All too soon we were huddled in a tiny cabin to get out of the piercing cold, and the chief guide was making a Knute Rockne speech. Shortly after midnight, he told us, we would set out by moonlight for the summit, and it would be tougher than we'd ever dreamed. Lying in my sleeping bag, I couldn't believe that it was possible to be so bone weary and yet unable to sleep. Others in the party seemed to be pitching around, too, and I wasn't the only one who heard the wake-up man open the cabin door at the witching hour.

Didi was cheerful and talkative, while everyone else was groaning. I kept watching and listening to her, thinking that in these circumstances she was acting weird. "What are you so happy about?" I growled.

"Oh, I'm not going any further," she said happily. "I don't need to. I've seen the promised land."

I understood, and I knew what she meant, because the view from Camp Muir was as awesome as I'd ever dreamed the summit could be. So she stayed in the warm cabin for some shut-eye. "So far I've enjoyed this," she said, "but if I go any farther, I won't."

Soon we were lined up and roped together under the moonlight, like convicts. At 11,000 feet we took our first break. It was four o'clock in the morning, and already you could see the first gray light before dawn. Everything was so still at that altitude that all the sounds of our climb were magnified. Every time someone took a step, you could hear the loud crunch of steel crampons driving into snow, and the sound seemed to drift off into nothingness for hundreds of miles. The other sound you heard was breathing, which was even louder. At that height you take a full, forced breath every time you put your foot forward; then you step, rest and blow the air out. It's called a lock-step, and it's a slow processional. I realized that the essence of mountain climbing is to keep putting one foot in front of the other, and that it takes all your concentration. Like so much else, all you have to do is to keep one step ahead, but it's hard to do. You keep bumping against the walls inside you, trying to push them back. My walls were mostly pain. There were a few thoughts, every one of which seemed brand new, but mostly it was pain. I could feel every ounce of weight in my pack, and kept kicking myself for all the extras I was carrying, like the collapsible golf club I'd brought so that I could hit a golf ball off the top. Nice thinking, Russell. I couldn't imagine the state of mind I'd been in when I'd put that thing in my pack.

During the next leg of the climb the sun came up, and the clouds down below looked small. I welcomed the light. We were passing cravasses of various sizes—some no larger than a desk, some larger than football fields. As you approached, they were white with black interiors, but when you looked directly down into them the white turned into a pale blue and then became a deep blue. If you lifted your eyes slightly, you found yourself looking out over the whole world.

We were still roped together, marching slower and slower in the deepening snow. My feet had long been numb from the cold night climb, but the morning sun baked me above the waist. At 12,200 feet, when we took our next break, I found myself collapsed on the ground. One guide was going back down from here, but thereafter no one could turn around. If you fell out, they'd just leave you in a sleeping bag and pick you up on the way down. I had just broken through to the fiftieth new level of fatigue, and I felt something giving way inside me that I'd been fighting for a long time. The sensation was one that I've encountered many times in life, when I've found myself asking, "What am I doing here?"

Usually on such occasions I have one of my infrequent conversations with God. I tell Him that if He'll just get me out of this one scrape, He'll never have to worry about me again. But this time I said, "Lord, you catch me next time. I can take care of this one myself." I was too weak to laugh, but I managed to tell the guide that I was turning back with him. I had visited so many places in my life that people had claimed was the mountaintop that I felt I'd already been there. By pushing myself and breaking barriers and experiencing that awe, I'd already done what I wanted to accomplish with Mount Rainier. To go on was not worth the pain, and I didn't mind getting my second wind on the downhill part of the mountain.